AFRICA-CHINA COOPERATION CHALLENGES AND PROSPECTS

Tongele N. Tongele, Editor

Thaddée M. Badibanga
Jean-Louis Peta Ikambana
Annie Kinwa-Muzinga
Ngamboko (Lawrence) P. Muzinga
Mutombo Nkulu-N'Sengha
John M. Ulimwengu
Ndasi Zialo

Copyright © 2025 TWF, Richmond, VA

All Rights Reserved

ISBN: 979-8-3492-0963-5

DEDICATION

This book is dedicated to men and women around the world who work at the grassroots level to do things right, to play by the rules, to sacrifice, and to lay the foundation upon which cooperation at regional and international levels is built. These men and women, often unknown and never recognized with national, regional, or international prizes, are the true heroes, the invisible pillars that support the malleable web of international cooperation.

Acknowledgment

The authors thank their families for the encouragement and support received during this work. They also thank researchers and writers whose publications are used to produce this book.

About the Authors

Thaddée M. Badibanga, PhD

Dr. Thaddée M. Badibanga earned a Master's degree in Economics from Western Illinois University, Macomb, IL, USA, and a PhD degree in Applied Economics, Macroeconomics, Economic Growth and Development from the University of Minnesota Twins Cities, MN, USA. His research foci include structural transformation, economic growth, development, and agricultural and rural development.

Jean-Louis Peta Ikambana, PhD

Dr. Jean-Louis Peta Ikambana holds multidisciplinary master's degrees in political science, criminal justice, and international relations, as well as a doctorate degree in African American Studies. His primary research interest is in a comparative look at the intersections of political systems and democracy. He is deeply committed to the intersectionality of academic theories and their application to social life. He has devoted his professional life to social justice issues such as human rights education, community organizing, education, democracy, youth civic engagement, and social justice advocacy.

Annie Kinwa-Muzinga, PhD

Dr. Annie Kinwa-Muzinga earned a Bachelor of Science degree in applied economics from the University of Kinshasa in the Democratic Republic of the Congo with a focus on financial management. She completed an MBA in Finance and her PhD in Agricultural and Consumer Economics, specializing in Food and Agribusiness Management and Strategic Management with a significant Marketing component from the University of Illinois at Urbana-Champaign, Illinois, USA. Her research interests cover various projects related to agriculture and scholarship of teaching, including Decision Analysis,

Financial Management, Marketing (pricing strategy), Strategic Management, Investment, and Economic Analysis of firms in the Agribusiness sector.

Ngamboko (Lawrence) P. Muzinga, PhD

Dr. Ngamboko (Lawrence) P. Muzinga earned a BS degree in Applied Economics from the University of Kinshasa in the Democratic Republic of Congo, with a concentration in Financial Management. He completed a Master of Arts in African Studies and a PhD in Agricultural and Consumer Economics with a specialization in Agricultural Finance and Economics Development from the University of Illinois, Champaign-Urbana, Illinois, USA. His research focuses on teaching effectiveness, accounting, taxes, farm firms' financial performances, higher education assessment, and reforms in emerging countries.

Mutombo Nkulu-N'Sengha, PhD

Dr. Mutombo Nkulu-N'Sengha is a poet, a teacher, and a human rights activist. He earned a Master's degree in Philosophy in the Democratic Republic of the Congo, a Master's degree in Theology in Rome, Italy, a Master's degree in African American Studies, and a doctorate in Religion and Human Rights at Temple University, Philadelphia, USA. His research and work focus on human rights and the dialogue between civilizations, especially in the field of religion and philosophy.

Tongele N. Tongele, PhD

Dr. Tongele N. Tongele earned a Bachelor of Science in mechanical engineering from California State Polytechnic University Pomona and a Master's and a PhD in Mechanical Engineering from the Catholic University of America, Washington, DC. His areas of research include dynamics and vibration control, renewable energy systems and technologies, science and society.

John M. Ulimwengu, PhD

Dr. John M. Ulimwengu earned master's degrees in development economics from Williams College and in economics from Ohio State University. He received his PhD in agricultural economics from Ohio State University. His research foci include poverty dynamics, food systems transformation, and rural development. He is involved in research and policy advisory work on sector policy and strategy issues related to the implementation of the AU's Comprehensive Africa Agricultural Development Program (CAADP).

Ndasi Zialo, PhD

Dr. Ndasi Zialo earned a Bachelor of Social Work (BSW) from the University of Maryland Baltimore County (UMBC), a Master's degree (MA) in Child Welfare from the Catholic University of America, and a PhD in Social and Behavioral Sciences from the Walden University. His areas of research include social welfare, crisis intervention, and human development.

Table of Contents

Dedication ii
Acknowledgment iii
About the Authors iv
INTRODUCTION viii
Chapter I Africa-China Involvement: A Preliminary Historical And Ideological Background 1
Chapter II A Review Of The Political Economy Of Africa-China Trade Relations 23
CHAPTER III Assessing The Economic Impact Of Chinese Foreign Direct Investment's Inflows Into African Countries 62
Chapter IV Sino-Congolese Trade: Impact On Higher Education Infrastructure 100
Chapter V China-Africa Science And Technology Cooperation 127
Chapter VI Science And Technology In Africa: From Cooperation To Revolution 186
Chapter VII Africa:From Deficit To Strength-Based Cooperation 227
Chapter VIII quo Vadis Africa? Rethinking Geopolitics In The Age Of Heightened Rivalry Between China And The West 238
CONCLUSION 340

INTRODUCTION

The relationship between Africa and China has evolved dramatically over the past several decades, growing from minimal contact to a strategic partnership encompassing economic, political, and technological dimensions. This transformation reflects broader shifts in global geopolitics and economic development strategies, positioning China as Africa's largest trading partner and a major source of foreign direct investment (FDI). This partnership, however, is not without its challenges and controversies. While it offers significant opportunities for development, infrastructure expansion, and economic diversification in Africa, it also raises concerns about debt sustainability, the quality of development projects, and the long-term impact on local economies and governance structures (Brautigam, 2020).

Historically, Africa-China relations have their roots in the ideological solidarity of the mid-20th century, particularly during the Cold War era. China, under Mao Zedong, positioned itself as a supporter of African liberation movements, offering political support and economic aid as part of its broader strategy to counter Western and Soviet influence in the developing world. This early engagement was characterized by symbolic gestures and limited economic interactions. However, the post-Cold War era, especially since the turn of the 21st century, marked a significant shift as China's economic rise necessitated greater access to natural resources, markets, and strategic partnerships, leading to an intensified focus on Africa.

The establishment of the Forum on China-Africa Cooperation (FOCAC) in 2000 signified a new era in Africa-China relations, providing a structured platform for dialogue and cooperation. Through FOCAC, China has committed to various development projects across Africa, ranging from infrastructure development to technological transfer and educational exchanges. This has been complemented by the Belt and Road Initiative (BRI), which further integrates African nations into global trade networks led by China.

These initiatives have resulted in massive inflows of Chinese FDI into Africa, with investments primarily concentrated in infrastructure, mining, and energy sectors (Ulimwengu, 2024).

Despite the mutual benefits, this relationship has attracted considerable scrutiny and criticism. One of the primary concerns revolves around the debt sustainability of African nations. Many Chinese-funded projects are financed through loans, which have contributed to increasing debt burdens in several African countries. Critics argue that these loans often come with opaque terms and conditions, potentially leading to a new form of economic dependency akin to neo-colonialism (Ergano & Rao, 2019). Furthermore, the heavy reliance on Chinese firms for the execution of these projects raises questions about the true extent of technology transfer and capacity building within African economies (Broadman, 2007).

Another area of concern is the impact on local industries and job markets. The influx of cheaper Chinese goods has often been blamed for undercutting local businesses, leading to deindustrialization in some sectors. Additionally, there are reports of preferential treatment towards Chinese labor in infrastructure projects, which limits the job creation potential for local populations. These issues are compounded by the environmental and social challenges associated with some Chinese investments, particularly in the mining and energy sectors, where there have been accusations of environmental degradation and insufficient regard for local communities' rights (Chaudhury, 2022).

On the geopolitical front, China's growing influence in Africa is reshaping the continent's international relations. While traditional Western powers have often attached political conditions to their aid, such as demands for governance reforms, China's approach has been markedly different, characterized by a policy of non-interference in domestic affairs. This has made China an attractive partner for many African governments, particularly those with authoritarian tendencies. However, this also raises concerns about the implications for democratic governance and human rights in Africa (Pham, 2006).

In conclusion, while the Africa-China partnership offers significant opportunities for economic development and infrastructure expansion, it also presents complex challenges that require careful management. The future of this relationship will depend on how both Africa and China navigate these challenges, ensuring that the benefits are broadly shared and that the long-term impacts are sustainable and equitable (Tongele, 2016). As Africa continues to seek pathways for development, the role of China as a partner and the terms of that partnership will remain a critical area of focus for policymakers, scholars, and stakeholders across the continent.

This book offers unique insights as the authors—renowned experts in their fields—bring to light perspectives from sons and daughters of Africa, living beyond its borders that no one else could articulate. It begins by exploring the evolution of Africa-China cooperation, followed by an analysis of the political economy driving this partnership. Subsequent chapters assess the economic impacts for both Africa and China, delve into the scientific and cultural exchanges between the two, and evaluate the broader implications of their cooperation in science and technology on a global scale. The final chapters provide strategic recommendations for how Africa can strengthen its position in global trade, military-security relations, and technological advancements, ensuring that it remains relevant and resilient in its partnerships, including those with China.

REFERENCES

Brautigam, D. (2020). *The Dragon's Gift: The Real Story of China in Africa*. Oxford University Press.

Broadman, H. (2007). *Africa's Silk Road: China and India's New Economic Frontier*. World Bank Publications.

Chaudhury, D. R. (2022). *China's Infrastructure Projects in Africa: A Double-Edged Sword*. International Journal of Development Studies.

Ergano, A., & Rao, A. (2019). *Africa-China Economic Relations: Benefits and Challenges*. Journal of International Development.

Pham, J. P. (2006). *China's African strategy and its implications for US interests*. American Foreign Policy Interests, 28(3).

Tongele, T.N. (2016). *Rise and Shine: Resilient People and Immense Resources in the Shadow of Death*. Green Ivy Publishing.

Ulimwengu, J. M. (2024). *A Review of the Political Economy of Africa-China Trade Relations*, chapter II in this book.

CHAPTER I

AFRICA-CHINA INVOLVEMENT: A PRELIMINARY HISTORICAL AND IDEOLOGICAL BACKGROUND

By

Jean-Louis Peta Ikambana, PhD

1. Introduction

It is no secret that Africa and China are involved in relationships and cooperation that span from economic to military to science and technology. The presence of China on the continent of Africa is noticeable. But what results can be observed from these relationships and cooperation? Is the presence of China on the continent of Africa helping or hurting the developmental interests of Africa? This paper will first look at the foundation and the historical timeline of China's foreign policy, then review and analyze China's pragmatic involvement in the continent of Africa, and look into the implication of China's presence in Africa as well as Africa's Western allies, including the United States of America. This will lead to a concluding remark with suggestions for Africa, China, and the West.

2. Ideological Foundations of Chinese Foreign Policy

US Foreign Policy experts have consistently credited China for its coherent and long-standing strategy guiding its foreign policy based on an implicit desire to replace the United States as a global hegemon (Pillsbury, 2022).

At the origin of China's Foreign Policy is what experts have described as the century of humiliation from 1839 to 1949, during which China experienced Western and Japanese domination. China has always considered that period as their country's loss of greatness.

Humiliation has always been at the core of China's emphasis on issues of sovereignty, national unity, and territorial integrity (Zhu, 2019).

3. Timeline of Chinese Foreign Policy

The Digital Archive of the Wilson Center has underlined the following Timeline for Foundations of Chinese Foreign Policy (digitalarchive.wilsoncenter.org):

3.1 April 23, 1945: 7th Congress of the Chinese Communist Party

During the 7th Congress of the Chinese Communist Party (CCP) held from 23 April through 11 June 1945, Mao Zedong was made leader of the Party, and "Mao Zedong Thought" was enshrined in the new constitution.

3.2 August 06, 1946: Mao Zedong's Intermediate Zone

During an interview with Anna Louise Strong, Mao Zedong introduced the theory of the "intermediate zone," asserting that the United States and the Soviet Union are separated by a vast zone, which includes many capitalist, colonial, and semi-colonial countries in Europe, Asia, and Africa."

3.3 June 30, 1949: Leaning to One Side

In a famous article entitled "On the People's Democratic Dictatorship," Mao Zedong announces that China will "lean to one side" in its foreign policy. He explicitly stated that China must "ally with the Soviet Union" and "form an international united front."

3.4 October 1, 1949: Founding of the People's Republic of China

Following three years of fighting against the Guomindang, Mao proclaims the founding of the People's Republic of China (PRC) from Tiananmen Square.

3.5 December 31, 1953: Five Principles of Peaceful Coexistence

Zhou Enlai announced the Five Principles of Peaceful Coexistence during a discussion over disputed Tibetan territory with a delegation from India on December 31, 1953, emphasizing mutual respect for sovereignty, non-interference, and peaceful coexistence. The Five Principles were enshrined in the Ten Principles of the Bandung Conference in 1955 and became a core set of principles underlying Chinese foreign policy throughout the Cold War and after.

3.6 September 15, 1956: 8th Congress of the Chinese Communist Party (CCP)

During the 8th Congress of the Chinese Communist Party, Deng Xiaoping was elevated to the near top of the Central Committee' Mao Zedong Thought was removed from the constitution, and Liu Shaoqi delivered an extensive political report on the state of China.

3.7 September 1, 1963: Two Intermediate Zones

Mao Zedong begins to espouse his theory of the "Two Intermediate Zones," with Asia, Africa, and Latin America constituting the first and Europe and North America constituting the second.

3.8 February 22, 1974: Mao's Three Worlds Theory

In February 1974, Mao officially proposed the theory of Three Worlds, claiming that the "First World" is made up of the rich and nuclear-armed USSR and US, the "Second World" refers to Japan, Europe, Australia, and Canada, and the "Third World" covers the undeveloped countries of Asia, Latin America, and Africa. Reflecting a new diplomatic orientation, China begins prioritizing the Third World in its foreign policy following Mao's speech.

3.9 June 27, 1981: Resolving "Certain Questions in the History of Our Party"

At the Sixth Plenary Session of the 11th Central Committee, the Chinese Community Party published an important document entitled *"Resolution on Certain Questions in the History of Our Party since the Founding of the People's Republic of China."*

The document assessed the legacy and shortcomings of Mao Zedong, criticized the Cultural Revolution, and called for Party unity.

3.10 September 1, 1982: China's "Independent Foreign Policy"

The Chinese Communist Party convenes its 12th National Congress from 1-11 September and proclaims an "independent foreign policy."

4. China-Africa relationships

4.1. China, crude oil, and Africa

In 2023, the United States and China led oil consumption globally, with the United States leading the way with 19 million barrels daily, followed by China with 14 million barrels.

Although most of its oil imports during the past year have come mainly from Russia, Saudi Arabia, and Brazil, Angola is among China's top 10 crude oil trading partners. In 2021 alone, it is estimated that the destination of 72% of Angola's oil exports was China. Underscoring China's continued increased presence in Africa, trade between China and Africa is estimated to have reached a record $282 billion in 2022 alone, according to China General Administration of Customs data compiled by Bloomberg, L.P.

The 2023 data confirms a trend that started in the early 2000, when China became the second largest consumer of crude oil, with more than 25% of its oil imports from the Gulf of Guinea and Sudan. It was estimated that by 2020, China would be forced to supply 60% of its energy needs from abroad, even from nations such as Chad that have maintained diplomatic relations with Taiwan[1]. Although in 2004, only 2% of Chinese trade was with Africa, the continent has done particularly well as China has opened to the world. For example, during the 1990s, China-Africa trade grew by 700%[2], and since the first China-Africa Forum celebrated in Beijing in 2000, more than 40 agreements have been signed, doubling the trade to more than 420 billion over the four years to the end of 2004. By the end of 2005,

---

[1] Le Monde Diplomatique, May 2005
[2] See Chine-Afrique: la cooperation fructueuse, in www.Chinafrique.com

China had become Africa's third most important trading partner, behind the US and France and ahead of the United Kingdom[3]. In 2005 alone, more than 674 Chinese state companies were involved in Africa, investing not only in flourishing sectors such as mines, fishing, precious woods, and telecommunications but also in others that the West has neglected or, in some cases, abandoned because they are less profitable. For example, Zambia's Chambezi copper mines are being worked on again, and supposedly exhausted oil reserves in Gabon are being explored. In 2004, Chinese investments represented more than $900 million of the 415 billion foreign direct investment in Africa. Of the thousands of projects underway in Africa during that period, 500 were exclusively directed by China Road and Bridge Corporation, a state enterprise. In Ethiopia, for example, China became involved in telecommunications. In the Democratic Republic of Congo, China became heavily involved in Gecamines, the lucrative state-owned mining company that contributes almost 60% of Congo's national budget. In Kenya, China repaired the road linking Mombasa and Nairobi, two major economic and political Kenyan cities. In Nigeria, China helped this major oil-rich country to build its first space satellite. This paper argues that Chinese presence in Africa has evolved from merely ideological interest (search for allies and political dependents) to more pragmatic (search for Chinese economic interest: natural and cheap resources, etc.). Harry Broadman (2007) affirms that Africa's "exports to China increased at an annual rate of 48 percent between 2000 and 2005, two and half times as fast as the rate of the region's exports to the United States and four times as fast as the rate of its exports to the European Union (EU) over the same period".

4.2 China's Ideological Partnership with Africa

Chinese interest in Africa before the end of the Cold War was seen as mainly ideological. China first became involved in Africa during the Cold War, when it wanted to make friends and do business in a region of the world overlooked by the West and the Soviet Union. China might have needed Africa to expand its ideological influence beyond its borders, and Africa's own quest for political independence

---
[3] Le Monde Diplomatique, May 2005.

from the Western hemisphere made the partnership easy, given the nominal U.S. presence in Africa. In fact, the U.S. interest in Africa before the Cold War was very limited. The only known American presence in Africa was limited to Liberia, a country founded by the free American slaves who decided to return to Africa.

Chairman Mao's pragmatism might have led him to consider Africa as an opportunity to build his legacy and influence China's reactions to Western colonialism and domination in Africa, Asia, and Latin America. China's presence provided the African nations with a certain moral support despite its weak diplomatic status.

Since China's attitudes to the African continent have largely remained quite constant as it has always considered Africa as a symbol of its stand against colonialism, for China, Africa's share of colonial circumstances and experiences has substantially marked their respective roles in the international political system and their global perception of the world. This could explain China's policy toward Africa during the 1960's and the 1970's. In fact, China's policy sought to win Africa and, in turn, the world recognition as a major global player.

In the 1970s, Africa was transformed into a major battleground in the conflict opposing China to the Soviet Union. As we will recall, that struggle was happening at two primary levels: first, at the level of the Chinese and Soviet political, economic, and military interaction with African states and movements (the case of Angola, Mozambique, Congo), and secondly their mutual fight as communist giants, on the other's motives and role related to Africa. Specifically, China wanted to challenge the Soviet Union on both levels by engaging in a major campaign to discredit the Union of Soviet Socialist Republics and, thus, make new friends and gain influence. China's strategy was to provide military, ideological, and technical support to nationalist governments in Africa and the rest of the so-called third-world countries with the goal of gaining influence among developing countries. Until the mid-1970s, cooperation between China and Africa consisted of building solidarity between two continents that belonged to the so-called underdeveloped world. China sent its technicians to Africa to boost nations newly liberated from colonialism. For example, China sent some 15,000 doctors and over 10,000 agricultural engineers[4] were sent to areas of Africa devastated by the economic effects of the Cold War. I remember, as a child, seeing hundreds and hundreds of hard-working Chinese nationals running our state-owned farms on national television and their products flooding our markets. In its role as an anti-imperialist counter-factor, China was able to infiltrate parts of the world neglected by the United States and the Soviet Union. As I mentioned before, China took on ambitious projects, such as the construction of the Tanzam railway between Tanzania and Zambia. China also concluded agreements for military cooperation, concentrating on countries that were ideologically close, mostly in East Africa, including Ethiopia, Uganda, Tanzania, and Zambia, and non-aligned countries such as Egypt. It is estimated that between 1955 and 1977, China sold $142 million of military equipment to Africa and received more than 15,000 African students in Chinese universities. By 1977, trade between China and Africa reached a record $817 million.[5] During the 1980s, when the Cold War powers were pulling out of Africa, and Western development aid became limited, China kept its contacts with Africa. That strategy was part of its world revolution. Also, China sought to accomplish this strategic objective by trying to prove that it had reached the status of a third-world power and thus, it could provide a balance between the two superpowers involved in an ideological war, the United States of America and the Union of Soviet Socialist Republics.

China has significantly increased its defense trade in Africa, with an estimated 55% growth between 2012 and 2017. In addition, China has strategically opened military bases, mostly in the Horn of Africa. Egypt has increased its exports to China, more than doubling it between 2010 and 2018, while also borrowing over $ 3 billion from China between 200 and 2017. Likewise, Kenya had to rely on China for credit to accomplish its dream of the Standard Railway project, while one-third of Zambian external debt in 2020 was also estimated to be held by China.

---

[4] Monde Diplomatique, May 2005
[5] Le Monde Diplomatique, May 2005.

4.3 China's pragmatism in Africa after the Cold War

Following the end of the Cold War, China adopted a more realistic approach in its foreign policy toward Africa. Simply put, China's foreign policy towards Africa has been in alignment with its economic policy and needs. Putting behind the quest for ideological expansion, China has become more pragmatic in search of natural resources dictated by its impressive economic growth. Peter Pham (2006) has argued that China's new objectives for its policy towards Africa can be translated as quests for resources, business opportunities, diplomatic initiatives, and building strategic partnerships. So, China is back in Africa, and the main incentive is no longer ideological but a more pragmatic and strategic objective that involves economic interests and access to energy. China's growing economy has triggered a demand for raw materials, and involvement in the African continent seems the most appropriate way to help China balance its growing trade deficit with exports of commodities and labor. In its interaction with Africa, China is offering an economic model different from that of Western powers, based on its cheap labor and products, stress on non-conditionality and non-interference, and a huge market for African oil and raw materials. For a continent that has grown suspicious of Western exploitation, China's offer sounds very appealing to African authoritarian leaders because, unlike the West, investment aid from China comes with no political strings attached.

Will such a partnership hurt or help Africa's development? We will consider a few examples of Chinese engagements in Africa to respond to this question.

In countries where relations with the West are problematic, China is benefiting from its policy of non-involvement in internal politics. For example, China's relations with Sudan, a country condemned by the United Nations over the situation in Darfur, and which former president was served with a war crime indictment by the International Court was supposed to be very problematic, but both countries still enjoy great partnership.

China was also involved in a political scandal in Zimbabwe, a country that plunged into a political crisis after then-President Mugabe's refusal to accept an electoral defeat and clung to a presidential seat he held for over four decades since his country's independence from Great Britain. It was widely believed that Mugabe's party did not only lose its majority in parliament but also in the presidential election. Results were not published three weeks after the elections despite public pressure from the opposition and Western powers, including the United States of America. China publicly backed then President Mugabe, despite his known poor economic and human rights records, by sending a cargo of combat ammunition[6] estimated at 77 tons of cartridges, AK-47 assault weapons, three million cartouches, and one thousand five hundred grenades. The arrival of the cargo, first revealed by a British newspaper, is a violation of the embargo imposed by Western powers. However, the African Union leaders remained silent and did little not only to stop the Chinese transaction but also to take any sanctions against Mugabe's government. Mugabe went on to "win" the run-off election, which was seen by the international community as unfair, as was the case with the African Union. He was the only candidate on the ballot after his rival withdrew his name because of political intimidation. Through the United Nations Security Council, the international community immediately called for sanctions against Mugabe and the non-recognition of his victory. China and Russia opposed the resolution, leading to its failure.

In Sudan, a country pointed out by the international community for its bad governance and human rights violations against innocent civilians, China has been the most powerful investor, according to certain sources[7]. The oil industry is the most visible example of Chinese investment in Sudan. China National Petroleum Company (CNPC) has its own operating stake in several oil blocks and owns exploration rights in others. This is secured through part-owned subsidiary companies such as Petrodar, the Greater Nile Petroleum Operating Company (GNPOC), and the Red Sea Petroleum Operating

---

[6] Source : *Le Figaro*, April 19, 2008
[7] African Development Information Service. July 2008.

Company (RSPOC). China Petrochemical Corporation (Sinopec) also holds a 6% stake in Petrodar through its Sudanese-registered subsidiary company. In the energy sector, there is a significant ongoing Chinese investment in electricity generation, transmission, and distribution. The most obvious illustration has been the Merowe Dam 69357, a $1.8 billion hydropower project that has been called both the pearl of the Nile and an environmental disaster. There are reports of several Chinese companies engaged at Merowe, including Harbin Power Equipment Company, Sinohydro, and China International Water and Electric Company, all contracted on the project, which aims for a peak output of 1250 MW. In addition, there are also reports of other Chinese companies working in the power sector, including Shandong Electric Power Construction Corp, which is engaged in the construction of plants at Port Sudan and Gaili, while Shanghai Power Transmission and Distribution Company has committed to build transformer sub-stations in White Nile and North Kordofan states.

In addition to the Oil and Energy sectors, Chinese investment in Sudan is also present in Engineering and Military, as suggested by the Sudan Divestment Task Force Sudan Company Report. AviChina Industry and Technology Company are alleged to have supplied military aircraft to the Sudanese government, while Dongfeng Automobile Company has been linked to the supply of military vehicles. The same report also links weapons produced by China North Industries Corporation to Chadian rebel movement activity in Western Darfur.

Khartoum's largest foreign investor and most significant international supporter is, without a doubt, China, according to the Sudan Tribune[8]. Over the past ten years, Beijing has courted Sudan's leadership in order to secure access to petroleum and other primary resources supplies needed to feed China's booming economy. While Western allies, including the US and Europe, have either imposed or considered imposing sanctions on Sudan, China has, in contrast, poured an estimated $15 billion into Sudan[9], and China's main oil

---

[8] See www.sudantribune.com/spip.php
[9] www.time.com/time/magazine

operator in Sudan, owned by China National Petroleum Corporation, has invested at least $5 billion in Sudan. In 2007, then-Chinese President Hu Jintao announced an interest-free loan of $13 million to help rebuild the Sudanese presidential palace[10], while in March 2007, the Sudanese Ministry of Finance also announced its intention to borrow $2 billion from China to cover Sudan's budget deficit[11]. In exchange, China benefited from its Sudanese investments and loans by securing a steady oil supply, avoiding a volatile open market purchase. Sudan supplied 7% of China's oil needs, representing between fifty and eight percent of Sudan's oil exportation. In exchange, Sudan's interests are protected by China at the United National, where China holds a veto power as a permanent member of the Security Council. In the security sector, a report published by the state-controlled China Business News quoted "a Chinese foreign official as saying that Beijing cooperates with the Sudan government on security and has asked Khartoum to send troops to areas in which Chinese companies operate[12].

Because Chinese investments are from government subsidies, it gives Chinese investors in Africa a competitive advantage over their counterparts from Europe and other countries. Addressing an audience of mostly American and African business leaders at a US-Africa Business Summit in Cape Town, South Africa, Professor Yang Guang of the Institute of West-Asian and African Studies of the Chinese Academy of Sciences argued that China possesses low-cost technology for resource development. He also added that China enjoys a low cost of labor, including engineers and managers, and employs cheap electrical machinery, all made in China. In 2004, it was estimated that China had more than 800 companies operating in Africa in a wide range of sectors. About one hundred are state-owned, and the rest are private, but they are still subsided by the Chinese government. In monetary terms, Professor Yang Guang of the Institute of West-Asian and African Studies of the Chinese Academy of

---

[10] Washington Post, February 4, 2007.
[11] www.boston.com/news
[12] www.energybulletin.net/3753.html

Sciences estimated the cumulative value of Chinese investment in Africa to be $11.7 billion by the end of 2006.

In 2007 alone, the Chinese government announced an economic aid package for the Democratic Republic of Congo estimated at nearly $10 billion dollars, to be invested not only in the resource development industries but also in other industries such as textiles, agro-industries, electricity, road constructions, tourism, telecommunications.[13]

The deal was designed to provide the African country with nearly $6 billion dollars, which is desperately needed to improve its national infrastructure, including about 2,400 miles of road, 2,000 miles of railway, 32 hospitals, 145 health centers, and two universities. In return, China was expected to get a share of the country's precious natural resources to feed its booming industries, including 10 million tonnes of copper and 400,000 tons of cobalt. It was recently announced that the deal was renegotiated by the Tshisekedi government because the original agreement proved to be economically non-profitable for the Democratic Republic of Congo.

In Nigeria, former President Obasanjo signed a multibillion-dollar contract with the Chinese Civil Engineering Construction Corporation (CCECC) for the rehabilitation of the Nigerian railways in exchange for Chinese access to Nigeria's oil.

The examples chosen above bring us to the central issue of Chinese involvement in Africa: is it in Africa's long-term interest?

A high-ranked African diplomat[14] was quoted as saying at the Cape Town summit that Africa should focus on its own interests while trying to meet China's needs.

It is true that Chinese economic investments in Africa have allowed Africans to have new partners with whom they can deal fairly with the prices of what they want to buy or sell.

---

[13] *Le Potential*, April 2008.
[14] *AllAfrica.com,* November 16, 2007.

But to echo the African diplomat, Africa should focus on its own interest, and it is not evident that Chinese involvement in Africa will serve Africa's long-term interests based on the following considerations: the real economic cost of contracts, lack of transparency involving the signing of these contracts, lack of consideration of democratic values, the negative Chinese attitude towards human rights violations. As pointed out by a representative of *Reporters Without Borders*, appearing on BBC News, the "influence of China in African Affairs has been very toxic for democracy."[15] The organization referred to the fact that China gave aid to Africa without asking for political reforms in return, thus compromising Africa's long-term interest in democratic stability and development.

China's relation with Sudan: The China-Sudan partnership involves weapons sales. With profits generated through production-sharing agreements with CNPC, the Sudanese government purchases assault helicopters, armored vehicles, and small arms from China.[16] According to William Hawkins, senior fellow for national security studies at the U.S. Business and Industry Council, " Beijing has also helped Sudan build its own factories to manufacture small arms and ammunition used in Khartoum's campaign of ethnic cleansing."[17] In addition, a U.N. investigation conducted in 2006 determined that the vast majority of weaponry used to attack civilians across Darfur was of Chinese origin. China continues to be one of the largest suppliers of arms to Sudan, reiterating in 2007 its pledge to boost military cooperation with Sudan.[18] This simply implies that Chinese investment in Sudan has not only helped China's economy but also supported the atrocity of human violations against innocent Sudanese civilians. Such practices have proven anti-democratic and have not promoted Sudan's long-term interests.

China's relations with Zimbabwe: We have indicated how China has supported the corrupt and authoritarian regime of Robert Mugabe of Zimbabwe. Furthermore, using its veto power as a permanent

---

[15] BBC News: February 13, 2008. From: www.genocideintervention.net
"www.genocideintervention.net"
[17] www.washtimes.com
[18] www.genocideintervention.net

member of the U.N. National Security Council, China joined Russia in rejecting the sanctions against Mugabe's regime despite the world's outrage against Mugabe's bad governance and authoritarian practices.

5. Implications for the US foreign policy

In Africa, the United States is officially committed to promoting good governance, democracy, and development. This objective could appear to be challenged by China's economic policy in Africa. According to Gal Luft, a specialist in energy security and executive director of a neoconservative thinktank, the Institute of the Analysis of Global Security, "The Chinese are much more prone to do business in a way that today Europeans and Americans do not accept- paying bribes and bonuses under the table. I think that it will be much easier for some African countries to work with Chinese companies, rather than American and European companies, which are becoming more and more restricted by the publish what you pay initiative and others calling for better transparency."[19] Former Rwanda's minister of finance and economic planning, Donald Kaberuka, was quoted saying: "It's a different way of doing business,"[20] meaning with fewer restrictions. Under these circumstances, it becomes more and more difficult, not only for the United States but also for NGOs and international organizations, such as the World Bank International Monetary Fund, to reinforce the principles of financial transparency and accountability. China poses a challenge to the ways in which the United States has dealt with Africa by using instruments and methods to advance its interests in ways that undermine the American message of good governance and democracy, open market, civil liberties, etc. For example, most of China's investments are through state-owned companies, whose individual investments do not have to be profitable if they serve Chinese objectives.

China's appeal to African leaders appeared to be driven by political and economic motivations. Unlike the usual constraints that come with aid from Europe and the US, China's economic package is

---

[19] See "Bottom of the barrel: Africa's oil boom and the poor", in www.Catholicrelief.com
[20] Ibidem

offered to African leaders with no political strings attached. This is very appealing to these leaders who struggle with good governance, human rights abuses, and lack of democracy. Ambassador Princeton Lyman of the U.S. Council on Foreign Relations declared [21] the U.S. could not compete with the packages offered by China because China is able to package its government programs, its state-owned enterprises, and its aid programs in ways that the United States can't. For example, the U.S. can't assist an African oil company in making a deal by saying if they win a contract, the U.S. will build a road for that African country. That's a challenge for the U.S. if it wants to do things differently in Africa. For a long time, U.S. strategic interests in Africa were unchallenged, given its overwhelming political and economic leverage over the continent. Through US-dominated financial institutions such as the World Bank and the IMF, the U.S. and the EU were successful in securing mechanisms that allowed the Western hemisphere to ensure their economic and political interests to the detriment of Africa's development. For example, these financial institutions were often used to exert powerful political pressure on African leaders. That's the case with the conditions imposed on African leaders under the name of structural adjustments. Dictators such as former President Mobutu of Zaire or Kerekou of Benin were typical illustrations of the U.S. strategic leverage on the continent.

Dealing with corrupt African leaders with no strings attached may not help the long-term African aspiration to democracy and development. African strong men are known for using their power not to promote democracy and the development of their people but to consolidate their personal power and perpetuate their self-interest. Personal power is characterized by the concentration of power in the hands of one individual and the personification of power in that individual. It often becomes political power when the state is confronted with seemingly overwhelming challenges. The concentration of power in one individual often leads to his becoming the personification of power. Individualization allows the person to substitute himself for the primary sovereign. Generally, the individual

---

[21] Ambassador Lyman was speaking at the U.S.- Africa Business Summit in Cape Town, South Africa.
Source: *allAfrica.com*, 16 November 2007.

initiates his ascent to power through a coup d'état, which often negates the legitimacy in the eyes of the people. However, the person becomes the basis of institutions and their leaders, who, therefore, receive their own legitimacy and raison d'être from him. Moreover, there is always a host of legal advisers for any dictators who help them create a legal framework for justifying their powers. This is compared to Machiavelli's providence that man is sent by destiny to establish enduring institutions. In fact, without endurance, instability could destroy the institutions. The Machiavellian vision endows this unique, lonely, and genius individual with a mission to provide the state with institutions and laws intended to survive through his drive and life, even after the individual's death. The consolidation of power is necessary to enforce order and maintain the peace of a state. People need unity, and therefore, one person must have all the power: sovereignty is not without unity. Only singular decision-making can guarantee harmony among the parts of the political body. From an ideological standpoint, scholars of the 18th century enlightened absolutism justified this type of power, arguing that it was necessary to achieve much-needed social reforms. In practice, the individual who incarnates personal power does not care alone. On the contrary, he governs with the support of numerous faithful followers who make sure that his orders are respected, reinforced, and executed. Loyalty to the chief is reinforced through financial incentives.

On the other hand, postcolonial African leaders utilized military power to claim legitimacy, gain recognition and credibility, and, worse, intimidate and deter political malcontents. When social and national conflicts arise, military solutions are often favored by the political elite. As an institution, the military has been presented as a modernizing factor for countries in transition from traditional to modern stages of political and economic development. Unfortunately, in Africa, militarization has become a door of opportunity for political elites to seize and maintain their power.

Thus, China's presence in Africa is challenging the universal premise of good governance and democracy promoted by the United States.

However, the China-Africa partnership is less likely to threaten China-US relations because these two economic and military powers still need and fear each other more than China would need or fear Africa. Although China-Africa relations may lead the US to readjust its role in Africa, it is unlikely that such relations will displace US hegemony.

After the Cold War era, the United States of America emerged as the sole superpower in the world, in general, and the western hemisphere, in particular. However, it is increasingly becoming a fact that the most dangerous scenario the United States might face in this century is the one in which China becomes a potential superpower in Northeast Asia.

Two major factors are making China a superpower: its expanding economy and its growing military capabilities. Since the start of economic reforms in 1978, the Chinese economy has impressively expanded and grown. Given the size of its population and the rising productivity of its workers, China may one day regain its historic position as the world's largest economy. Some experts have predicted that China's economy could overtake that of the United States as early as 2015, but that remains to be seen. China's economic growth comes with the potential to sustain a large and expanding military effort. In fact, China's speed on arms and military equipment has grown at an impressive pace. In addition, its arsenal of nuclear weapons constitutes another value-added element to China's military power and its quest for regional hegemony. This is so true that since 2006, the Pentagon recognized that of the major and emerging powers, China has the greatest potential to compete militarily with the United States. As a matter of fact, the United States has been taking China's military potential seriously to the point where its growing counterforce power reflects its concerns about China's emergence as a peer competitor.

It is now clear that economic and military growth is transforming China into an Asiatic superpower. Most analysts point out that Beijing is preparing to take the lead in the future dominance of East Asia. Should this materialize, China's unstated goal to replace the United States as the chief influence in East Asia could materialize. From a comparative perspective, we should recall that the external expansion of the United Kingdom and France, Germany, Japan, the Soviet Union, and the United States coincided with phases of intense industrialized and economic development. As a rising power, China may have legitimate aspirations to expand and seek its place in the international arena, just like Germany did at the turn of the twentieth century or the United States in the late nineteenth and early twentieth centuries. China may eventually seek to regain its place as the preponderant force in Asia and the hub of a Sino-centric Asia international system.

As China's economy booms and its armed forces grow, the United States will seek to curb Chinese military power and influence. Therefore, China is a serious threat to the U.S. hegemony, and as such, it may attempt to use forces preemptively to destroy a rising power before it can achieve its full potential.

What most worries the United States is the unpredictable nature of China's political system and, thus, its use of its potential hegemonic power, which creates potential insecurity in the region and in the international community. China's rising power threatens the United States' preponderance in East Asia, as well as its economic and military hegemony.

Despite its impressive military and economic growth, China would not measure up to the United States. China's rising power could be limited. Economically, China's major enemies are on its own turf. Air and water pollution and land degradation are creating global environmental problems that can eventually substantially slow Chinese economic growth. In fact, pollution poses a risk to public health and social stability, which eventually will hurt Chinese productivity and its international reputation. Furthermore, China needs to define itself politically as a potential economic hegemony: as a modern democracy or a communist empire.

On the other hand, its military power may not measure up to the United States in the long run, despite the nuclear arsenal. Some experts argue that after the Cold War ended, China showed little interest in modernizing its nuclear weapons, and the small strategic force that China built and deployed in the 1970s and early 1980s is essentially the same one it has today. Meanwhile, the United States has steadily improved its counterforce capabilities, including nuclear weapons most effective at targeting the enemy's nuclear arsenal. Consequently, the United States seems to possess a clear nuclear supremacy over China, making any military confrontation between both uneven.

Despite serious factors constantly pointing out a possible armed conflict between the United States and China, their relationship would likely remain that of strategic deepening cooperation with inevitably increased open competition. An armed conflict seems to be a reasonably remote option for both powers, for the time being, except in the extreme but plausible scenario of an unexpected crisis involving one of the major trigger factors, such as a Taiwanese declaration of independence from China coupled with an ideological radicalization of Chinese communist leaders, a belligerent US leader inclined to use the current preemptive war doctrine given the American's nuclear supremacy.

A prominent international relational analyst probably has put it better than anyone when he asked whether Washington can adjust and adapt to a world in which others have moved up and whether the U.S. can respond to shifts in economic requirements and political power. He argued that the world would not stay unipolar for decades, and then suddenly, one afternoon, it would become multipolar. The U.S. will most likely lose its status as a hegemon, including in Africa. The distribution of power is shifting and moving away from U.S. dominance, but the analyst thinks that the world is changing, but it is going in the United States' way because the countries that are rising are embracing American ideas and ideals, and the rising partnership between China and Africa will do little to change that.

6. Conclusion and Recommendations

Chinese presence in Africa has evolved from merely ideological interest. The presence of China on the continent of Africa is noticeable. We tried to analyze whether such partnerships hurt or help Africa's development. From a US-China rivalry perspective, China's appeal to African leaders appeared to be driven by political and economic motivations. Unlike the usual constraints that come with aid from Europe and the US, China's economic package is offered to African leaders with no political strings attached.

Regardless of any global dynamics between China and the West, and particularly the United States, the best interest of the African people must be at the center of African leaders when positioning their countries on one side or another. The quest for full humanity, which has been at the center of the African struggle since the experience of enslavement, must be the raison d'être of any partnership between Africa and its external partners, including China. This quest is legitimate because, like any other people, Africans aspire to be recognized as fully human and invested with the same rights and dignity. Africans have been denied their humanity, alienated, and remolded to fit in certain strategically designed ideological, political, military, or economic schemes. However, dehumanization should not and cannot define African destiny. African people must continue to rise from the valley of the exploited to claim their destiny. As Ibrahim (2022) pointed out, "Africans need to look forward, not backward, and take responsibility for and ownership of our destiny. That means continuing to fight for better governance, the rule of law, and decent leadership... Africa needs allies in its development, not accomplices to its plunder."

The best metric for measuring the success of the Africa-China partnership should not be to replace China's hegemonic Western rivals but to the well-being of the African people, as measured by the restoration of their full humanity and dignity.

REFERENCES

Broadman, H. *China and India Go to Africa.* In Foreign Affairs. March/April 2008.

Cheng, Joseph Yu-Shek. 2016. *China's Foreign Policy: Challenges and Prospects.* Singapore: World Scientific Publishing.

Economy, E. *"The Great Leap Backward?"* Foreign Affairs, September/October 2007.

Friedberg, A., *"The Future of U.S. –China Relations: Is Conflict Inevitable?"* International Security, fall 2005.

Kankwenda, M. & Cie. 2004. *Dynamiques des conflits et crises de développement en Afrique Centrale,* Paris : Editions Duboiris.

Lieber, K. and Press, D., *"Supremacy Complex. Why America's growing nuclear supremacy may make war with China more likely".* The Atlantic, July/August 2007.

Machiavelli, Nicolo. 1916. *The Prince.* The Macmillan Company.

National Security Strategy of the United States of America. Washington DC: Office of the President, November 2017.

Pham. J. Peter. *China's African strategy and its implications for US interests.* In American Foreign Policy Interests. June 2006, Vol.28 Issue 3.

Pillsbury, Michael. 2015. *The 100-Year Marathon: China's Soviet Strategy to Replace America as Global Superpower.* New York: St Martin's Griffin.

Terril, R, *"What Does China Want"* Wilson Quarterly, autumn 2005.

www.allAfricam.com

www.lefigaro.com

www.lepotentiel.com

www.lemondediplomatique.com

www.digitalarchive.wilsoncenter.org

Yu, George T. *Africa in Chinese foreign policy.* In Asian Survey. August 88, Vol. 28 Issue 8.

Zakaria, F. 2008. *The Post-American World.* W.W. Norton & Company, Inc.

CHAPTER II

A REVIEW OF THE POLITICAL ECONOMY OF AFRICA-CHINA TRADE RELATIONS

by

John M. Ulimwengu, PhD

1. Introduction

The political economy of Africa-China trade relations has emerged as a pivotal area of study due to the profound implications these interactions have on global trade, economic development, and geopolitical dynamics. The political economy of Africa-China trade relations is a multifaceted and dynamic field that reflects broader shifts in the global economic landscape. It encompasses a complex interplay of economic growth, development strategy, and geopolitical interests that shape the contemporary relationship between Africa and China.

Over the past few decades, the relationship between Africa and China has undergone significant transformation, evolving from minimal engagement to a comprehensive strategic partnership characterized by extensive trade, investment, and infrastructure development projects. This relationship has been driven by China's demand for natural resources to fuel its economic growth and Africa's need for infrastructure development and direct foreign investment to spur its economic development and diversification efforts.

As a result, trade volumes between Africa and China have seen remarkable growth, making China Africa's largest trading partner. This surge is attributed to China's aggressive investment in African infrastructure, mining, and oil sectors, alongside its participation in various sectors of Africa's economy, including agriculture, manufacturing, and technology. For instance, Mbuya and Mphahlele

(2021) highlight China's significant role in Africa's infrastructure development, emphasizing the impact of these projects on the continent. Ergano and Rao (2019) further analyze the nature and perspectives of Sino-Africa economic relations, discussing the benefits and challenges, including governance and environmental concerns.

The engagement has been mutual, with African countries benefiting from improved infrastructure, job creation, and access to new technologies, while China gains access to critical raw materials and new markets for its goods. However, this relationship has also attracted scrutiny and debate. Critics argue about the sustainability of debt levels, the quality of infrastructure projects, and the broader implications for domestic industries and environmental sustainability in African countries.

The purpose of this paper is to meticulously examine the nature, drivers, challenges, and implications of Africa-China trade relations within the broader context of the global political economy. This analysis is critical, given the rapid expansion of Sino-African relations and their consequential impact on the international economic landscape, regional development patterns, and global power dynamics. By delving into the multifaceted dimensions of this relationship, the paper aims to unravel the complex interplay between economic strategies, geopolitical interests, and development policies that underpin the burgeoning partnership between Africa and China.

The scope of this investigation extends to assessing the strategic motivations behind China's engagement with Africa, including access to natural resources, market expansion, and the projection of its geopolitical influence. Simultaneously, it explores the African perspective, seeking to understand the continent's objectives in diversifying its economic partners, attracting foreign investment, and securing infrastructure development. Through this dual lens, the paper will address the critical challenges that have emerged, such as the sustainability of debt, the environmental impact of infrastructure projects, and the socio-economic consequences of these trade relations on local industries and communities.

Furthermore, the paper will evaluate the broader implications of these trade relations on global economic governance, the redistribution of global economic power, and the potential reshaping of international trade norms and policies. By integrating theoretical frameworks with empirical data, this study aims to provide a comprehensive analysis of the political economy of Africa-China trade relations, contributing valuable insights to policymakers, scholars, and stakeholders engaged in or affected by these interactions.

2. Theoretical framework

The political economy of Africa-China trade relations is a rich field for analysis, intersecting with several theoretical frameworks that can illuminate the motivations, benefits, and consequences of this burgeoning relationship. At the core, political economy theories provide tools for understanding how economic policies and practices are influenced by and, in turn, influence political structures, power dynamics, and historical contexts. In the case of Africa-China relations, these theories help elucidate the strategic economic interests and political motivations driving both parties, the distribution of benefits and challenges arising from their interactions, and the broader implications for the global economic order.

Dependency theory offers a critical lens through which to examine Africa-China trade relations, positing that the economic conditions of poorer nations are largely shaped by their relationships with wealthier countries. Within this framework, concerns are raised about the potential for new forms of dependency to emerge from Africa's engagement with China, particularly through resource extraction and debt-financed infrastructure projects. Critics argue that such dynamics may perpetuate unequal economic structures, wherein Africa supplies raw materials while importing manufactured goods, thus hindering the continent's industrialization and sustaining a cycle of dependency (Mbatu & Otiso, 2012). However, the relationship also challenges traditional dependency theory narratives by offering African countries alternatives to Western economic models and sources of capital, suggesting a more complex interdependency.

World-systems theory expands on dependency theory by analyzing the global economy as a complex system characterized by core, semi-peripheral, and peripheral countries. China's rise to core status and its engagement with peripheral African nations can be seen as an attempt to reconfigure global trade networks, where Africa-China trade relations serve to diversify the economic interactions of African countries beyond their traditional Western partners (Ergano & Rao, 2019). This diversification is posited as a way for African countries to enhance their leverage in the global economy, potentially shifting some dynamics of the world system.

Realist theories in international relations emphasize the role of state power and security interests in shaping economic policies, suggesting that China's engagement with Africa is driven by strategic considerations, including access to resources and geopolitical influence. From this perspective, trade and investment are tools for China to expand its global influence and secure its economic interests (Antwi-Boateng, 2017).

Conversely, liberal theories highlight the potential for economic interdependence to foster peace and cooperation between nations. In the context of Africa-China relations, this theory suggests that increased trade and investment can lead to mutually beneficial outcomes, enhancing economic growth and development in African countries while securing resources and markets for China. This perspective underlines the importance of institutions like FOCAC in facilitating these positive-sum interactions.

Structuralist perspectives focus on how global economic structures and institutions shape the interactions between countries, with particular attention to how these dynamics affect development outcomes. In the analysis of Africa-China trade relations, structuralist theories draw attention to the ways in which global trade rules, financial systems, and development policies influence the nature and impact of Sino-African economic ties. These theories question whether existing global economic institutions adequately accommodate the interests of developing countries or if new structures, possibly influenced by emerging powers like China, are needed to ensure more equitable development outcomes (Ergano & Rao, 2019).

The political economy analysis of Africa-China trade relations, through the lens of these theories, reveals a multifaceted relationship shaped by historical legacies, economic imperatives, and strategic interests. While offering significant opportunities for economic development and diversification in Africa, this relationship also poses challenges related to dependency, equity, and sustainability. The evolving nature of these ties underscores the need for careful negotiation and policy formulation to maximize benefits and mitigate risks for African countries.

This theoretical framework provides a nuanced understanding of the complex dynamics at play in Africa-China trade relations, drawing on a range of political economy theories to highlight the intricate interplay of economic and political factors.

Chinese aid, with its focus on infrastructure and economic projects, is tied to the use of Chinese goods and services and avoids the 'good governance' conditionality typical of Western aid. The impact of such aid varies by sector and is contingent upon the recipient's institutional and structural conditions. For instance, Chinese monetary aid is connected to physical infrastructure projects and shows positive correlations with economic development (McCormick, 2008; Xu, Zhang, & Sun, 2019). China's non-interventionist and multipolar strategy offers an attractive alternative to conditional Western aid for African elites, supporting a range of initiatives from infrastructure to debt cancellation. However, it has been criticized for reinforcing asymmetrical relationships and supporting authoritarian regimes, potentially leading to mixed economic consequences and possibly harmful political outcomes (Tull, 2006).

The influence of Chinese aid models on traditional donors is significant but not universal. China's aid model is distinct in its explicit links between aid and economic activity and is executed through specific projects rather than broader programs (Deyassa, 2019). Chinese development projects have sometimes been seen as self-serving and potentially conflict-provoking. However, the presence of Chinese aid projects can also foster a positive view of Chinese engagement among the local population, depending on the types of aid and recipients' socioeconomic status (Xu & Zhang, 2020).

Chinese aid can serve as a complement to Western aid by filling gaps in physical infrastructure and productive sectors left by Western donors' shift towards capacity building and good governance. However, the effectiveness of both models can be hindered by factors such as insufficient state capacity or poor governance, leading to similar challenges in achieving sustainable development (Broich, Szirmai, & Adedokun, 2019). There are differences in norms and the intended outcomes of Chinese and Western aid models. For instance, while both aim at stability, Chinese aid is associated with the acceptance of authoritarian norms, whereas Western projects, like those of the World Bank, reinforce democratic values (Gehring, Kaplan, & Wong, 2019).

In summary, both Chinese and Western aid models present unique opportunities and challenges. The impact of these aid models is complex and is influenced by a myriad of factors, including the governance capacity of recipient countries, the nature of the aid provided, and the conditions attached to the aid.

3. Historical context and evolution

The historical evolution of Africa-China economic ties encapsulates a trajectory from sporadic initial contacts to a comprehensive strategic partnership that has become a cornerstone of the global political economy. This journey reflects broader shifts in international relations, economic paradigms, and geopolitical strategies, marking a significant departure from traditional North-South dynamics to a more diversified and multipolar global landscape.

The genesis of Africa-China relations can be traced back to ancient times, with the Silk Road facilitating early indirect contacts between Chinese and African civilizations. However, it was not until the mid-20th century that these interactions began to formalize, coinciding with the decolonization of Africa and the establishment of the People's Republic of China. In the 1950s and 1960s, as newly independent African nations sought international partnerships to navigate the Cold War landscape, China emerged as a supportive ally, offering political solidarity and aid to Africa's anti-colonial movements and nascent states. This period laid the foundational ethos of solidarity, with China positioning itself as a fellow developing country offering an alternative to the influence of Western powers and the Soviet Union.

By the 1970s and 1980s, the relationship began to shift towards economic cooperation, albeit modestly, with China engaging in infrastructure projects, agricultural development, and the exchange of technical expertise in several African countries. These efforts were emblematic of China's South-South cooperation approach, aiming to foster mutual development while consolidating diplomatic ties. Despite these early economic engagements, trade volumes remained relatively low, and China's presence in Africa was primarily characterized by its political and ideological support for liberation movements and newly independent states.

The turn of the 21st century marked a significant escalation in Africa-China economic ties, driven by China's booming economy and its insatiable demand for natural resources to fuel its industrialization and urbanization. Concurrently, African countries sought investment and development partners to address their infrastructure deficits, stimulate economic growth, and reduce poverty. The Forum on China-Africa Cooperation (FOCAC), established in 2000, became a pivotal mechanism for deepening this relationship, providing a structured platform for dialogue, trade agreements, and investment commitments.

China's engagement strategy has been multifaceted, encompassing state-led investments, private-sector ventures, and a broad spectrum of aid initiatives. Infrastructure projects, including roads, railways, ports, and telecommunications networks, have been particularly prominent, funded through concessional loans and, in some cases, resource-backed financing arrangements. Trade between Africa and China has surged, with China surpassing the United States and European countries to become Africa's largest trading partner. This economic engagement is not limited to resource extraction; it also includes manufacturing, services, and technology, reflecting a diversification of mutual interests.

The contemporary phase of Africa-China relations is characterized by its strategic depth, economic breadth, and increasing complexity. China's Belt and Road Initiative (BRI) has further intensified these ties, with several African countries participating in the ambitious global infrastructure and connectivity project. While the economic benefits of this partnership are tangible, including infrastructure development and increased trade, it has also raised concerns regarding debt sustainability, environmental impact, and the long-term implications for local industries and employment.

Critics argue that the relationship risks entrenching a neo-colonial pattern of resource extraction and economic dependency. However, proponents highlight the principles of mutual respect and win-win cooperation that purportedly underpin China's approach to its engagement with Africa. Moreover, the dynamic nature of this partnership has prompted a reevaluation of global economic governance, challenging existing norms and institutions.

The evolution of Africa-China economic ties from initial contacts to a strategic partnership encapsulates a broader narrative of shifting global power dynamics and the search for alternative development paradigms. As this relationship continues to evolve, it will undoubtedly shape the contours of the global political economy, offering both opportunities and challenges for Africa, China, and the world at large.

4. Brief on economic impacts

The economic impacts of Africa-China trade relations have been profound, reshaping trade flows, altering the balance of trade, and raising critical discussions on market access and trade imbalances. These dynamics underscore the complex nature of the economic engagement between Africa and China, reflecting both the opportunities and challenges inherent in their rapidly evolving relationship.

Trade between Africa and China has experienced exponential growth, with China becoming Africa's largest trade partner. This surge in trade has been driven by China's demand for African natural resources, including oil, minerals, and metals, which support China's industrial growth. Conversely, Africa imports a wide range of manufactured goods from China, from machinery and electronics to textiles and consumer goods. While this trade has contributed significantly to economic growth and development in African countries, it has also led to debates on the balance of trade. Many African countries run trade deficits with China, importing more than they export, raising concerns about the sustainability of these trade patterns and the potential for increased indebtedness (Ergano & Rao, 2019).

Figure 1: China-Africa trade

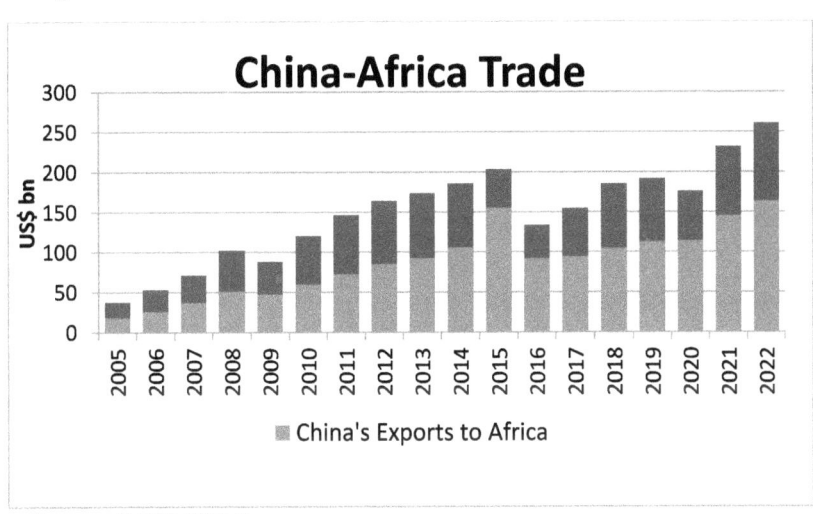

Source: CARI (2024)

As shown in Figure 1, over the past two decades, China-Africa bilateral trade has shown a consistent upward trajectory, reflecting the deepening economic ties between the vast continent and the global powerhouse. The trade relationship between China and Africa can be explained by a number of factors. China's economic growth has been a major driver of increased demand for African exports, especially raw materials and natural resources, supporting higher trade volumes (Zafar, 2007; Besada, Wang, & Whalley, 2008). The commodities boom, driven in part by China's industrialization, led to an increase in prices for oil and metals from Africa, which benefitted African economies but also made them vulnerable to price shocks (Jenkins & Edwards, 2006). The real appreciation of most African currencies relative to the Chinese yuan favored China's exports to Africa but did not significantly impact imports from Africa, contributing to trade imbalances (Jeanneney & Hua, 2015). However, trade between the two-faced challenges, notably due to weak commodity prices since 2014, which significantly impacted the value of African exports to China (CARI, 2024). This downturn was further exacerbated by the global supply chain disruption caused by the COVID-19 pandemic, illustrating the vulnerability of this trade relationship to external shocks. Including data from North Africa, our analysis provides a comprehensive view of the trade dynamics.

In 2020, the pandemic's impact was starkly visible as the value of China-Africa trade decreased to US$176 billion, down from US$192 billion the previous year. This decline underscored the fragility of international trade networks amidst global crises. However, demonstrating the resilience and robustness of the China-Africa economic relationship, trade value impressively rebounded to US$251 billion in 2021. This recovery signals not only the adaptability of these economies but also suggests a strengthening of trade ties in the post-pandemic world.

South Africa emerged as the leading African exporter to China in 2021, with Angola and the Democratic Republic of Congo also playing significant roles in the trade landscape. These countries, rich in natural resources, highlight the commodity-dependent nature of African exports, which, while profitable, also exposes these economies to global price fluctuations and economic volatility.

On the import side, Nigeria retained its position as the largest African consumer of Chinese goods, followed by South Africa and Egypt. This reflects China's strategic investment in African infrastructure, technology, and consumer markets, further intertwining their economic fortunes.

The significance of these trade patterns extends beyond mere numbers. For African economies, the reliance on commodity exports to China presents both opportunities and challenges. While it drives economic growth and generates revenue, it also underscores the need for diversification to mitigate the risks associated with commodity price volatility. For China, the sustained investment in Africa not only secures necessary raw materials but also opens up emerging consumer markets, supporting its long-term economic objectives.

Moreover, the quick recovery of trade volumes post-pandemic highlights the potential for further growth and collaboration, suggesting an increasingly interdependent relationship. As these nations navigate the post-COVID economic landscape, understanding the nuances of this trade dynamic becomes crucial for policymakers, businesses, and researchers alike.

This analysis, grounded in the latest available data, sheds light on the evolving nature of China-Africa trade relations, offering insights into its complexities and the strategic considerations at play. As the global economy continues to recover and adapt, the resilience and growth of China-Africa trade will undoubtedly have significant implications for the future of international trade and economic development.

The debate on trade imbalances is central to discussions on the economic impacts of Africa-China relations. Critics argue that the current trade patterns perpetuate a colonial-style extraction model, where Africa exports raw materials, and imports finished goods, hindering industrialization and value addition on the continent. These imbalances raise questions about the equitable distribution of benefits from trade and the long-term sustainability of these economic ties.

Since 2003, Chinese foreign direct investment (FDI) into Africa, officially termed "Overseas Foreign Direct Investment" (OFDI) in Chinese government reports, has experienced a remarkable upward trajectory. Beginning at a modest US$75 million in 2003, these investments soared to an impressive US$5 billion by 2021. A notable spike occurred in 2008, when investment peaked at US$5.5 billion, largely driven by the Industrial and Commercial Bank of China's (ICBC) strategic acquisition of a 20% stake in Standard Bank of South Africa, one of the continent's largest banking groups (CARI, 2024).

The accompanying Figure 2 vividly illustrates that starting in 2013, Chinese FDI flows into Africa consistently outpaced those from the United States, which, in contrast, have shown a general decline since 2010. This shift underscores China's growing economic influence in Africa compared to traditional Western investors.

Figure 2: Chinese FDI vs. US FDI to Africa, Flow

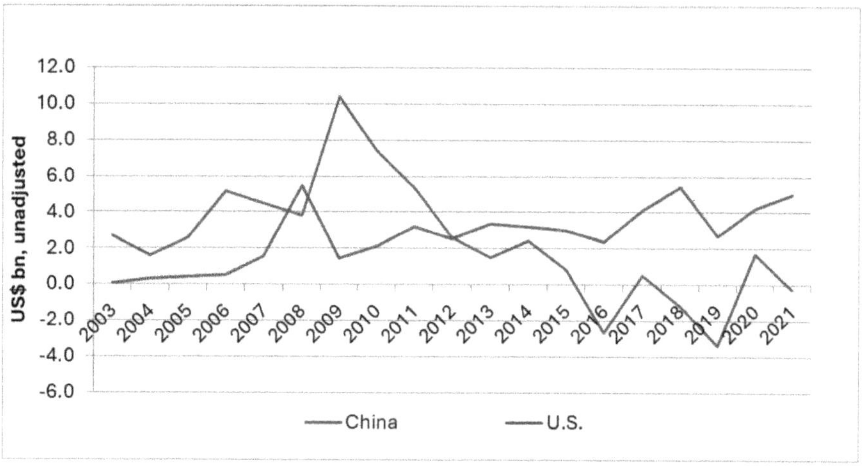

Source: CARI (2024).

In 2021, the primary beneficiaries of Chinese FDI were the Democratic Republic of Congo, Zambia, Guinea, South Africa, and Kenya, highlighting a diverse range of investment destinations across the continent. These countries have attracted significant Chinese interest, reflecting China's strategic focus on Africa's rich natural resources and burgeoning markets.

Conversely, American investment has been concentrated in South Africa, Egypt, Nigeria, Ethiopia, and the Republic of the Congo. It's important to note, however, that the U.S. government has withheld FDI data for nine African nations, including the Democratic Republic of Congo, citing the need to protect the commercial confidentiality of individual companies' operations.

This pattern of investment reveals much about the evolving landscape of international relations and economic priorities in Africa.

While China's investment strategy appears to be broad and encompassing a wide array of sectors and countries, U.S. investments are more selective, with an emphasis on traditional economic powerhouses and strategic partners in the continent.

In 2021, Chinese engineering and construction firms generated an impressive US$37 billion in gross annual revenues from their projects across Africa. This figure represents 24.0% of their global revenues, marking a notable shift from 2010—the peak year—when Africa's share, including Libya, soared to 38.9%. The decline to the 2021 level reflects a broader trend of diversification and global market dynamics affecting Chinese overseas construction ventures.

The lion's share of these revenues was concentrated in five key African nations: Nigeria, Algeria, Kenya, Angola, and the Democratic Republic of Congo. Together, these countries contributed to 39% of the total gross annual revenues from Chinese construction projects on the continent in 2021. This statistic underscores the significant role that these nations play in China's construction industry footprint in Africa.

However, it's worth noting that 2021 marked the sixth year of consecutive decline in the gross annual revenues of Chinese construction companies operating in Africa. This trend suggests a complex interplay of factors, including market saturation, increased competition, geopolitical shifts, and perhaps adjustments in China's foreign investment strategies. Despite the downturn, the enduring presence of Chinese construction firms in Africa highlights their long-term commitment to the continent's infrastructure development. The focus on Nigeria, Algeria, Kenya, Angola, and the Democratic Republic of Congo also illustrates strategic interests in regions with robust economic potentials and significant infrastructure needs.

As the global economic landscape continues to evolve, the dynamics of Chinese construction activities in Africa will remain a critical area of interest. Observing how these companies adapt to changing market conditions and geopolitical environments will provide valuable insights into the future of Africa's infrastructure landscape and China's role within it.

Finally, market access remains a critical issue in Africa-China trade relations. African countries seek greater access to China's vast market for their agricultural and manufactured goods, aiming to move beyond raw materials exports and diversify their economic base. However, barriers such as tariffs, standards, and regulatory hurdles can limit the ability of African countries to penetrate the Chinese market, affecting the potential benefits of trade. Moreover, the influx of Chinese goods into African markets has sparked debates about the impact on local industries and jobs, with some sectors facing competition from cheaper imports (Mbuya & Mphahlele, 2021).

The economic impacts of Africa-China trade relations highlight the need for a balanced approach that ensures mutual benefits, addresses trade imbalances, and promotes sustainable development. As Africa and China continue to deepen their economic ties, strategies to enhance market access, encourage value addition, and achieve more equitable trade outcomes will be critical.

The economic impacts of Chinese investment in Africa's infrastructure are profound, reshaping the continent's development landscape. This investment has been both lauded for its potential to catalyze economic growth and critiqued for its implications on debt sustainability and environmental integrity. By examining the role of Chinese investment in Africa's infrastructure, we can glean insights into its multifaceted effects on economic growth and development.

Chinese investment has significantly accelerated infrastructure development in Africa, addressing a critical bottleneck to economic growth. Through initiatives like the Belt and Road Initiative (BRI), China has become a leading financier and constructor of a wide array of infrastructure projects across the continent, including roads, railways, ports, and power plants. This investment has the potential to enhance connectivity, reduce transportation and energy costs, and improve access to markets, thereby facilitating trade and investment flows within Africa and with the rest of the world (Mbuya & Mphahlele, 2021).

The direct impact of improved infrastructure on economic growth cannot be overstated. By lowering the cost of doing business and easing the movement of goods and people, Chinese-funded projects have the potential to significantly boost productivity and economic efficiency. Moreover, infrastructure development is pivotal for industrialization, a key priority for many African countries. Access to reliable power and transportation networks is essential for developing manufacturing sectors and moving up the value chain away from dependence on raw material exports (Ergano & Rao, 2019).

Chinese investments often come with the promise of job creation and skill development for local populations. The construction phase of infrastructure projects typically generates a considerable number of jobs, providing both employment and opportunities for skill acquisition among local workers. However, the extent to which these opportunities are realized has been a point of debate, with concerns raised about the preference for Chinese labor and the quality of skills transferred (Antwi-Boateng, 2017).

One of the most contentious aspects of Chinese investment in Africa's infrastructure is the issue of debt sustainability. Many Chinese-funded projects are financed through loans that increase the debt burden of African countries. While these investments are critical for development, there are growing concerns about the ability of countries to manage and repay these debts without compromising their financial stability and sovereignty. The terms of Chinese loans, often shrouded in secrecy, have sparked debates on transparency and the potential for debt distress (Brautigam, 2020).

The environmental and social impacts of infrastructure projects are also significant considerations (Chaudhury, 2022). Critics argue that some Chinese-funded projects have proceeded with inadequate attention to environmental sustainability and social implications, including displacement and land rights issues. The need for stringent environmental assessments and safeguards to protect local ecosystems and communities is increasingly recognized as a critical component of sustainable development (Debongo et al., 2022).

Chinese investment in Africa's infrastructure has undeniably contributed to addressing the continent's critical development needs, offering opportunities for economic growth, industrialization, and job creation. However, these investments also present challenges, including concerns about debt sustainability, environmental and social impacts, and the equitable distribution of benefits. Addressing these challenges requires enhanced cooperation between African countries and China, focusing on sustainable financing models, capacity building, and inclusive development strategies.

5. Potential for factor productivity growth.

The economic relationship between China and Africa, including trade and investment, is a significant aspect of the broader dynamics of global economic interactions and its impact on factor productivity in African countries. This relationship, underpinned by substantial Chinese foreign direct investment (FDI) and an ever-growing trade volume, has the potential to significantly influence the efficiency with which labor and capital are utilized across the African continent. However, the realization of these benefits is deeply intertwined with the quality of domestic institutions within African countries, emphasizing the crucial role of governance in leveraging the China-Africa economic relationship for enhanced factor productivity.

China's engagement with Africa has been marked by a dramatic increase over the past two decades, making it one of the continent's largest trading partners and a key source of investment. Chinese investments, notably in infrastructure, mining, and manufacturing sectors, are often highlighted for their potential to fill critical infrastructure gaps and, by extension, potentially enhance the productivity of African economies. The efficacy of these investments, along with trade, in boosting factor productivity hinges on several dynamics, including the transmission of technology, infrastructure development, and the provision of capital to underfunded sectors (Miao et al., 2020).

The direct and indirect effects of China's economic activities in Africa on factor productivity are multifaceted. Infrastructure investments, for example, can significantly reduce transaction costs and improve market accessibility, thereby enhancing both labor and capital productivity. Moreover, the transfer of technology and management practices through Chinese FDI has the potential to increase the efficiency and competitiveness of African firms. Nonetheless, the extent to which these benefits materialize depends largely on the prevailing institutional landscape within the host countries (Miao et al., 2020).

The interplay between the China-Africa economic relationship and factor productivity is significantly modulated by domestic institutional quality. Strong legal frameworks, regulatory quality, and governance structures are paramount for ensuring that foreign investment and trade lead to sustainable development outcomes rather than exacerbating rent-seeking or environmental degradation. In essence, robust institutions act as a facilitator, amplifying the productivity gains from foreign investment and trade, thereby underscoring the importance of governance in the efficacy of the China-Africa economic relationship (Miao et al., 2020).

The imperative for African countries to harness the potential productivity gains from their economic relations with China necessitates a concerted effort to enhance governance and institutional quality. This involves reforming legal and regulatory frameworks, improving public sector transparency and accountability, and ensuring that investment agreements are equitable and promote sustainable development. Furthermore, strategic engagement with China, targeting sectors with high potential for productivity improvements, is crucial for maximizing the benefits of this relationship for sustainable economic growth and development (Miao et al., 2020).

The economic relationship between China and Africa presents a unique opportunity to drive factor productivity across the continent. While the potential benefits are significant, their realization is contingent upon the quality of domestic institutions within African countries. Enhancing governance and institutional quality emerges as a critical precondition for leveraging the China-Africa economic relationship effectively, highlighting the need for African countries to adopt strategic and informed approaches to engagement with China.

6. Potential for economic growth

The trade relations between China and Africa have significantly evolved over the past few decades, marking a profound impact on the economic growth of African countries. This relationship is part of a broader strategy by China, often referred to as its "Going Out" policy, which seeks to enhance its global presence through foreign investment, trade, and infrastructure development. The impact of China-Africa trade on economic growth can be analyzed through various lenses, including trade balance, investment in infrastructure, technology transfer, and the role of Chinese aid.

China has become Africa's largest trading partner, with trade volumes soaring from approximately $10 billion in the year 2000 to over $200 billion by 2019. This exponential growth in trade has been facilitated by China's demand for raw materials and energy to fuel its own economic boom and, in return, Africa's need for manufactured goods. While this trade dynamic has contributed to economic growth in African countries through increased export revenues, it has also raised concerns about trade imbalances and the sustainability of such growth. African economies have become increasingly reliant on exporting raw materials, which are subject to volatile global prices, while imports from China are mostly manufactured goods, leading to concerns about deindustrialization in some African countries (Sun, 2014).

One of the most significant impacts of China-Africa trade relations on economic growth is the investment in infrastructure. Through initiatives like the Belt and Road Initiative (BRI), China has financed and built a wide range of infrastructure projects in Africa, including roads, railways, ports, and power plants. These investments have been crucial in addressing the infrastructure gap in Africa, which is estimated to be around $130-170 billion annually by the African Development Bank. Improved infrastructure facilitates trade by reducing transportation costs and opening up landlocked countries to international markets, thereby enhancing economic growth (Cheru & Obi, 2010).

Technology transfer and capacity building are critical components of the China-Africa trade relationship. Chinese firms have not only invested in physical infrastructure but have also contributed to skills development and technology transfer in various sectors, including agriculture, telecommunications, and manufacturing. This transfer of knowledge and technology has the potential to enhance productivity and spur innovation in African economies. However, critics argue that the level of technology transfer has been limited and that more needs to be done to ensure that African countries can move up the value chain and diversify their economies (Brautigam, 2009).

Chinese aid to Africa, often linked to trade and investment agreements, has also played a role in economic growth. Unlike traditional Western aid, which is mostly grant-based and tied to conditions related to governance and human rights, Chinese aid is primarily provided in the form of concessional loans tied to infrastructure projects carried out by Chinese companies. This model of aid has been criticized for increasing debt levels in some African countries but has also been praised for its focus on infrastructure development, which is crucial for economic growth (Corkin, 2013).

The China-Africa trade relationship presents both challenges and opportunities for economic growth in Africa. On the one hand, it has provided African countries with much-needed infrastructure, access to affordable manufactured goods, and increased export revenues. On the other hand, concerns about sustainability, debt levels, and the impact on local industries cannot be ignored. For sustainable economic growth, African countries need to leverage their trade relations with China to diversify their economies, enhance value addition, and ensure technology transfer and capacity building.

The impact of China-Africa trade on economic growth is multifaceted, involving complex dynamics that offer both opportunities and challenges. While the trade relationship has undoubtedly contributed to economic growth in Africa through infrastructure development, increased exports, and technology transfer, it is crucial for African countries to adopt policies that will enable them to benefit more sustainably from this relationship. This includes negotiating more balanced trade agreements, promoting local industries, and ensuring that investments are aligned with their long-term development goals.

7. Political and strategic implications

The political and strategic implications of Africa-China trade relations extend far beyond the economic domain, positioning Africa within the broader context of US-China geopolitical rivalry. This dynamic introduces a complex layer of strategic considerations, influencing not only the continent's development trajectory but also the balance of global power.

Africa's strategic importance in the US-China rivalry stems from several factors, including its vast natural resources, growing consumer markets, and geopolitical positioning. China's engagement with Africa, characterized by substantial investments in infrastructure and deepening trade relations, is often viewed through the lens of expanding its global influence, challenging the traditional influence of the United States and other Western powers on the continent (Brautigam, 2020).

China's approach to Africa is multifaceted, involving economic, diplomatic, and military dimensions. Economically, Africa serves as a source of vital raw materials and a market for Chinese goods. Diplomatically, China leverages its relationships with African countries to bolster its international standing, often gaining support in multilateral forums. Militarily, although less pronounced, China's establishment of its first overseas military base in Djibouti signals a growing interest in projecting its power and protecting its interests in the region (Antwi-Boateng, 2017).

The United States has viewed China's expanding footprint in Africa with increasing concern, framing it as a challenge to its interests and to the liberal international order it seeks to uphold. In response, the US has sought to strengthen its economic and security ties with African nations, emphasizing governance, economic development, and counterterrorism. The rivalry has led to a competitive environment where African countries often find themselves navigating between US and Chinese interests, seeking to maximize their benefits from both partnerships (Ergano & Rao, 2019).

The strategic positioning of Africa within the US-China rivalry has implications for African sovereignty and autonomy. African countries face the challenge of leveraging their relationships with these global powers without becoming entangled in their geopolitical contests. The potential for dependency on external powers raises concerns about the continent's ability to pursue its own development agendas and maintain its policy independence (Debongo et al., 2022).

The geopolitical interest of both China and the US in Africa presents opportunities and risks. On the one hand, competition can lead to increased investment and support for development. On the other hand, it risks making African countries pawns in global power plays, with potential negative impacts on governance, peace, and security. The challenge for African nations is to navigate this complex landscape strategically, ensuring that engagement with both powers supports their national interests and development goals (Gavin, 2021).

The political and strategic implications of Africa-China trade relations within the context of the US-China geopolitical rivalry highlight the continent's growing importance on the global stage. African countries have the opportunity to leverage this interest to their advantage, but this requires careful diplomacy and strategic foresight to ensure that their engagement with global powers enhances their sovereignty, development, and security.

The political and strategic implications of Africa-China trade relations are multifaceted, with one of the most contentious issues being accusations of neo-colonialism in Chinese engagement with Africa. These accusations stem from concerns about the asymmetrical nature of trade relations, debt dependency, and the impact of Chinese investments on local industries and sovereignty. Analyzing these accusations requires a nuanced understanding of neo-colonialism within the context of contemporary international relations and economic globalization.

Neo-colonialism, in the context of Africa-China relations, refers to a form of influence that, while not colonial in the traditional sense, still allows one country to exert significant control over the economy and politics of another. Critics argue that China's approach to Africa, characterized by massive loans for infrastructure projects tied to Chinese contractors and companies, resource extraction agreements, and a trade imbalance favoring Chinese manufactured goods, mirrors a neo-colonial pattern. This pattern is said to bind African countries in a dependent relationship, limiting their economic autonomy and perpetuating a cycle of dependency on external powers for development (Antwi-Boateng, 2017).

A central concern is that Chinese loans and investments create a debt trap for African nations, undermining their sovereignty and forcing them into economic and political concessions. The terms of Chinese loans, often not transparent, and the use of Chinese labor and companies in infrastructure projects have raised alarms about the extent to which these arrangements benefit African countries versus serving China's strategic interests. This situation has led to a reevaluation of the sustainability and fairness of such economic partnerships (Brautigam, 2020).

The emphasis on natural resource extraction in China's engagement with Africa has also been critiqued for replicating colonial exploitation patterns. Large-scale mining and extraction projects, often with significant environmental and social impacts, have sparked debates about the long-term benefits for local communities versus the immediate gains for Chinese investors and African elites. This dynamic raises questions about whether such engagements facilitate development or exploit Africa's natural wealth to fuel China's economic growth with minimal reinvestment in local economies (Debongo et al., 2022).

In response to these accusations, Chinese and African officials often highlight the principle of mutual benefit and respect for sovereignty that underpins their cooperation. China positions itself as a development partner, offering much-needed infrastructure and economic opportunities without the political conditions attached to Western aid. Moreover, the concept of African agency is crucial; African leaders and policymakers are active participants in negotiating these relationships, seeking to leverage Chinese engagement for development objectives while navigating the complexities of global geopolitics (Gavin, 2021).

African actors, including state elites and social actors, have demonstrated the ability to negotiate and shape Chinese engagement in significant ways. The extent of African agency is, however, uneven and deeply embedded in the political landscape of each country, suggesting that while agency exists, its exercise is conditioned by the internal political dynamics of the countries involved (Mohan & Lampert, 2013). The growing economic relationship with China has given African countries, including the DRC, better leverage and negotiating power relative to Western countries. However, the level of agency is not uniform; countries like Angola have been able to exercise stronger bargaining power than others like Niger. This indicates that while African countries can assert more agency in their relationships with China, the outcomes can be quite different depending on each country's strategic resources and governance structures (Thiombiano & Zhang, 2020).

The ability of the DRC to benefit optimally from Chinese investments and partnerships depends greatly on the functionality of its state and governance. The question remains as to whether the 'win-win' principle effectively contributes to state-building and long-term development in the DRC (Kabemba, 2016). African governments can strengthen regulations for foreign direct investment (FDI) if they understand the motives behind foreign investments. In the case of Chinese ODI, considering a range of push, pull, intervening, and firm-specific factors could provide African countries, such as the DRC, with better insights into their capacity to manage and mitigate environmental and social impacts of these investments (van der Lugt, 2016).

While China's engagement presents opportunities for investment and infrastructure development, it has also been criticized for reinforcing the role of African countries as primary commodity suppliers with little impact on industrial development or diversification. This situation reflects the complex nature of the Sino-Congolese economic relationship and raises questions about the real benefits of the DRC's development (Marysse & Geenen, 2009).

The accusations of neo-colonialism in Chinese engagement with Africa reflect broader concerns about the nature of international economic relations and the challenges of achieving equitable and sustainable development. While Chinese investments have contributed to infrastructure development and economic growth in some regions, the need for greater transparency, fairness, and environmental and social responsibility remains paramount. Ensuring that Africa-China trade relations are genuinely mutually beneficial requires continuous dialogue, better negotiation strategies by African countries, and a commitment to sustainable development practices.

8. Governance and Human Rights Considerations

China's approach to economic cooperation in Africa, marked by its near absence of governance conditionality, has sparked considerable debate regarding its impact on African governance and human rights conditions. This approach contrasts with Western models of development assistance, which often tie economic aid to governance reforms and human rights improvements. The implications of China's stance are multifaceted, influencing African countries' governance landscapes in diverse and complex ways.

Non-Interference Policy: China's policy of non-interference in the domestic affairs of African countries is a cornerstone of its engagement on the continent. While this policy is welcomed by many African governments as respect for their sovereignty, it has raised concerns among international observers about the potential for reinforcing authoritarian regimes and overlooking governance deficiencies (Brautigam, 2020).

The Chinese model emphasizes economic growth without preconditioning it on democratic governance or human rights standards. Some argue that this model presents an attractive alternative for African leaders, potentially diverting focus from necessary political reforms and undermining efforts to promote transparency, accountability, and human rights (Antwi-Boateng, 2017). The influx of Chinese investments and loans has significant implications for governance structures in Africa. In some instances, these investments have been associated with increased corruption and rent-seeking behaviors, as large-scale projects are negotiated and implemented with limited public scrutiny (Debongo et al., 2022).

Concerns have also been raised about the human rights implications of some Chinese-funded projects in Africa. Reports of labor rights violations, displacement of communities without adequate compensation, and environmental degradation have prompted calls for greater attention to human rights in the context of China-Africa economic relations (Gavin, 2021).

African countries should prioritize enhancing transparency in their dealings with Chinese partners. This includes public disclosure of loan terms, project agreements, and implementation processes to ensure accountability and safeguard against corruption (Ergano & Rao, 2019). Strengthening legal and regulatory frameworks governing foreign investments is crucial. African nations need robust laws and institutions to protect labor rights, community lands, and the environment, ensuring that Chinese investments adhere to international human rights standards (Debongo et al., 2022).

Policies should aim to ensure that the benefits of China-Africa economic cooperation are broadly shared. This includes involving local communities in decision-making processes and ensuring that development projects do not exacerbate social inequalities or undermine human rights (Antwi-Boateng, 2017). Both African governments and Chinese investors should commit to responsible investment practices that respect governance norms and human rights. This can be facilitated through adherence to international guidelines on responsible business conduct, such as those outlined by the OECD (Brautigam, 2020).

The governance and human rights considerations in Africa-China trade relations are critical issues that require careful attention and strategic action from both African governments and Chinese stakeholders. By addressing these considerations, the partnership can contribute more effectively to sustainable development that respects the rights and dignity of African populations.

This analysis underscores the importance of integrating governance and human rights considerations into the economic partnership between Africa and China, ensuring that this relationship promotes not only economic development but also the well-being and dignity of African societies.

9. Sustainability of African debt to China

The sustainability of African debt to China has emerged as a critical issue in the discourse on Africa-China trade relations, reflecting broader concerns about the long-term economic implications of these debts for African countries. As China has become a major lender to Africa, financing infrastructure projects through loans rather than grants, the debt levels of African countries have surged. This section examines the sustainability of this debt, considering factors such as the terms of Chinese loans, debt servicing challenges, and the impact of these debts on Africa's economic autonomy and development prospects.

The Boston University Global Development Policy Center (2023) database estimates that from 2000-2022, 39 Chinese lenders provided 1,243 loans amounting to $170.08 billion to 49 African governments and seven regional institutions (Figure 3). At $170.08 billion, China's estimated total lending from 2000-2022 is 64 percent of the World Bank's $264.15 billion and almost five times the African Development Bank's (AfDB) $36.85 billion in sovereign loans to Africa.

Figure 3: Chinese Loans to Africa, 2000-2022

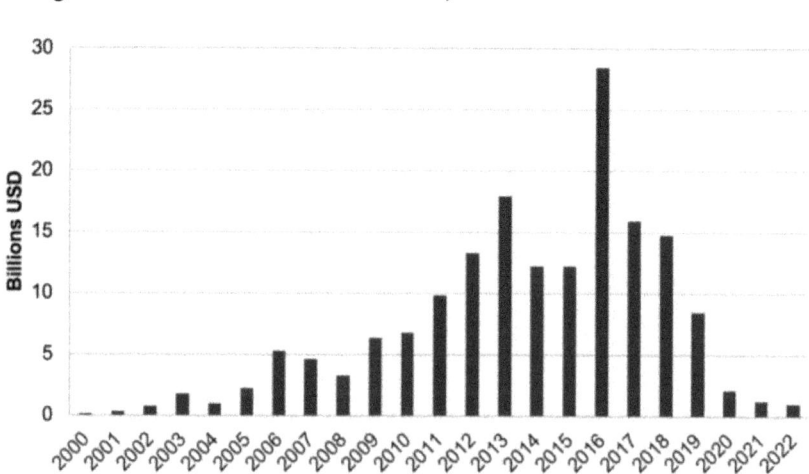

Source: Boston University Global Development Policy Center (2023).

Chinese loans to African countries are often characterized by their concessional nature, with lower interest rates and longer repayment periods compared to market-based loans. However, the volume of these loans, directed primarily towards infrastructure projects, has raised Africa's debt levels significantly. Unlike Western lenders, who typically offer grants or loans with stringent conditions tied to governance and human rights, Chinese financing is generally considered "no-strings-attached," focusing on infrastructure development without direct interference in domestic policies (Brautigam, 2020).

A major concern with the rising debt levels is the ability of African countries to service their debts. The structure of some Chinese loans, requiring repayment in commodities or revenues generated from the financed projects, poses risks if these projects do not generate the expected returns. Moreover, the depreciation of local currencies against the dollar, in which most loans are denominated, exacerbates debt servicing costs, potentially leading to debt distress. The COVID-19 pandemic has further strained the fiscal capacities of many African countries, highlighting the fragility of their debt sustainability (Gort and Brooks, 2023).

The opacity of loan agreements between China and African countries complicates the assessment of debt sustainability. The lack of transparency regarding the terms of these loans, including interest rates, maturity periods, and collateral requirements, poses challenges for debt management and risk assessment. This opacity hinders the involvement of international financial institutions in debt restructuring efforts, as precise liabilities are difficult to ascertain (Acker, Brautigam, & Huang, 2020).

The sustainability of African debt to China is also intertwined with concerns about economic autonomy and the long-term development prospects of African countries. Critics argue that high debt levels could lead to a dependency on Chinese financing, limiting the policy space of African governments and potentially compromising their sovereignty over key assets and sectors. Furthermore, the focus on infrastructure, while crucial for development, needs to be balanced with investments in health, education, and social services to ensure inclusive and sustainable growth (Carmody, 2019).

To mitigate the risks associated with high debt levels, African countries and their Chinese partners are exploring various strategies. Debt relief initiatives, such as the suspension of debt service payments under the G20 Debt Service Suspension Initiative (DSSI), offer temporary relief but do not address long-term sustainability. Restructuring agreements, aiming for longer repayment periods or lower interest rates, and increasing the grant component of financing could alleviate debt burdens. Moreover, improving the transparency of loan agreements and strengthening debt management practices are critical for sustainable debt levels (World Bank, 2021).

The sustainability of African debt to China is a complex issue, reflecting broader challenges in the Africa-China trade and financing relationship. While Chinese loans have contributed to infrastructure development in Africa, concerns about debt sustainability, economic autonomy, and long-term development prospects cannot be overlooked. Addressing these concerns requires a concerted effort from African governments, China, and international stakeholders to ensure that debt financing supports sustainable development goals without compromising the economic stability and autonomy of African countries.

10. Social and environmental considerations

The political and strategic implications of Africa-China trade relations extend beyond economic exchanges, significantly impacting social structures, employment, and local communities across the African continent. These effects are multifaceted, reflecting both the opportunities and challenges presented by China's engagement in Africa. This section explores how the deepening trade relations between Africa and China influence social dynamics, labor markets, and community well-being.

China's investments in African infrastructure, mining, and manufacturing sectors have profound implications for social structures and community dynamics. Infrastructure projects, while crucial for economic development, often necessitate large-scale land acquisitions and the relocation of communities, disrupting traditional livelihoods and social networks. While such projects promise development, the manner in which they are implemented can strain local communities, sometimes leading to social displacement without adequate compensation or resettlement support (Debongo et al., 2022).

On the employment front, Chinese investments have the potential to create numerous jobs, contributing to economic growth and poverty reduction. However, the reality on the ground is complex. There are concerns regarding the quality of employment provided, with reports of low wages, poor working conditions, and limited transfer of skills to local workers. Moreover, the preference for Chinese labor in some projects has sparked tensions, as local populations often feel sidelined in employment opportunities, exacerbating unemployment issues and not fully leveraging the potential for skill development among the local workforce (Brautigam, 2020).

The influx of Chinese goods and services into African markets has a dual impact on local industries. While consumers benefit from access to affordable products, local manufacturers can suffer from the competition, potentially undermining industrialization efforts and stifling the growth of fledgling local enterprises. This dynamic raises questions about the long-term sustainability of such trade patterns and the need for policies that protect and promote local industries, ensuring that trade relations contribute to diversified and resilient economies (Gavin, 2021).

The direct investment by Chinese companies in sectors such as agriculture, mining, and telecommunications has led to improved infrastructure and access to services, positively affecting community well-being and development. However, the environmental impact of some of these projects, including land degradation, pollution, and depletion of natural resources, poses risks to the health and sustainability of local communities. Ensuring that community rights and environmental standards are respected is crucial for mitigating adverse impacts and enhancing the positive outcomes of China-Africa trade relations (Antwi-Boateng, 2017).

The impact of Africa-China trade relations on social structures, employment, and local communities is a testament to the complex nature of international economic engagement. While there are clear benefits in terms of infrastructure development and access to affordable goods, significant challenges remain, particularly concerning employment practices, the sustainability of local industries, and community well-being. Addressing these challenges requires a concerted effort from African governments, Chinese investors, and international stakeholders to ensure that trade and investment policies are aligned with the goals of sustainable development and social equity.

11. Future prospects and policy recommendations

The future prospects of Africa-China trade relations hinge on the ability of both partners to navigate the complexities of their engagement toward more sustainable and mutually beneficial outcomes. Given the dynamic nature of these relations, there is a critical need for strategic policies that address current challenges while capitalizing on future opportunities. This section outlines proposals aimed at enhancing the sustainability and mutual benefits of Africa-China trade relations.

A key proposal for improving Africa-China trade relations is the diversification of trade and investment. African countries should leverage Chinese investments to develop a broader range of sectors beyond natural resources, including manufacturing, technology, and services. This diversification can help African economies move up the value chain, reduce vulnerability to commodity price fluctuations, and create more sustainable growth patterns (Brautigam, 2020).

Enhancing local capacity and participation is crucial for ensuring that Africa-China trade relations lead to inclusive growth. Policies should focus on skill transfer, local employment quotas in Chinese-funded projects, and support for local enterprises to participate in supply chains. Strengthening the capacity of local industries not only fosters economic resilience but also ensures that the benefits of trade and investment are more widely distributed within African societies (Debongo et al., 2022).

To address concerns over debt sustainability, African countries and China should work together to strengthen infrastructure financing mechanisms. This includes exploring alternative financing models such as public-private partnerships (PPPs), concessional loans with more favorable terms, and grants. Ensuring transparency in loan agreements and project bidding processes can also help mitigate the risk of debt distress and enhance the accountability of infrastructure projects (Ergano & Rao, 2019).

Improving environmental and social governance (ESG) standards in Chinese investments is essential for safeguarding African communities and ecosystems. Both African governments and Chinese investors should commit to higher ESG standards, including rigorous environmental impact assessments, community engagement processes, and adherence to international labor standards. Implementing robust ESG frameworks can help ensure that development projects are sustainable and socially responsible (Antwi-Boateng, 2017).

Strengthening bilateral and multilateral collaboration can enhance the governance of Africa-China trade relations. This includes regular dialogues, joint economic forums, and collaboration within international platforms to address global challenges such as climate change, health crises, and economic instability. Through collaborative efforts, Africa and China can develop strategies that align with their long-term development goals and global responsibilities (Gavin, 2021).

The future of Africa-China trade relations presents both challenges and opportunities. By implementing these policy recommendations, Africa and China can foster a partnership that is more equitable, sustainable, and beneficial for both parties. The success of this relationship will depend on the willingness of both sides to engage in open dialogue, mutual respect, and shared commitment to development goals.

12. Policy Implications

The evolving landscape of Africa-China trade relations presents both challenges and opportunities for policymakers in Africa and

China. To navigate these dynamics effectively, targeted policy recommendations are essential. These recommendations should aim to maximize the developmental benefits of trade relations, mitigate risks, and ensure equitable outcomes for both parties. Below are key recommendations for policymakers:

12.1 For African policymakers

Diversify economic partnerships: African countries should diversify their economic partnerships to reduce over-reliance on any single partner. By engaging with a broad array of international partners, African nations can enhance their bargaining power and ensure more balanced trade relations (Gavin, 2021).

Promote value addition: Policymakers should prioritize the development of local industries capable of adding value to raw materials before export. This approach can help shift away from the export of unprocessed resources, fostering industrialization and creating higher-value employment opportunities.

Strengthen negotiation capacities: Investing in the development of robust negotiation capacities is crucial. African nations need skilled negotiators who can ensure that trade agreements and investment projects are structured in ways that maximize benefits for the continent (Ergano & Rao, 2019).

Enhance regulatory frameworks: Strengthening regulatory frameworks to govern foreign investments, including environmental protections, labor laws, and corporate governance standards, is essential for safeguarding African interests and promoting sustainable development (Debongo et al., 2022).

12.2 For Chinese policymakers

Ensure sustainable investment practices: Chinese policymakers and investors should commit to sustainable investment practices that respect environmental standards and community rights. This includes conducting thorough environmental impact assessments and engaging with local communities throughout the project lifecycle (Antwi-Boateng, 2017).

Promote local employment and capacity building: Chinese companies operating in Africa should prioritize hiring local workers and investing in capacity building. Providing training and skill development opportunities can help ensure that investments contribute to long-term economic development in African countries.

Enhance transparency: Increasing the transparency of loan agreements, investment projects, and trade deals is vital. Clear and accessible information about the terms of engagement can help build trust and ensure that all stakeholders understand the benefits and obligations involved (Ergano & Rao, 2019).

Foster equitable trade relations: Chinese policymakers should work towards more equitable trade relations by addressing trade imbalances. This includes opening Chinese markets to a wider range of African products, particularly in sectors where Africa can offer competitive advantages (Gavin, 2021).

Addressing the challenges and leveraging the opportunities in Africa-China trade relations require concerted efforts from both African and Chinese policymakers. By implementing these recommendations, both parties can work towards a more balanced and mutually beneficial partnership. The success of these trade relations will depend on the commitment to principles of equity, sustainability, and shared prosperity.

13. Conclusion

The political economy of Africa-China trade relations encompasses a complex and multifaceted relationship that has evolved significantly over the past few decades. This paper has provided a comprehensive analysis of the economic, political, and strategic dimensions of the relationship between Africa and China, highlighting both the opportunities and challenges that arise from this dynamic engagement. As we conclude, it is imperative to summarize the key findings from our analysis and identify areas for further research and the necessity for ongoing monitoring of this evolving economic partnership.

Africa-China trade relations have led to significant economic impacts across the African continent, including accelerated infrastructure development and increased trade flows. While these developments have the potential to catalyze economic growth and development, concerns regarding debt sustainability, trade imbalances, and the impact on local industries have been raised. The strategic positioning of Africa within the US-China geopolitical rivalry has underscored the continent's growing importance on the global stage. Accusations of neo-colonialism in Chinese engagement with Africa highlight the complexities of navigating international economic relations and ensuring equitable outcomes.

Chinese investments have influenced social structures, employment patterns, and local communities in Africa. While there are opportunities for job creation and community development, issues related to labor practices, environmental sustainability, and the displacement of local communities present significant challenges. Enhancing the sustainability and mutual benefits of Africa-China trade relations requires strategic policies that address current challenges while leveraging future opportunities. Recommendations for African and Chinese policymakers include diversifying trade, promoting local capacity, ensuring sustainable investment practices, and fostering equitable trade relations.

Further research is needed to assess the long-term economic outcomes of Chinese investments in Africa, particularly in terms of industrialization, value addition, and technological transfer. The socio-political implications of Africa-China relations, including the impact on governance structures, civil society engagement, and the promotion of human rights, warrant deeper investigation.

Given the environmental concerns associated with some Chinese-funded projects, studies focusing on the implementation of environmental safeguards and the promotion of green development practices are crucial. The issue of debt sustainability remains a critical area for research, necessitating detailed analyses of loan agreements, debt management strategies, and the implications of debt distress.

The role of cultural and educational exchanges in shaping Africa-China relations represents an underexplored area that could provide insights into the soft power dimensions of the partnership. The evolving nature of the Africa-China economic partnership necessitates continued monitoring and analysis. As global economic and political landscapes shift, the relationship between Africa and China will undoubtedly undergo further transformations. Monitoring these developments is essential for identifying emerging trends, understanding the implications of new policies, and ensuring that the partnership remains beneficial to both parties.

In conclusion, the political economy of Africa-China trade relations offers a rich field of study with significant implications for both continents. By addressing the identified challenges and capitalizing on the opportunities presented by this partnership, Africa and China can work towards a future characterized by shared prosperity and sustainable development.

REFERENCES

Acker, Kevin, Deborah Brautigam, and Yufan Huang (2020). *Debt Relief with Chinese Characteristics*. Working Paper No. 2020/39. China Africa Research Initiative, School of Advanced International Studies, Johns Hopkins University, Washington, DC. https://papers.ssrn.com/sol3/papers.cfm?abstract_id=3745021

Antwi-Boateng, O. (2017). *New World Order Neo-Colonialism: A Contextual Comparison of Contemporary China and European Colonization in Africa*. The Journal of Pan-African Studies. vol.10, no.2. https://www.jpanafrican.org/docs/vol10no2/10.2-13-Antwi-Boateng.pdf

Boston University Global Development Policy Center (2023). *Chinese Loans to Africa Database*. Retrieved from http://bu.edu/gdp/chinese-loans-to-africa-database.

Brautigam, D. (2009). *The Dragon's Gift: The Real Story of China in Africa*. Oxford University Press.

Brautigam, D. (2020). *A critical look at Chinese 'debt-trap diplomacy': the rise of a meme*, Area Development and Policy, 5:1,1-14,https://www.tandfonline.com/doi/full/10.1080/23792949.2019.1689828

Broich, T., Szirmai, A., & Adedokun, A. (2019). *Chinese and Western Development Approaches in Africa: Implications for the SDGs*. Sustainable Development Goals Series.

CARI (China-Africa Research Initiative) (2024). *China-Africa Trade*. John Hopkins University. https://www.sais-cari.org/data-china-africa-trade

Carmody, P. (2019). *The New Scramble for Africa*. The Economist. https://www.economist.com/leaders/2019/03/07/the-new-scramble-for-africa.

Chaudhury, D. R. (2022). *Rising environmental costs of Chinese Investments in Africa*. The Economic Times. https://economictimes.indiatimes.com/news/international/world-news/rising-environmental-costs-of-chinese-investments-in-africa/articleshow/89467384.cms?from=mdr

Cheru, F., & Obi, C. (2010). *The Rise of China and India in Africa: Challenges, Opportunities and Critical Interventions*. Zed Books.

Corkin, L. (2013). *China's Emerging Strategy in International Development: The African Angle*. Routledge.

Debongo Devincy Yanne Sylvaire, Wu Hua Qing, Chang He Ran, Diane Laure Kassai, Nzabana Vincent, Djossouvi Adjoa Candide Douce, Osei-Kusi Frank, Nguefio Prince Nicaise, Fatoumata Traore, Awadji Fabrice Boris (2022). *The impact of China's foreign direct investment on Africa's inclusive development*, Social Sciences & Humanities Open, Volume 6, Issue 1. https://doi.org/10.1016/j.ssaho.2022.100276.

Deyassa, K. (2019). *Does China's Aid in Africa Affect Traditional Donors?* International Studies. Interdisciplinary Political and Cultural Journal, 23, 199-215.

Deyassa, K. (2019). *To what extent does China's aid in Africa affect traditional donors?* International Journal of Sociology and Social Policy.

Ergano, D., & Rao, S. (2019). *Sino–Africa Bilateral Economic Relation: Nature and Perspectives*. Insight on Africa, 11(1), 1-17. https://doi.org/10.1177/0975087818814914

Gavin, M. D. (2021). *Major Power Rivalry in Africa*. Council on Foreign Relations. Discussion Paper Series on Managing Global Disorder No. 5. https://cdn.cfr.org/sites/default/files/report_pdf/dpgavinmay21.pdf

Gehring, K., Kaplan, L., & Wong, M. H. L. (2019). *China and the World Bank - How Contrasting Development Approaches Affect the Stability of African States*. International Finance eJournal.

Gort, J., & A. Brooks (2023). *Africa's Next Debt Crisis: A Relational Comparison of Chinese and Western Lending to Zambia*. Antipode, Volume 55, Issue 3. https://doi.org/10.1111/anti.12921

Jeanneney, S., & Hua, P. (2015). *China's African Financial Engagement, Real Exchange Rates and Trade between China and Africa*. Journal of African Economies, 24, 1-25. https://doi.org/10.1093/JAE/EJU020.

Jenkins, R., & Edwards, C. (2006). *The economic impacts of China and India on sub-Saharan Africa: Trends and prospects*. Journal of Asian Economics, 17, 207-225. https://doi.org/10.1016/J.ASIECO.2006.02.002.

Kabemba, C. (2016). *China-Democratic Republic of Congo Relations: From a Beneficial to a Developmental Cooperation*. African Studies Quarterly, 16, 73.

Marysse, S., & Geenen, S. (2009). *Win-win or unequal exchange? The case of the Sino-Congolese cooperation agreements*. The Journal of Modern African Studies, 47(3), 371-396.

Mbuya, J., & Mphahlele, A. (2021). *Assessing the role of China in Africa's infrastructure development and its impact on the African continent*. The Business and Management Review, Volume 12 Number 2. https://cberuk.com/cdn/conference_proceedings/2022-01-20-18-22-33-PM.pdf

McCormick, D. (2008). *China & India as Africa's New Donors: The Impact of Aid on Development*. Review of African Political Economy, 35, 73-92.

Miao, M., Lang, Q., Borojo, D. G., Yushi, J., & Zhang, X. (2020). *The Impacts of Chinese FDI and China–Africa Trade on Economic Growth of African Countries: The Role of Institutional Quality*. Economies, 8(3), 53.

Mohan, G., & Lampert, B. (2013). *Negotiating China: Reinserting African agency into China–Africa relations*. African Affairs, 112(446), 92-110.

Sun, I. Y. (2014). *The Next Factory of the World: How Chinese Investment is Reshaping Africa*. Harvard Business Review Press.

Tan-Mullins, M., Mohan, G., & Power, M. (2010). *Redefining 'Aid' in the China-Africa context*. Development and Change, 41, 857-881.

Thiombiano, D., & Zhang, Z. (2020). *The impact of China on the agency and negotiating power of African countries: Cases of Angola and Niger*. African Journal of Political Science and International Relations, 14(1), 1-12.

Tull, D. (2006). *China's engagement in Africa: scope, significance and consequences*. The Journal of Modern African Studies, 44, 459-479.

Van der Lugt, S. (2016). *Exploring African Host Countries' Agency to Strengthen Local FDI Regulations: The Case of Chinese Investments in the Infrastructure Sector of the DRC*. Cornell International Law Journal, 49, 179.

World Bank (2021). *Global Economic Prospects*, June 2021: Sub-Saharan Africa. World Bank: Washington, DC.

Xu, Z., & Zhang, Y. (2020). *Can Chinese aid win the hearts and minds of Africa's local population?* Economic Modelling, 90, 322-330.

Xu, Z., Zhang, Y., & Sun, Y. (2019). *Will Foreign Aid Foster Economic Development? Grid Panel Data Evidence from China's Aid to Africa*. Emerging Markets Finance and Trade, 56, 3383-3404.

Zafar, A. (2007). *The growing relationship between China and Sub-Saharan Africa: macroeconomic, trade, investment, and aid links*. World Bank Research Observer, 22, 103-130. https://doi.org/10.1093/WBRO/LKM001.

CHAPTER III

ASSESSING THE ECONOMIC IMPACT OF CHINESE FOREIGN DIRECT INVESTMENT'S INFLOWS INTO AFRICAN COUNTRIES

by

Thaddée M. Badibanga, PhD

1. Introduction

African countries have been known until recently as the least developed and the poorest. Their under-development and extreme poverty are explained by their excessive reliance on low-productivity agriculture and exports of minerals and other raw products. Most of the policies designed over decades to lift them out of poverty have prescribed the development of strong manufacturing industries expected to transform their mineral and natural resources into high-value products, create jobs, and generate revenues for all segments of their populations.

Developing a manufacturing base in those countries has proved difficult due to their extremely low levels of investment. They have tried to attract foreign investment through more inducing policies. While several countries in the OECD group, in particular have responded positively to these policies, the results have been overall very disappointing. In fact, traditional bilateral and multilateral partners of Africa have failed to increase trade and investment after six decades of promises. For instance, the net inflows of foreign direct investment (FDI) into Africa represented, on average, 1.4% of its GDP over the period 1970-2021.[22] In per capita terms, net FDI inflows were, on average, 18.40 current US$ over the same period.[23]

It is in this context that China, helped by its fast economic growth and in search of strategic resources and market shares to sustain it, started to invest massively in Africa in the early 2000s. Today, China is the first foreign direct investor in Africa after dethroning the U.S. in 2013 (see Figure 1 below). Two sets of events may explain the emergence of China as a global foreign direct investor in Africa. First, the use of the conditionality principle by the countries of Western Europe and North America in their economic relations with Africa has held back the financial support needed by this continent for its development. In the case of the U.S., for instance, several initiatives have been developed since the end of the 1950s to promote trade with and investment in Africa, including the African Growth and Opportunity Act (AGOA), Doing Business in Africa, Power Africa, Trade Africa, Prosper Africa, and others. More than 60 years later, the U.S. trade with and investment in Africa are still insignificant. The U.S. trade with Africa in 2021 totaled US$ 83.6 billion (UN-COMTRADE 2023), which represented 1.19% of all U.S. trade in goods and services. [24] Furthermore, the net flows of the U.S. investment into Africa in 2018 and 2019 were negative (Faria, 2021) but turned positive in 2022 at US$ 2 billion (WDI, 2023). Long-standing biases and preconceived notions about the region, skepticism about market opportunities, stereotypes about corruption, and investment challenges have contributed to reinforcing the conditionality principle.

---

[22] This figure is calculated using Foreign Direct Investment, net inflows (BoP, current US$) and GDP (current US$) of 54 African countries from 1970 to 2021 from the 2023 World Development Indicators.

[23] This figure is calculated using Foreign Direct Investment, net inflows (BoP, current US$) and total population of 54 African countries from 1970 to 2021 from the 2023 World Development Indicators.

[24] This figure is calculated from the statistics on the U.S. trade published in 2022 in The White House's Fact Sheet on U.S. – Africa Partnership in Promoting Two Way Trade and Investment in Africa.

Second, China and Africa have developed more pragmatic economic cooperation motivated by the economic complementarities and win-win principle without any interference in domestic policies (Koumou and Manyi, 2016). Chinese FDI inflows into and trade with Africa increased substantially in the last decade.

Figure 1. Chinese FDI versus US FDI to Africa, Flow (billions of U.S. Dollars)

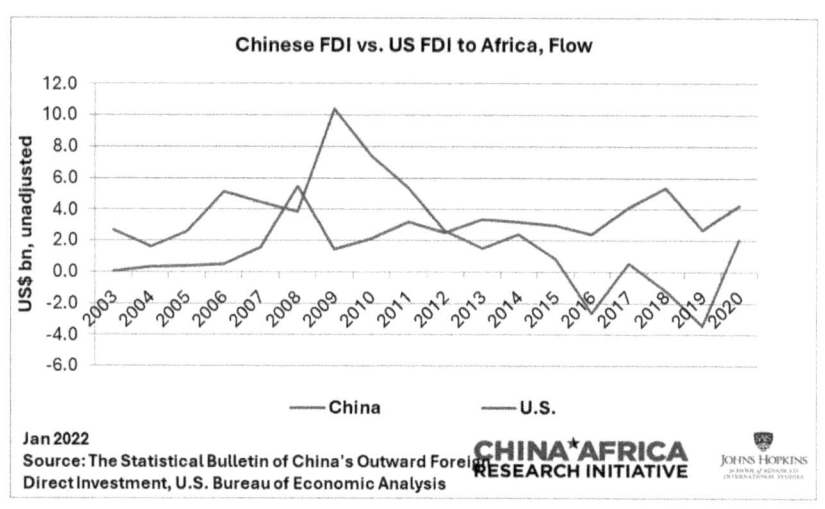

Chinese FDI inflows into Africa reached more than US$5 billion in 2018 before dropping to US$ 4.5 billion in 2022 (WDI 2023), while Chinese trade with Africa in goods and services totaled US$ 282 billion in 2022 (UN-COMTRADE 2023).Increasing FDI inflows to Africa may have contributed to transferring technology to and industrializing African Countries, not to mention possible rises in incomes of the African population, labor training, and business management knowledge transfer. In return, China has taken advantage of opportunities offered by Africa, including the use of the young, dynamic, and low-cost African labor force to expand its labor-intensive manufacturing sector, the development of the agricultural trade to satisfy the Chinese food needs, and the expansion of markets of Chinese products and services to satisfy the demand of the rising African middle class estimated to 350 million people in 2019 (Ze Yu, 2021).

Is there any evidence that Chinese FDI inflows into African countries have contributed to income rises in, technology transfer to, and industrialization of Africa? In this study, we investigate the impact of the Chinese FDI inflows on economic growth in African countries. Specifically, we use data on yearly Chinese FDI inflows into African countries and on the per capita GDP annual growth of Africa over the period 2003-2022 to create the scatter plot, which we use to detect the existence of the relationship between the two variables. Next, we build on trends observed in the scatter plot to specify three alternative regression models, and then estimate each of them to assess the economic impact of Chinese FDI inflows into Africa. Finally, we disaggregate Chinese FDI inflows at the country level to determine whether the results obtained at the continental level replicate at the country level, too.

Several studies have recently attempted to examine the effects of Chinese FDI inflows on the economic growth of Africa. Some have reached conclusions in line with the views of the bilateral and multilateral partners of Africa of the OECD group, that is, Chinese Investment in Africa is predatory in nature as it targets raw materials without any positive contribution to the development of this continent (Ademola et al., 2009; Giovannetti and Sanfilippo, 2009). Koumou and Manyi (2016) reached mixed conclusions from their qualitative analysis of the impact of Chinese FDI inflows on the economic growth of the African economy. Accordingly, Chinese FDI inflows may have contributed to the economic development of the African economy through the increase in demand for raw materials, development of infrastructure, creation of jobs, and facilitation of access to products considered luxurious before (i.e., mobile phones, computers, and others). However, those economic advantages may have been outweighed by economic distortions introduced by Chinese interventions in Africa. In fact, the low quality of Chinese products and their low prices may have destroyed local industries and displaced local firms, not to mention the violation of environment standards, the non-compliance with labor standards, and the exploitation of the labor force.

Obviously, the lack of data-based evidence on the Chinese FDI – African economic growth relationship is the reason for the long-lasting controversy. Unclear predictions from the FDI – economic growth literature, as well as the unavailability of data, have been the justification. This study fills the gap in the literature by building on the current availability of Chinese FDI inflow data over 20 years in 53 African countries to quantitatively assess the effects of Chinese investment into African countries on their economies.

The results indicate that the Chinese FDI inflows into Africa have a negative impact on the economic growth of Africa. Indeed, per 1% increase in Chinese FDI inflows in GDP, the annual rate of growth of per capita GDP decreases by 7.61%. Furthermore, disaggregating Chinese FDI inflows at the country level and assessing their economic impact for each country show mixed results. In fact, of 51 African countries for which Chinese FDI data are available, nine countries experienced a negative economic impact of Chinese FDI inflows, seven countries experienced a positive economic impact of Chinese FDI inflows, and 35 countries have not experienced any impact at all.

The rest of the paper is organized as follows: Section 2 reviews the literature on the relationship between economic growth and FDI. Section 3 describes data as well as the methodology for assessing the growth impact of Chinese FDI inflows into African countries. Section 4 conducts the empirical analysis. Section 5 discusses the results of the study. Section 6 presents policy recommendations and concludes the study.

2. Literature Review

In recent years, economists have devoted much effort trying to understand and describe the FDI–economic growth relationship. Two issues have been central to such effort, namely, the existence or not of such a relationship and the description of the mechanisms through which FDI affects the economic growth of the host country. Several theories have been developed to address those issues; however, none has provided a unified explanation of how FDI impacts economic growth. One of the theories that have dominated the literature in the last two decades is known as the classical theory.

The classical theory has been pioneered by a certain number of scholars, including Toone (2013), Denisia (2010), Gorg and Greenaway (2004), Javorcik (2004), Rappaport (2000); Aitken and Harrison (1999), and Romer (1993). This theory sees the FDI as a source of spillover benefits that contribute to the economic development of the host country. Such positive effects are exerted through a certain number of channels, including the transfers of capital, advanced technology, and skills from the foreign investor country to the host country; the expansion of the tax base, and foreign exchange earnings; the integration of the host economy into international markets; the infrastructure development and job creation, the increase in productivity of domestic firms, and others.

The classical theory, however, has not shown some regularity in empirical studies. Evidence of growth effects of FDI from cross-country analyses has been either inconclusive or weak. Ashraf et al. (2016), Herzer (2012), Herzer et al. (2008), Adewumi (2006), Mencinger (2003), Carcovic and Levine (2002), Lipsey (2002), Lichtenberg and Van Pottelsberghe De La Potterie (1998), Young and Lan (1997), Haddad and Harrison (1993), Mansfield and Romeo (1980), and Germidis (1977) find no evidence of any independent impact of FDI inflows on economic growth in cross-country studies using either a mix of developing, in transition, and developed countries or countries at the same level of development. Further, Türkcan et al. (2008) observe a bidirectional causality between FDI inflows and economic growth, where economic growth stimulated the rate of FDI inflows more than the rate of FDI inflows affected economic growth.

Some other cross-country studies have reported mixed evidence of a growth-FDI relationship. For instance, Gui-Diby (2014) finds a positive impact of the FDI inflows on the economic growth of Africa in the later period of investigation (1995-2009) but a negative impact in the early period (1980-1994). Yabi (2010) observes a positive impact of FDI in countries with high economic growth but no FDI impact in countries with low economic growth. Johnson (2006) documents the positive effects of FDI on economic growth in developing countries but not in developed ones. Alfaro (2003) finds a positive contribution of FDI to growth in countries with inflows in the manufacturing sector, a negative contribution in countries with inflows in the primary sector, and an ambiguous contribution in countries with inflows in the service sector. Balasubramanyam et al. (1996) find a larger economic growth impact of FDI in countries that promote exports of products rather than in those implementing import substitution policies. Blomstrom et al. (1992) indicate similar mixed empirical evidence, that is, FDI affect positively economic growth in higher-income developing countries but not in lower-income countries.

As for cross-country studies, the economic growth effects of FDI inflows are controversial in single-country studies, too. Mun et al. (2008) document a positive impact of FDI inflow on economic growth in Malaysia over the period 1970-2005. Frimpong and Oteng-Abayie (2006) find no causality between FDI and economic growth in Ghana during the pre-Structural Adjustment Program period, but FDI caused GDP growth during the post – Structural Adjustment Program period. Smarzynska (2002) documents a positive growth impact of FDI in the case of Lithuania. Castellani and Zanfei (2003) found positive productivity effects of FDI in Italy but no such effects in Spain and France. Djankov and Hoekman (2000) report significant negative spillovers of foreign investment on domestic companies that do not have foreign partnerships in the Czech Republic. Blomström and Sjöholm (1999) find that domestic firms benefit from spillovers of FDI in Indonesia. Blomstrom and Wolff (1994) find a positive impact of FDI on the competitiveness of domestic companies in Mexico and Indonesia. Aitken and Harrison (1999) find mixed effects in panel data of Venezuelan plants; that is, FDI inflows are correlated positively with the productivity of FDI-owned plants but have a negative impact on the productivity of domestically owned plants.

Furthermore, causality issues arise in single-country studies. In fact, Chowdhury and Mavrotas (2006) find unidirectional causality from economic growth to FDI inflows in the case of Chile but bidirectional causality between the two indicators for the cases of Malaysia and Thailand.

The controversy on the economic growth effects of FDI has prompted further evaluation to determine why the classical theory seems not to be empirically a unified theory of the economic growth – FDI relationship. Some scholars have documented that FDI inflows may create distortions (i.e., price, trade, or financial) in the host country's economy that end up decelerating its economic growth (Taylor and Thrift, 2013; Jensen, 2008; Boyd and Smith, 1992; Brecher, 1983; and Brecher and Diaz-Alejandro, 1977). They have provided three explanations for those distortions. First, multinational corporations, which are the vehicles of FDI, exploit profit-making opportunities in their host countries but distribute unequally the FDI benefits by repatriating profits to the foreign investor countries. Second, multinational corporations crowd-out domestic investments and use inappropriate capital-intensive technologies that result in job losses and distort the distribution of incomes. Third, FDI is prone to the political and economic elite capture, which results in distorted policies that end up marginalizing the majority of citizens of the host country.

Whether or not FDI creates distortions in the host country's economy is still to be proved. However, efforts have been amplified lately for further evaluation of the FDI – economic growth relationship. The predictions from those additional efforts are obvious. The host country needs to satisfy minimum requirements for the FDI inflows to positively impact its economy. Those requirements have varied from study to study. In Li and Liu (2005), Alfaro et al. (2004), Reisen and Soto (2001), and Olofsdotter (1998), each country's characteristics have determined the size of the positive effect of FDI inflows on its economic growth. More specific preconditions for such positive impact include the minimum threshold of a stock of human capital (Batten and Vo, 2009; Prasad et al., 2007; Li and Liu, 2005; Bengoa and Sanchez-Robles, 2003; and Borensztein et al., 1998), the financial sector development (Alfaro et al., 2004; and Hermes and Lensink, 2003), the macroeconomic stability (Zhang, 2001; and De Gregorio, 1992), the trade openness (Balasubramanyam et al., 1996), the absorptive capacity of the economy (Carbonell and Werner, 2018; Alege and Ogundipe, 2014; and Durham, 2004), the level of local capacity and competition (Blomström and Kokko,

1998), and the country-specific factors (i.e. economic environment, institutions and policies) that contribute to eliminating the technological gaps between foreign investing and host countries (De Mello, 1999).

Among the strands of the literature described above, the one that emphasizes the satisfaction of preconditions by a country prior to its opening to FDI seems more appealing in capturing the true effect of FDI on the economy. This is the strand that will guide our analysis. Indeed, most countries in general and developing countries in particular see FDI as an economic opportunity to accumulate capital stocks. However, they ignore the distortions that investment can create as well as their negative effects on the economy when a country doesn't meet the minimum threshold of human capital stock to adopt advanced technology from foreign investors. Further, weak institutions in those FDI host countries prevent the design and implementation of appropriate policies to prevent or limit economic distortions, including the repatriation of revenues generated through FDI and the elimination of domestic competition.

3. Data and Methodology

In this section, we develop a methodology for assessing the economic impact of Chinese FDI inflows into African countries. Different models suggested by different strands of the literature on FDI – economic growth relationship have been used in different studies to verify empirically this relationship. We depart here from the adoption of any existing model or assumption of a specific functional form ex-ante. Instead, we create a scatter plot using data on Chinese FDI inflows and African economic growth to detect the existence and nature of the relationship at the continental level. Furthermore, we disaggregate data at the country level to assess how each African country's growth process has responded to Chinese FDI inflows.

The data we use in this study was collected from two sources, namely, the 2023 World Development Indicators (World Bank, 2023) for per capita GDP annual growth rate (percent) and annual GDP (current US$), and the Statistical Bulletin of China's Outward Foreign Direct Investment from the U.S. Bureau of Economic Analysis (2022) for the Chinese FDI inflows into African countries (current US$). The data covers all African countries and the African continent over the period 2003-2022. The per capita GDP growth rate (annual %) will be used as a measure of economic growth for the country or for the continent (PCGDPG). For the indicator of the FDI inflows, we divide the Chinese FDI Inflow of the country or the continent in a particular year (in current US$) by the corresponding GPP (in current US$) of the country or the continent in that year. We then multiply the ratio by 100 to express it as a percent of GDP (FDIC_RATIO).

Figure 2. Scatter Plot of Per Capita GDP Growth Rate (%) Versus Chinese FDI to GDP Ratio (%)

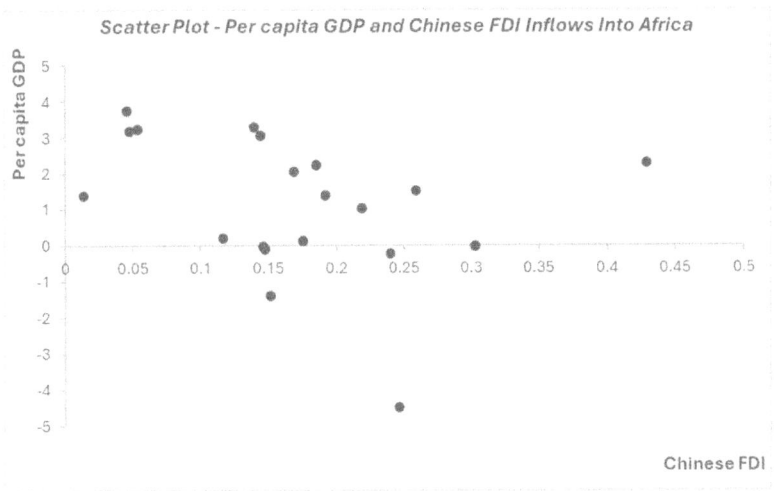

We use data on the per capita GDP growth rate of the African economy and Chinese FDI inflows to GDP ratio (for the continent) to create the scatter plot shown in Figure 2 (above). Chinese FDI Inflows to GDP ratio is plotted on the horizontal axis and per capita GDP is plotted on the vertical axis. In this two-dimensional graph, any trend from the origins of axes towards the North-East reflects a positive relationship between the two variables. A trend moving from the North-West towards the South-East reflects a negative relationship between the two variables. Any North to South or South to North and any East to West or West to East describe the absence of any relationship between the two variables. At a glance, Figure 2 shows a less obvious relationship between the two variables. However, a close look at this figure reveals the possibility of a downward relationship between the per capita GDP annual growth rate and Chinese FDI inflows to GDP ratio. That is, as FDI_ratio increases, PCGDPG may decrease.

To remove any doubt about the nature of this relationship, let's add alternative trendlines to this scatter plot in Figure 3. Those trendlines includes the linear (Figure 3 - Panel A), the logarithmic (Figure 3 - Panel B), the quadratic (Figure 3 - Panel C), and the moving average (Figure 3 - Panel D). Clearly, Panel A and Panel B show each a downward-sloping relationship, while Panel C reveals a mixed relationship, that is, a downward-sloping relationship up to the inflection point and then an upward-sloping relationship. Panel D shows a trendline that is not revealing. Thus, we will not include it in our analysis.

Figure 3. Trendlines of Per Capita GDP Growth Rate (%) Versus Chinese FDI Inflows To GDP Ratio (%)

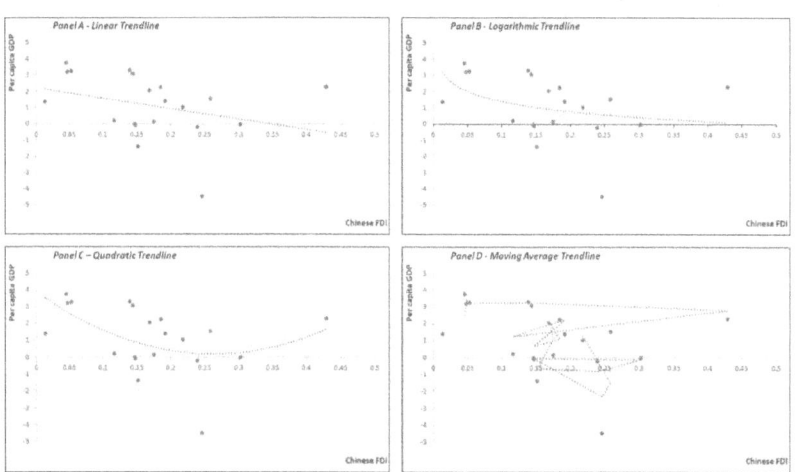

A further examination of Panels A, B, and C shows that the three trendlines seem comparable in detecting the relationship between the two variables. We are going to use them to specify three alternative models, which we will estimate to assess the economic impact of Chinese FDI inflows into Africa. We should emphasize that a model with only Chinese FDI inflows as a sole explanatory variable will not have sufficient explanatory power since a per capita GDP growth is determined by several variables, including labor, physical capital, human capital, FDI, domestic investment, government spending, financial development, inflation, exchange rate premium, quality of institutions, and others. At the same time, including all the variables mentioned above is not feasible for two reasons. First, given the size of our sample (n = 20), estimating a model with more than ten explanatory variables will significantly affect our statistical results and their economic relevance. Second, data on most of those variables is not available. To avoid a model misspecification with all its issues, we are going to include in each specification a composite variable, call it Z, to account for all those known variables that are not included in the model. In the next section, we will describe our strategy for generating that variable. The three model specifications are as follows.

Linear Specification

$$PCGDPG_t = \beta_0 + \beta_1 FDI\_Ratio_t + \beta_2 Z_t + \varepsilon_t \quad (1)$$

Logarithmic Specification

$$PCGDPG_t = \beta_0 + \beta_1 \ln(FDI\_Ratio)_t + \beta_2 Z_t + \varepsilon_t \quad (2)$$

Quadratic Specification

$$PCGDPG_t = \beta_0 + \beta_1 FDI\_Ratio_t + \beta_2 FDI\_Ratio_t^2 + \beta_3 Z_t + \varepsilon_t (3)$$

where $PCGDPG_t$ and FDI_Ratio_t are defined as before, Z_t is a composite variable included to capture the effects of known but not incorporated input and policy variables, and ε_t is the usual random variable included to account for all factors more likely to influence the dependent variables but which are not introduced in the systematic part of the model. ε_t is assumed to be normally distributed with mean zero, $E(\varepsilon_t) = 0$, and a constant variance, $E(\varepsilon_t^2) = \sigma_\varepsilon^2$. $\beta_0, \beta_1, \beta_2$, and β_3 are the parameters of our models. β_0 has the same interpretation across the three models, that is, it measures the value of PCGDPG when all explanatory variables are set to zero. Likewise, β_2 in the linear and logarithmic specifications and β_3 in the quadratic specification have both the same interpretation. Each measures the marginal effect of the composite variable Z_t on PCGDPG. β_1 in the linear specification measures the marginal effect of Chinese FDI_Ratio, that is, $\frac{\partial PCGDPG}{\partial FDI\_Ratio} = \beta_1$. In the logarithmic model, β_1 is not the marginal effect of the Chinese FDI_Ratio. It is instead used to calculate such effect as follows:

$$\frac{\partial PCGDPG}{\partial FDI\_Ratio} = \frac{\partial PCGDPG}{\partial \ln(FDI\_Ratio)} \times \frac{1}{PCGDPG} = \beta_1 \times \frac{1}{PCGDPG}.$$

Finally, β_1 and β_2 are used to calculate the marginal effect of Chinese FDI_Ratio in the quadratic specification as follows:

$$\frac{\partial PCGDPG}{\partial FDI\_Ratio} = \beta_1 + 2\beta_2 \times \overline{FDI\_Ratio}.$$

where $\overline{FDI\_Ratio}$ and $\overline{PCGDPG}$ are the averages of FDI_Ratio and $PCGDPG$, respectively.

The three models will be estimated in the next section and the one yielding the best results on both the statistical and economic grounds will be retained/selected.

4. Estimation

To conduct our estimations, we need data on the composite variable Z_t. This data is however not available. We can generate its instrument as the residuals from the estimation of the following equation:

$$PCGDPG_t = \gamma_0 + \gamma_1 FDI\_Ratio_t + \gamma_2 T_t + \epsilon_t \quad (4)$$

$$Z_t = PCGDPG_t - \hat{\gamma}_0 - \hat{\gamma}_1 FDI\_Ratio_t - \hat{\gamma}_2 T_t \quad (5)$$

where Z_t is the residual of the estimation of the equation (4), T_t is the time variable, which takes on the value 1 in year 1 (i.e. 2003) and value 20 in year 20 (i.e. 2022). $\hat{\gamma}_0, \hat{\gamma}_1,$ and $\hat{\gamma}_2$ are estimates of parameters $\gamma_0, \gamma_1,$ and γ_2, respectively.

We implemented all our estimation procedures using Stata/SE 17.0. We first estimate equations (1), (2) and (3) using the Ordinary Least Squares (OLS) technique. The results of our estimation[25] show the superiority of the quadratic model over the linear and logarithmic models in fitting the data. In fact, the coefficient of determination (R^2) is the highest in the quadratic specification. Specifically, the

---

[25] We do not display the results at this step since they may be subject to changes justified by data transformations required to correct for econometric problems.

FDI_Ratio, its square, and Z explain 82.68% of the variability in PCGDPG. The corresponding values of (R^2) in the linear and logarithmic specifications are 68.67% and 70.38%, respectively. Further, the estimated coefficients associated with the FDI_Ratio, its square, and its log are both statistically significant in the three specifications.

Next, we conduct econometric tests, including multicollinearity, heteroscedasticity, and autocorrelation tests. Starting with the mutlicollinearity test, we regress the variable Z_t on FDI_Ratio_t in the linear specification, Z_t on $ln(FDI\_Ratio)_t$ in the logarithmic specification, and Z_t on FDI_Ratio_t and $FDI\_Ratio_t^2$ in the quadratic specification. The R^2 value in the three specifications is close to zero, indicating the absence of correlation between the independent variables in each specification or no multicollinearity.

Turning to the heteroscedasticity test, we use the Breusch-Pagan/Cook-Weisberg test for heteroscedasticity. The $\chi^2_{(1)}$ statistic is 0.16 in the linear specification, 0.01 in logarithmic specification, and 0.06 in quadratic specification. The P-value to observe the value of the test statistic greater than $\chi^2_{(1)}$ if the null hypothesis is true is 68.64% in the linear specification, 91.12% in the logarithmic specification, and 81.36 in the quadratic specification. As a result, we do not reject the null hypothesis of homoscedasticity since the P-value in each specification is greater than the 5% significance level.

Finally, the autocorrelation test is conclusive. The Breusch-Godfrey LM test for autocorrelation returns values of $\chi^2_{(1)}$ that lead both to the rejection of the null hypothesis of no autocorrelation in both specifications. Those $\chi_{(1)}$ values are 10.89, 11.28, and 7.76 in the linear, logarithmic, and quadratic specifications, respectively. The P-value to observe a value of the test statistic greater than $\chi^2_{(1)}$ under the true null hypothesis is 0.001 in the linear specification, 0.008 in the logarithmic specification, and 0.0053 in the quadratic specification. In addition to the LM test, we also conducted the Durbin Watson test of autocorrelation. The Durbin Watson (DW) statistic - d-statistic (3, 20) is 0.53 in the linear specification and 0.46 in the logarithmic specification. Those d-statistic (3, 20) fall in the region of a negative autocorrelation built using the critical values of dl and du at 5% (with $n = 20$ and $k = 3$). Likewise, the d-statistic (4, 20) is 0.76 in the quadratic specification, falling into the region of a negative autocorrelation using the critical values of dl and du at 5% (with $n = 20$ and $k = 4$).

Next, we try to correct for the autocorrelation using the Prais – Winsten transformations with several options, including the Cochrane–Orcutt transformation (corc), the suppression of the constant option (noconstant), the has user-defined constant (hascons), the ssesearch option, and the twostep option. Most of those options failed to achieve the convergence. However, the Prais –Winsten transformations with the twostep option yields the desired results. Accordingly, the autocorrelation has persisted after the transformation in both the linear and logarithmic specifications. The values of d-statistic (3, 20) after the transformation are 0.46 and 0.62 for the linear and logarithmic specifications, respectively. Those values still fall in the region of negative autocorrelation. However, the value of d-statistic (4, 20) after the transformation is 0.98 in the quadratic specification, which changes the issue from the negative autocorrelation to the indeterminate autocorrelation.

We display the results corrected for autocorrelation with the Prais – Winston transformation in Table 1 (see Appendix). A look at the results indicates that they are statistically satisfying across the three specifications. The Adjusted R^2 is above 90% in each of the three models, reflecting a good fit of each to the data. Furthermore, the *P-value* to observe the value of the test statistic greater than $F(k, 20 - k - 1)$ under the true null hypothesis is zero. Therefore, we reject the null hypothesis that all independent variables do not jointly explain the variability of PCGDPG. Also, heteroscedasticity and multicollinearity are absent across the three specifications.

Turning now to the estimated coefficients, we can see from Table 1 that the one associated with FDI_Ratio in the linear specification and the one associated with the LN_FDI_Ratio in the logarithmic specification are not statistically significant at a 5% or a 10% level of significance. Their signs seem, however, consistent with the downward trend detected in the scatter plot of the PCGDPG and

FDI_Ratio. The no significance of those coefficients affects negatively the economic relevance of the two models. In contrast, all coefficients and in particular those associated with the FDI variables are statistically significant at 5% or 10% significant level in the quadratic model. In addition, they have the expected signs, that is, the estimate of β_1 is negative and that of β_2 is positive.

The regression results described above show clearly that the appropriate specification for analyzing the Chinese FDI – African economic growth is the quadratic model. This modeling and its estimation results satisfy the statistical regularity and the economic relevance. We use those results and the following formula to assess the marginal effect of Chinese FDI inflow on economic growth of Africa.

$$\frac{\partial PCGDPG}{\partial FDI\_Ratio} = \hat{\beta}_1 + 2\hat{\beta}_2 \times \overline{FDI\_Ratio} \qquad (6)$$

Based on the calculated marginal effect, Chinese FDI inflows have a negative impact on the economic growth of African countries. In fact, a 1.00% increase in Chinese FDI inflows in African GDP results in a 4.04% decrease in African per capita GDP annual growth rate. This result comes without any surprise since a negative relationship between Chinese FDI inflows and the economic growth of Africa was detected from the scatter plot of the two variables. Next, we use the disaggregated Chinese FDI inflows at the country level as well as the per capita GDP annual growth rate to assess the economic impact of Chinese investment in each African country.[26] We tried both specifications, that is, linear specification (equation (1)), logarithmic specification (equation (2)), and quadratic specification (equation (3)).

We use the same estimation procedure as for the continental regression. Specifically, we estimate the equation (4) for each African

---

[26] Three African countries are not included into the analysis due to the unavailability of Chinese FDI data. Those countries are Eswatini, Somalia, and South Sudan.

country, recover the residuals, and then use them in each of the three specifications as the composite variable Z_t.

The estimation of each country model using the three specifications yields mixed results.[27] Indeed, six African countries have experienced a positive economic impact of Chinese FDI inflows (see Table 2 in APPENDIX), nine African countries have experienced a negative economic impact of Chinese FDI inflows (see Table 3 in APPENDIX), and 36 countries have not experienced any economic impact of FDI inflows (see Table 4 in APPENDIX).[28]

Of those countries with a positive economic impact (see Table 2), Senegal has experienced a large impact, that is, per 1% increase in Chinese FDI inflows in its GDP, its per capita GDP annual growth rate increases by 7.52%. Kenya has experienced a moderate response of per capita GDP annual growth rate of 3.63% to 1% increase in Chinese FDI inflows in its GDP. In contrast, the last four countries in this group have experienced each a very small impact. Per a 1% increase in Chinese FDI inflows in their GDP, per capita GDP annual growth rate increases only by 0.79% for Uganda, 0.62% for Cote d'Ivoire, 0.39% for Guinea, and 0.03% for Chad.[29]

Turning now to the group of nine countries with a negative economic impact, Table 3 in APPENDIX reveals that three have experienced each a large impact while five have experienced each a very small impact. Lesotho is at the top of the group with a strong response to the per capita GDP annual growth rate of -11.17% to 1% increase in Chinese FDI inflows in its GDP. It is followed by Angola

---

[27] The estimation results are not displayed but are available upon request.

[28] The economic impact of Chinese FDI inflows is interpreted as the marginal effect on per capita GDP annual growth rate of a country of 1% increase in Chinese FDI inflow in GDP of that particular country.

[29] The specification that better works for each country in this group can be found in the last column of Table 2.

with -9.08%[30] and by Madagascar with -8.58%.[31] The remaining six countries in this group have each a very small response of the per capita GDP annual growth rate to a 1% increase in Chinese FDI inflows in GDP. The response is -1.13% for Congo, -0.89% for Tunisia, -0.57 for Sierra Leonne, -0.47% for Sao Tome & Principe, -0.41% for Zimbabwe, and -0.15% for Tanzania.[32]

Finally, the list of the 36 countries that have not experienced any economic impact of Chinese FDI inflows is displayed in Table 4 in APPENDIX. None of the three specifications works for any country in this group.

5. Discussion

The African economy has been on the sustained economic growth path for the last twenty years, growing on average at an annual rate of 4.25%. Initially attributed to increases in the foreign development assistance from the Africa's bilateral and multilateral partners as well as to the FDI inflows (Dahou et al., 2009), such performance has proved over time to be the result of structural and institutional reforms and prudent monetary and fiscal policies that have contributed to improving significantly the business environment, the quality of institutions, and the mobilization of internal resources in African countries (African Development Bank, 2023; Tupy and Rohac, 2014). The results of estimation of our model provide further evidence that Africa is itself the owner of its growth performance. As it is obvious from the results displayed in Table 1 in APPENDIX, the estimate of the coefficient of the composite variable Z is not only statistically significant, but also, it is positive. While we cannot interpret this estimate given that it includes several input and policy variables that have either a positive or a negative effect on PCGDPG, we can at least

---

[30] This response for Angola is obtained with the linear specification. The logarithmic specification works too. However, its response is small (i.e. 1.92%).

[31] As for Angola, the linear and logarithmic specification work for Madagascar. The result reported here is the one obtained under the linear specification. The response associated with the logarithmic specification is small, that is, -1.09%.

[32] The specification that better works for each country in this group can be found in the last column of Table 2.

isolate a few to demonstrate their possible positive effects. Let us consider the domestic investment and government spending. Data on African national income and product accounts reveals that the start of the African sustained economic growth coincides with the fast growth of domestic investment in Africa. The annual investment growth rate was, on average, 9.50% between 2003 and 2008, and 5.36% between 2017 and 2022.[33] During those two periods, however, Africa's partners (including the U.S.) disinvested in Africa (see figure 1). As for domestic investment, data also reveal that the continent experienced an improvement in government expenditures. Although the fiscal pressure fluctuated around 15% during the period under analysis (2000-2022), government expenditures grew on average at an annual rate of 3.95%.[34] Among those expenditures, the ones that improve the efficiency of the economy also increased. This is the case of educational and health expenditures. The share of health expenditures in total government expenditures (expressed as a percent) increased by 18.41% between 2000 and 2020.[35] Likewise, government educational spending in Africa increased during the same period too. This figure expressed as a percentage of GDP increased from 15.61% in 2000 to 17.00% in 2018 or an 8.9% increase.[36]

Going back to the negative impact of Chinese FDI inflows on the economic growth of Africa, these results are not surprising. Indeed, they provide additional evidence to the nuanced aspects of this relationship that may help to solidify its empirical regularity. The level

---

[33] These figures are constructed using gross capital formation (annual % growth) from 2022 World Development Indicators (World bank, 2023). The 2020 data point was not included in calculation since it is an outlier.

[34] The fiscal pressure and the average annual growth rate of government expenditures are calculated using general government final consumption expenditure (% of GDP) and general government final consumption expenditure (annual % growth) from the 2023 World Development Indicators (World Bank, 2023).

[35] This figure was constructed from domestic government spending on health as a percent of total government spending from Global Health Expenditure Database (WHO, 2023).

[36] This figure is calculated using Sub-Saharan Africa Education Spending 2000-2024 from Macrotrends (World Bank, 2024).

of complexity that has characterized this relationship, in combination with the controversial nature of its debate, have prevented a consensus among policymakers. According to most bilateral and multilateral partners of Africa, Chinese investment in Africa is predatory. For instance, the US former Secretary John Bolton accused China of using strategically the debt to hold African countries captive to Beijing's wishes and demands, while the former President Bill Clinton warned against this new form of colonialism established through predatory investment (Jones et al., 2022). Criticisms of Chinese investments in Africa are unjustified since they have allowed those countries to diversify their economies and exports as well as to achieve economic growth and improve overall prosperity (de Freitas, 2023).

More and more empirical evidence has helped to go beyond the above qualitative debate. A study by Cudjoe et al. (2021) suggests that FDI, trade, and aid from China have a nonlinear relationship with Africa's economic growth, emphasizing the role of Chinese FDI in the manufacturing sector. Conversely, Miao et al. (2021) highlight that the impact of Chinese FDI on economic growth is contingent upon the improvement of governance quality in African countries, suggesting that governance plays a mediating role in harnessing the benefits of FDI for domestic investment and economic growth.

Furthermore, Shetewy and Jiang (2019) find that Chinese FDI inflows have no significant impact on the economic growth of North African countries, aligning with the argument that domestic factors might play a more pivotal role in driving economic outcomes. This is corroborated by Koomson-Abekah and Nwaba (2018), who report a negative or declining effect of China's FDI on African economic growth in both the short and long run, suggesting that investments are allocated to capital-intensive activities with less labor employability, thus having limited direct effects on broad-based economic growth.

The negative impact of Chinese FDI may also be explained by the failure of the Chinese FDI to increase capital stock per worker in Africa. Evidence suggests that this figure has remained constant after more than 20 years of Chinese economic intervention in Africa. In fact, Chinese FDI inflows were the highest in 2018 and 2022, with the figures of 5 billion US$ and 4.5 billion US$, respectively. Dividing each of the two figures by 54 countries in which China has intervened yields the average FDI inflows per each African country of 92.6 million in 2018 and 83.3 million in 2022. This amount is too small to have any impact on the capital stock of each country. In per capita terms, the Chinese FDI inflows are very insignificant; that is, they were 3.59 US$ in 2018 and 3.24 US$ in 2022.[37] Clearly, the per capita FDI inflows decreased between 2018 and 2022. To better understand the relatively small scale of Chinese FDI inflows, let's analyze the 2018 figures. Taking the Chinese FDI of $5 billion and dividing it by Africa's GDP for the same year, then multiplying the result by 100, we get 0.16%. This means that even at its peak in 2018, Chinese FDI accounted for less than 1% of Africa's GDP.

Besides the small size of the Chinese FDI inflows, the sectoral destination of those investments is another factor that may explain their limited or negative impact. According to figures constructed using statistics reported in Galal (2023), the distribution of Chinese FDI inflows into Africa by sector has been on average as follows: 37.05% for construction, 22.73% for mining, 13.41% for manufacturing, 9.55% for financial intermediation, 4.55% for leasing and commercial services, and 12.73% for other. Clearly, construction and mining received 60% of those investments. However, the two sectors are weakly connected to the local economy to have any lingering impact on it. Further, the lack of strong regulation on the sharing of FDI benefits results in an unequal exploitation of profit-making opportunities in the African countries through the repatriation of profits to China.

The other sector, which includes agriculture, attracts only 12.73% of Chinese FDI inflows. However, the agricultural sector, that should be the destination of FDI inflows, given its high potential for rapid economic growth, has received less attention for FDI. In fact, more than 60% of the sub-Saharan African population is smallholder farmers with the GDP contribution of only 23% (Goedde et al., 2019). This low performance has been explained by the use of rudimentary

---

[37] The per capita FDI is obtained by dividing the FDI of each year by the African population of was 1.39 billion in 2018 and 1.43 billion in 2022. The population figures are from the 2023 World Development Indicators (World Bank, 2023).

technology and insufficient capital stock, including basic infrastructure (Badibanga and Ulimwengu, 2019). Attracting more Chinese FDI inflows into this sector can boost the sector's productivity and induce economic growth by facilitating the transfer of technology and increasing capital stock, the two missing pieces for Africa to become the major player in the global food networks and ensure global food security.

Furthermore, the negative impact of Chinese FDI inflows on the economic growth of Africa may also be explained by their subjection to political and economic elite capture in African countries. This behavior may have created distortions in policies that may have ended up marginalizing the majority of people in those countries. Several elite capturing cases have been reported in African countries. The most recent is the 2008 agreement between the Democratic Republic of Congo and China that led to a joint venture through a company named Sicomines in which the shareholding has been 68% for Chinese partners and 32% for the Gecamines[38] (Reuters, 2024). Under this agreement, Chinese investors committed to investing 3 billion US$ in infrastructures in the Democratic Republic of Congo in exchange for the exploitation of copper and cobalt through Sicomines. Fifteen years later, an audit of this agreement indicates that only infrastructures worth 822 million US$ were built. In addition, Chinese partners have transferred back to China the revenue of 10 billion US$ from exports of copper and cobalt. This audit also exposed the Civil Servants who initially signed and managed this agreement to enrich themselves at the expense of millions of Congolese. It also led to the revisitation of the agreement, which, under its updated version includes 7 billion US$ of investments in infrastructures by Chinese construction companies (i.e. 7,000 miles of roads), the increase in the share of the Democratic Republic of Congo in the Busanga hydroelectric dam[39] from 25% to 40%, and the granting to the

---

[38] Gecamines is a Congolese state-owned company engaged in the exploration, research, exploitation, and production of mineral deposits including copper and cobalt.

[39] Busanga is a 240 MW hydroelectric power plant located in Lualaba Province in the Democratic Republic of Congo. The plant is owned 40% by Gecamines and

Gecamines of the responsibility for marketing 32% of the Sicomines' annual production in addition to its 1.2% of royalties on the Sicomines' annual sales.

Overall, while Chinese FDI has been perceived as a potential catalyst for economic growth in Africa, evidence suggests that its impact might not be as substantial as that of domestic investments and government expenditures in driving the observed increases in income levels across the continent. This underscores the importance of enhancing domestic investment climates and governance structures to fully leverage FDI for the economic development of the continent.

6. Conclusion

In this study, we used alternative model specifications as well as the data on Chinese FDI inflows into African countries over the period 2003 – 2022 to estimate their economic impact. Next, we compared the alternative results of estimation to identify the best of the three models, that is, the one whose estimation results are statistically satisfying and economically relevant.

The results indicate that the quadratic model is the appropriate specification for investigating the relationship between Chinese FDI inflows into Africa and its economic growth. Accordingly, the economic impact of Chinese FDI inflows into African countries is negative. In fact, a 1.00% increase in Chinese FDI inflows in African GDP results in a 4.04% decrease in its per capita GDP annual growth rate. This result comes without any surprise since a negative relationship between Chinese FDI inflows and the economic growth of Africa was detected from the scatter plot of the two variables. Furthermore, disaggregating Chinese FDI inflows at the country level and assessing the economic impact for each country show mixed results. In fact, of 51 African countries for which Chinese FDI data are available, nine countries experienced a negative economic impact of Chinese FDI inflows, six countries experienced a positive economic impact of Chinese FDI inflows, and 36 countries did not experience any impact at all.

60% Sinohydro and China Railway Group.

This study investigates further the reasons why Chinese FDI inflows have a negative impact on the African economy. The small size of the Chinese FDI inflows, the less impactful sectoral destination of those investments, and their subjection to the elite capture may have created obstacles to the economic impact of those investments. Meanwhile, Chinese multinational firms have benefited from preferential tax policies in several African countries, which have deprived governments of those countries of important tax revenues. Coincidently, government expenditures and domestic investments seem to have moved in the same direction as the economic growth of the African continent during the period under study. The co-movements of the above two variables and economic growth indicate that they may be the main drivers of the African healthy economic growth performance in the last twenty years.

Where should African countries go from here? It would be utopic to believe that Chinese investors will leave Africa soon. They seem to be there to stay. However, African countries need to design policies that will prevent the displacement of local firms and allow an equitable distribution of FDI benefits. First, they need to determine the minimum amount of foreign investment that makes it eligible in the host country. It does not make sense to observe Chinese investors spreading just 5 billion US$ over multiple projects in 54 countries and expect a positive outcome. Further, African governments need to design preferential tax policies to attract foreign investment into the agricultural sector. This sector has a high potential for job creation, revenue generation, and strong economic growth because it employs more than 60% of the African population but contributes less than 23% to the African GDP.

Further, the governments of African countries need to prioritize FDI that facilitates the transfer of new technology and capital accumulation. In particular, those governments have to prevent FDI from being the means through which multinational firms in the mining sector come to Africa to extract minerals and ship them abroad without transforming them or creating any value chain. In addition, governments in those countries need to involve research institutions in the FDI activities to ensure that all technologies developed and used by FDI will be adopted and disseminated. Finally, legislation that limits the amounts of profits to be repatriated so as to allow a portion of those profits to be reinvested in the host country must be developed.

As we are about to end this study, it is worth emphasizing that there is still much to learn about the relationship between African economic growth and the Chinese FDI inflows. The results obtained here inform us in the particular context of our modeling and the size of the dataset in our hands. We can still improve our understanding of this relationship by investigating it in a broad context where additional policy and control variables are incorporated. Indeed, some important policy variables were not included in this study because of the unavailability of data. This is the case of the black-market premium on foreign exchange, the measure of political instability (political assassinations and wars), the measure of political rights, the measure of quality of institutions, and others. Furthermore, as more data become available, more stable estimations can be conducted to prevent the shortfalls of small data sizes.

REFERENCES

Ademola, O., Bankole and Adewuyi A. O (2009), "China-Africa trade relation: insight from AERC Scoping Studies," *European Journal of Development Research* 21(4), pp. 485-505.

Adewumi, Sarumi (2006). The impact of FDI on growth in developing countries: An African experience. Jönköping international business school.

African Development Bank (2023). Africa's Economic Growth to Outpace Global Forecast in 2023-2024 – African Development Bank Biannual Report, January 19, 2023 (https://www.afdb.org/en/news-and-events/press-releases/africas-economic-growth-outpace-global-forecast-2023-2024-african-development-bank-biannual-report-58293).

Aitken, Brian J., and Ann E. Harrison (1999). "Do Domestic Firms Benefit from Direct Foreign Investment? Evidence from Venezuela." *American Economic Review 89(3),* 605-618.

Alege, Philip O.; and Adeyemi A. Ogundipe (2014). Foreign Direct Investment and Economic Growth in ECOWAS: A System-GMM Approach (SSRN Scholarly Paper No. ID 2476365). Social Science Research Network, Rochester, NY.

Alfaro, Laura (2003). Foreign direct investment and growth: Does the sector matter. ? Harvard Business School 1–31.

Alfaro, Laura; Areendam Chanda; Sebnem Kalemli-Ozcan; and Selin Sayek (2004). FDI and Economic Growth: The Role of Local Financial Markets. *Journal of International Economics 64(1)*, 89–112. doi:10.1016/S0022-1996(03)00081-3

Ashraf, Ayesha; Dierk Herzer; and Peter Nunnenkamp (2016). The effects of greenfield FDI and cross-border M&As on total factor productivity. World Economy 39 (11): 1728–55. doi:10.1111/twec.2016.39.issue-11.

Badibanga, Thaddée and John Ulimwengu (2019). "Optimal investment for agricultural growth and poverty reduction in the democratic republic of congo - a two-sector economic growth model." *Applied Economics, DOI: 10.1080/00036846.2019.1630709.*

Balasubramanyam, Vudayagi; Mohammed Salisu; and David Sapsford (1996). Foreign Direct Investment and Growth in EP and IS Countries. *The Economic Journal 106(434)*, 92-105.

Batten, Jonathan A., and Xuan Vinh Vo (2009). An analysis of the relationship between foreign direct investment and economic growth. *Applied Economics 41 (13):* 1621–1641. doi:10.1080/00036840701493758

Bengoa, Marta; and Blanca Sanchez-Robles (2003). Foreign direct investment, economic freedom and growth: new evidence from Latin America. *European Journal of Political Economy 19 (3)*, 529–545

Blomström, Magnus, and Edward N. Wolff (1994). Multinational corporations and productivity convergence in Mexico. In Baumol William, Nelson Richard R., Wolff Edward N. (Eds), Convergence of productivity: Crossnational studies and historical evidence. 263–84. Oxford: Oxford University Press.

Blomström, Magnus; and Fredric Sjöholm (1999). Technology transfer and spillovers: Does local participation with multinationals matter? *European Economic Review 43 (4–6):* 915–23. doi:10.1016/S0014-2921(98)00104-4.

Blomstrom, Magnus; and Ari Kokko (1998). Multinational corporations and spillovers. *Journal of Economic Surveys 12 (3):* 247–77. doi:10.1111/1467-6419.00056.

Blomstrom, Magnus; Robert Lipsey and Mario Zegan (1992): "What explains developing country growth?" NBER Working Paper No. 4132, National Bureau for Economic Research, Cambridge, Massachusetts.

Borensztein, Eduardo ; José De Gregorio ; and Jong-Wha Lee (1998). How does foreign direct investment affect economic growth? *Journal of International Economics 45(1998)*, p. 115-135;

Boyd, John H. and Bruce D. Smith (1992). "Intermediation and the Equilibrium Allocation of Investment Capital: Implications for Economic Development," Journal of Monetary Economics, 30, 409-432.

Brecher, Richard (1983). "Second-Best Policy for International Trade and Investment," *Journal of International Economics 14*, 313-320.

Brecher, Richard and Carlos Diaz-Alejandro (1977). "Tariffs, Foreign Capital and Immiserizing Growth," *Journal of International Economics 7*, 317-322.

Bureau of Economic Analysis (2022). The Statistical Bulletin of China's Outward Foreign Direct Investment. Johns Hopkins University SAIS China – Africa Research Initiative (2022).

Carbonell, Jorge Bermejo and Richard A. Werner (2018) Does Foreign Direct Investment Generate Economic Growth? A New Empirical Approach Applied to Spain, *Economic Geography 94(4)*, 425-456 DOI: 10.1080/00130095.2017.1393312 (https://doi.org/10.1080/00130095.2017.1393312).

Carkovic, Maria, and Ross Levine (2002). Does Foreign Direct Investment Accelerate Economic Growth? Institute of International Economics Press, Washington DC, p. 195-221.

Castellani, Davide; and Antonello Zanfei, A. (2003). Technology gaps, absorptive capacity and the impact of inward investments on productivity of European firms. *Economics of Innovation and New Technology 12 (6)*, 555–576. doi:10.1080/714933761.

Chowdhury, Abdur; and George Mavrotas (2006). FDI and Growth: What Causes What? *World Economy 29 (1)*, 9–19. doi:10.1111/j.1467-9701.2006.00755.x

Cudjoe, Derrick A., He Yumei, and Hanhul Hu (2021). The impact of China's trade, aid and FDI on African economies. *International Journal of Emerging Markets*. https://doi.org/10.1108/ijoem-10-2020-1180.

Dahou, Karim; Haibado Ismael Omar; and Mike Pfister (2009). "Deepening African Financial Markets for Growth and Investment."

Paper presented at the Ministerial and Expert Roundtable of the NEPAD-OECD Africa Investment Initiative on November 11-12, 2009.

De Freitas, Marcus V. (2023). The Impact of Chinese Investments in Africa: Neocolonialism or Cooperation? Policy August 2, 2023. Policy Center For the New South. https://www.policycenter.ma/publications/impact-chinese-investments-africa-neocolonialism-or-cooperation#:~:text=Through%20Chinese%20investments%2C%20 African%20countries,growth%2C%20and%20improved%20overall %20prosperity.

De Gregorio, José (1992). Economic growth in Latin America. *Journal of Development Economics, 39(1)*, 59-84 (https://doi.org/10.1016/0304-3878(92)90057-G).

De Mello, Luiz R. (1999). Foreign direct investment-led growth: evidence from time series and panel data. *Oxford Economic Papers 51 (1)*, 133–151. doi:10.1093/oep/51.1.133.

Denisia, Vintila (2010). "Foreign Direct Investment Theories: An Overview of the Main FDI Theories." *European Journal of Interdisciplinary Studies 2(2)*, 104-110.

Djankov, Simeon; and Bernard Hoekman (2000). Foreign investment and productivity growth in Czech enterprises. *World Bank Economic Review 14 (1)*, 49–64. doi:10.1093/wber/14.1.49.

Durham, Benson J. (2004). Absorptive capacity and the effects of foreign direct investment and equity foreign portfolio investment on economic growth. *European Economic Review 48 (2)*, 285–306. doi:10.1016/S0014-2921(02)00264-7.

Faria, Julia (2021). Foreign Direct Investment (FDI) Flows from China and the United States to Africa Between 2003 to 2019. *Statista, October 19, 2021* (https://www.statista.com/statistics/1270433/fdi-flows-from-china-and-the-us-to-africa/).

Frimpong, Joseph Magnus; and Eric Fosu Oteng-Abayie (2006). Bivariate causality analysis between FDI inflows and economic growth in Ghana. MPRA Paper No. 351 (http://mpra.ub.uni-muenchen.de/351/)

Galal, Saifaddin (2023). Foreign Direct Investment (FDI) Stock from China into African Countries in 2021, By Sector. Statista 2024. (https://www.statista.com/statistics/1222749/fdi-flow-from-china-into-africa-by-sector/).

Germidis, Dimitri (1977). Transfer of technology by multinational corporations. Paris: Development Centre of the Organization for Economic Cooperation and Development, 1977.

Giovannetti, G. and Sanfilippo, M. (2009) "Do Chinese exports Crowd-out African Goods? An Econometric Analysis by country and sector", *The European Journal of Development Research 21(4),* pp. 506-530.

Goedde, Lutz, Amand Ooko-Ombaka, and Gillian Pais (2019). Private-sector Companies Can Find Practical Solutions to Enter and Grow in Africa's Agricultural Market. Winning in Africa's Agricultural Market (February 2, 2019). McKinsey & Company. (https://www.mckinsey.com/industries/agriculture/our-insights/winning-in-africas-agricultural-market#/)

Gorg, Holger; and David Greenaway (2004). Much ado about nothing? do domestic firms really benefit from foreign direct investment? The World Bank research observer 19 (2), 171–197.

Gui-Diby, Steve (2014). Impact of foreign direct investments on economic growth in Africa: Evidence from three decades of panel data analyses. Research in Economics 68 (3), 248–256. doi:10.1016/j.rie.2014.04.003.

Haddad, Mona and Ann Harrison (1993). Are there positive spillovers from direct foreign investment? Evidence from panel data for Morocco. *Journal of Development Economics 42*, 51-74.

Hermes, Niels; and Robert Lensink, (2003). Foreign direct investment, financial development and economic growth. *Journal of Development Studies 40 (1),* 142–63. doi:10.1080/00220380412331293707.

Herzer, Dierk (2012). How Does Foreign Direct Investment Really Affect Developing Countries' Growth? *Review of International Economics 20 (2)*, 396–414. doi:10.1111/j.1467-9396.2012.01029.x

Herzer, Dierk; Stephen Klasen; and Felicitas Nowak-Lehmann D. (2008). "In search of FDI-led growth in developing countries: The way forward." *Economic Modelling 25 (5)*, 793–810. doi:10.1016/j.econmod.2007.11.005

Javorcik, Beata Smarzynska (2004). Does Foreign Direct Investment Increase the Productivity of Domestic Firms? In Search of Spillovers Through Backward Linkages. *American Economic Review 94(3)*, 605–627.

Jensen, Nathan M. (2008). *Nation-States and the Multinational Corporation: A Political Economy of Foreign Direct Investment.* Princeton University Press.

Johnson, Andreas (2006). The effects of FDI on host country economic growth. Working Paper 58. Stockholm, Sweden: Royal Institute of Technology, Centre of Excellence for Studies in Science and Innovation.

Jones, Carla D., Hermann A. Ndofor, and Mengge Li (2022). Chinese Economic Engagement in Africa: Implications for U.S. Policy. Foreign Policy Research Institute. https://www.fpri.org/article/2022/01/chinese-economic-engagement-in-africa/#:~:text=More%20recently%2C%20U.S.%20Secretary%20of,that%20encompasses%20several%20African%20countries.

Koomson-Abekah, Isaac, and Eugene C. Nwaba (2018). Africa-China investment and growth link. *Journal of Chinese Economic and Foreign Trade Studies.* https://doi.org/10.1108/JCEFTS-11-2017-0034.

Koumou, Roquia Fane Madouka and Wang Manyi (2016). Effects of Chinese Foreign Direct Investment in Africa. *Journal of Finance and Accounting 4(3)*, pp. 131-139. doi: 10.11648/j.jfa.20160403.15

Li, Xiaoying; and Xiaming Liu (2005). Foreign direct investment and economic growth: An increasingly endogenous relationship. *World Development 33 (3)*, 393–407. doi:10.1016/j.worlddev.2004.11.001.

Lichtenberg, Frank, and Bruno Van Pottelsberghe De La Potterie (1998). International R&D spillovers: A comment. *European Economic Review 42 (8)*, 1483–1491. doi:10.1016/S0014-2921(97)00089-5.

Lipsey, Robert E. (2002), "Home and Host Country Effects of FDI", National Bureau of Economic Research, Working Paper 9293 (http://www.nber.org/papers/w9293).

Mansfield, Edwin and Anthony Romeo, (1980), Technology transfers to overseas subsidiaries by US-based firms. *Quarterly Journal of Economics 95(4)*.

Mencinger, Jože (2003). Does Foreign Direct Investment Always Enhance Economic Growth? *Kyklos 56(4)*, 491-508.

Miao Miao, Dinkneh Gebre Borojo, Jiang Yushi, and Tigist Abebe Desalegn (2021). The impacts of Chinese FDI on domestic investment and economic growth for Africa, Cogent Business & Management, 8:1, 1886472, DOI: 10.1080/23311975.2021.1886472. https://doi.org/10.1080/23311975.2021.1886472

Mun, Har Wai; Teo Kai Lin, and Yee Kar Man (2008). FDI and Economic Growth Relationship: An Empirical Study on Malaysia. *International Business Research 1(2)*, 11-18. DOI:10.5539/ibr.v1n2p11

Olofsdotter, Karin (1998). "Foreign direct investment, country capabilities and economic growth." *Review of World Economics Vol. 134 (3)*, 534-547.

Prasad, Eswar; Raghuram Rajan; and Arvind Subramanian, A. (2007). Foreign capital and economic growth. *Brookings Papers on Economic Activity 2007 (1)*, 153–230. doi:10.1353/eca.2007.0016.

Rappaport, Jordan (2000). "How Does Openness to Capital Flows Affect Growth?" Mimeo, Federal Reserve Bank of Kansas City, (June).

Reisen, Helmut; and Marcelo Soto (2001). Which types of capital inflows foster developing country growth? *International Finance 4 (1)*, 1–14. doi:10.1111/infi.2001.4.issue-1.

Reuters (2024). Chinese Companies to Invest Up to $7 billion in Congo Mining Infrastructure. January 27, 2024, 12:04 PM EST (https://www.reuters.com/markets/commodities/chinese-invest-up-7-bln-congo-mining-infrastructure-statement-2024-01-27/).

Romer, Paul (1993). Idea gaps and object gaps in economic development. *Journal of Monetary Economics 32(1993)*, 543-573.

Shetewy, Nsreen, and L. Jiang (2019). The Impact of Chinese FDI on Economic Growth in North Africa. Journal of Poverty, Investment and Development. https://doi.org/10.7176/cmr/11-3-01.

Smarzynska, Beata (2002): "Spillovers from Foreign Direct Investment through Backward Linkages: Does Technology Gap Matter?" Mimeo, World Bank.

Taylor, Michael; and Nigel Thrift (2013). The Geography of Multinationals: Studies in the Spatial Development and Economic Consequences of Multinational Corporations. Routledge.

Toone, Jordan E (2013). Mirage in the Gulf?: Examining the Upsurge in FDI in the GCC and Its Legal and Economic Implications for the MENA Region (SSRN Scholarly Paper No. ID 2150603). Social Science Research Network, Rochester, NY.

Tupy, Marian L., and Dalibor Rohac (2014). Sustaining the Economic Rise of Africa. Economic Development Bulletin *(22)*, August 1, 2014. Center For Global Liberty & Prosperity. Cato Institute. (https://www.cato.org/sites/cato.org/files/pubs/pdf/economic-development-bulletin-22.pdf).

Türkcan, Burcu, Alper Duman, and I. Hakan Yetkiner (2008). "How Does FDI and Economic Growth Affect Each Other? The OECD Case," Papers of the Annual IUE-SUNY Cortland Conference in Economics, in: Oguz Esen & Ayla Ogus (ed.), Proceedings of the Conference on Emerging Economic Issues in a Globalizing World, pages 21-40, Izmir University of Economics.

United Nations Statistics Division, UN COMTRADE (2023). International Merchandise Trade Statistics. Available online at http://comtrade.un.org/

World Bank (2023). World Development Indicators -WDI 2023. The World Bank Group - Washington, DC.

Yabi, Olakounlé Gilles (2010). *Investissements directs étrangers et croissance: Théories et analyse économétrique appliquée aux pays en développement.* Editions universitaires europeennes EUE.

Young, S., and Lan, P. 1997. Technology transfer to China through foreign direct investment. *Regional Studies 31 (7),* 669–79. doi:10.1080/00343409750130759.

Zhang, Kevin (2001). Does Foreign Direct Investment Promote Economic Growth? Evidence From East Asia And Latin America. Contemporary Economic Policy 19 (2), 175–185.

Ze Yu, Shirley (2021). Why Substantial Chinese FDI Is Flowing Into Africa. *China-Africa Initiative, April 2, 2021* (https://blogs.lse.ac.uk/africaatlse/2021/04/02/why-substantial-chinese-fdi-is-flowing-into-africa-foreign-direct-investment/).

APPENDIX

Table 1. Ordinary Least Squares' Estimation of the three models

Dependent Variable: Per Capita GDP Growth Rate (PCGDPG)

Independent Variable	Linear (P-values in parentheses)	Logarithmic (P-values in parentheses)	Quadratic (P-value in parentheses)
FDI_RATIO	-0.2879 (0.7950)	-	-11.1799* (0.0810)
LN_FDI_RATIO	-	-0.0929 (0.5960)	-
FDI_RATIOSQUARE	-	-	20.8574* (0.0990)
Z	0.9790* (0.0000)	0.9856* (0.000)	0.9818* (0.0000)
Constant	1.0950 (0.2400)	0.8226 (0.1800)	2.1414* (0.0050)
R^2	0.9463	0.9583	0.9222
Adjusted R^2	0.9400	0.9534	0.9076
$httest(\chi^2_{(1)})$	0.1600 (0.6864)	0.0100 (0.9312)	0.0600 (0.8136)
$LM\ test(\chi^2_{(1)})$	10.8840 (0.0010)	11.2790 (0.0008)	7.758 (0.0053)
dw-stat (original)	0.5300	0.4600	0.7209
dw-stat (transformed)	0.4632	0.6206	0.9628
$F(k, 20-k-1)**$	149.75 (0.0000)	195.21 (0.0000)	63.23 (0.0000)
Observations	20	20	20

The * symbol indicates the estimated coefficient is statistically significant at 5% or 10% significance level.

**k is 2 in the linear and logarithmic specifications but 3 in the quadratic specification

Table 2. List of Countries with Positive Economic Effect of Chinese FDI Inflows

Number	Country	Marginal Effect (%)	Model
1	Chad	0.03	Quadratic
2	Cote d'Ivoire	0.62	Logarithmic
3	Guinea	0.39	Logarithmic
4	Kenya	3.63	Quadratic
5	Senegal	7.52	Quadratic
6	Uganda	0.79	Logarithmic

Table 3. List of Countries with Negative Economic Effect of Chinese FDI Inflows

Number	Country	Marginal Effect (%)	Model
1	Angola	-1.92	Logarithmic
		-9.08	Linear
2	Congo	-1.13	Quadratic
3	Lesotho	-11.17	Linear
4	Madagascar	-8.58	Linear
		-1.09	Logarithmic
5	Sao Tome & Principe	-0.47	Logarithmic
6	Sierra Leonne	-0.57	Quadratic
7	Tanzania	-0.15	Logarithmic
8	Tunisia	-0.89	Logarithmic
9	Zimbabwe	-0.41	Logarithmic

Table 4. List of Countries with Non-Economic Effect of Chinese FDI Inflows

Number	Country	Marginal Effect (%)	Model
1	Algeria	0.00	All
2	Benin	0.00	All
3	Botswana	0.00	All
4	Burkina Faso	0.00	All
5	Burundi	0.00	All
6	Cameroon	0.00	All
7	Cape Verde	0.00	All
8	Central African Republic	0.00	All
9	Comoros	0.00	All
10	Democratic Republic of Congo	0.00	All
11	Djibouti	0.00	All
12	Egypt	0.00	All
13	Equatorial Guinea	0.00	All
14	Eritrea	0.00	All
15	Ethiopia	0.00	All
16	Gabon	0.00	All
17	Gambia	0.00	All
18	Ghana	0.00	All
19	Guinea Bissau	0.00	All
20	Liberia	0.00	All
21	Libya	0.00	All
22	Malawi	0.00	All

23	Mali	0.00	All
24	Mauritania	0.00	All
25	Mauritius	0.00	All
26	Morocco	0.00	All
27	Mozambique	0.00	All
28	Namibia	0.00	All
29	Niger	0.00	All
30	Nigeria	0.00	All
31	Rwanda	0.00	All
32	Seychelles	0.00	All
33	South Africa	0.00	All
34	Sudan	0.00	All
35	Togo	0.00	All
36	Zambia	0.00	All

CHAPTER IV

SINO-CONGOLESE TRADE: IMPACT ON HIGHER EDUCATION INFRASTRUCTURE

by

Ngamboko P. Muzinga, PhD

Annie Kinwa-Muzinga, PhD

1. Background

The Democratic Republic of the Congo, hereafter DRC, is among the poorest countries in the world. Its Gross Domestic Product (GDP) per capita was estimated at $544.0[40] in 2020, dropping from $560.8 and $580.7 (in current US$) in 2018 and 2019, respectively. In 2018, it was estimated that 73% of the Congolese population, equaling 60 million people, lived on less than $1.90 a day (the international poverty rate). As such, almost 14% — or one out of six people living in extreme poverty in Sub-Sahara Africa (SSA) — live in DRC[41].

These figures have decreased despite (1) the DRC's effort to improve public resources management and service delivery and (2) the World Bank's commitment to building human capital and inclusive development. What seems to be paradoxical regarding DRC is the fact that it possesses an abundance of natural resources, including minerals such as diamonds, gold, cobalt and copper, cassiterite, coltan, timber, coffee, oil as well as, hydropower potential,

---

[40] The World Bank, World Development Indicators (2020). Retrieved from http://data.worldbank.org/indicator/NY.GDP.PCAP.CD

[41] The World Bank, World Development Indicators (2021). Retrieved from https://www.worldbank.org/en/country/drc/overview#1

significant arable land, immense biodiversity, and the world's second-largest rainforest. Note that coltan (short for columbite-tantalite) is a valued input in producing several electronic devices, including cameras, mobile phones, printers, and refractive lenses for glasses[42]. DRC is one of the top two world producers of coltan, producing roughly more than 30% of the world's tantalum (370 Metric Tons (MT) in 2017).[43]

Given this gigantic resource endowment, how could the DRC fight against this alarming poverty and trigger economic growth? What financial strategies, trade agreements, or economic development policies has the DRC government undertaken recently to ensure wealth has been created and distributed relatively among its population?

Literature suggests many ways to attain economic development, including consumer spending and investment, tax cuts, deregulation, innovation, infrastructure spending, and foreign direct investment, to name a few. Despite various ways to trigger economic growth and development, many experts in development theories and policymakers firmly posit that education is one of the forces mentioned frequently but has yet to receive serious consideration in emerging markets. Azturk (2001)[44] best describes the role of education in economic development. According to Azturk, education, in every sense, is one of the fundamental factors of development. Every country can achieve sustainable economic development with substantial investment in human capital. Education enriches people's understanding of themselves and the world. It improves the quality of their lives and leads to broad social benefits for individuals and society. Education raises people's productivity and creativity and

---

[42] "Commodity Report 2008: Tantalum" (PDF). United States Geological Survey. Retrieved 2008 - 10 - 24

[43] https://investingnews.com/daily/resource-investing/critical-metals-investing/tantalum-investing/2013-top-tantalum-producers-rwanda-brazil-drc-canada/

[44] Ozturk, Ilhan, 2001. "The role of education in economic development: a theoretical perspective," MPRA Paper 9023, University Library of Munich, Germany.

promotes entrepreneurship and technological advances. In addition, it plays a very crucial role in securing economic and social progress and improving income distribution.

Education's unquestionable role in economic development would be at the core of negotiations between the DRC government and its financial partners. In recent years, China has become a major DRC partner in several infrastructure-building projects. In fact, in 2007, the DRC government and a group of state-owned enterprises signed the 2007 Sino-Congolese agreement[45], in which both countries agreed that several public infrastructure projects would be constructed with Chinese loans. To guarantee reimbursement, a Congolese/Chinese joint venture was created to extract and sell Congolese minerals, including cobalt, copper, and gold, making it the most prominent trade investment China made back then in Africa[46]. Indeed, China agreed to finance the realization of some of these projects; however, China decided to carry them out. For 10 billion dollars, China was to build roads, the Kinshasa-Ilebo railway, schools, and hospitals and electrify some towns and cities[47].

The main objective of this mega agreement was to reduce poverty by targeting the five construction sites, including infrastructure, employment, education, health, and electrification of the country.

How has the Sino-Congolese agreement been assessed regarding its infrastructure component in higher educational settings? In other words, have substantial buildings been constructed or renovated due to the Sino-Congolese agreement's educational component (building universities or school infrastructure)? If yes, were these constructions

---

[45] Stefaan, M & Sara G, (2009). Win-win or unequal exchange. The case of the Sino-Congolese cooperation agreement. *Journal of Modern African Studies*, 47 (3), 371 - 396. doi:10.1017/Soo22278

[46] Stefaan, M & Sara G, (2009). Win-Win or unequal exchange. The case of Sino-Congolese cooperation agreement. *Journal of Modern African Studies*, 47 (3), 371 - 396. doi:10.1017/Soo22278

[47] Kabaka, P.I, (2018). La Chine en RD Congo : relecture du contrat infrastructures contre minerais. Ffhal-01711338ff

based on the vision and mission statements of Congolese colleges and universities? What is the current state of DRC higher education in terms of its competitiveness locally, regionally, or continentally after the Sino-Congolese trade agreement? If no, what lessons can be learned from this experience?

An abundant body of literature and communications exists, ranging from journal articles, seminars, and conference proceedings to political debates, theses, and dissertations discussing the merits or failures of the Sino-Congolese agreement. Still, thus far, it has yet to thoroughly investigate its implications in higher education despite its undeniable role in economic development.

2. Research Questions

The main objective of this paper is to assess whether or not the Sino-Congolese agreements have improved the infrastructure of higher education in the DRC. Specifically, this study evaluates how many new or renovated university buildings or schools have been built across the country under the Sino-Congolese agreement.

The paper uses two research methods: (1) secondary data and (2) focus groups of Congolese involved in the Sino-Congolese trade agreement, educators, and those indirectly involved.

3. Literature Review

The present section reviews significant conversations surrounding higher and university education about (1) the state of higher education and university in the RDC and the background related to the Sino-Gongolese trade, especially on the construction of the two universities.

3.1 State of Higher Education and University in the DRC

3.1.1 General Context

There exists a vast body of literature about the historical perspective of higher education in the DRC (Wattenberg & Smith,

1963; Parelius, R . & Parelius, A. 1987, and Hill, J. 2006)[48] and Bashonga, Y., R. (2008)[49] For this particular paper, we focus our literature review on higher and university education from the 1971 reform and after that. Higher and university education in the DRC, represented by the National University of Zaire (UNAZA), went very quickly from being one of the elite universities in Africa around the 1970s (the 3rd place in Africa) to becoming a mediocre higher and university education. Worse, it is not even on the list of the top 200 universities in Africa (2020 Ranking of the Top 200 Universities in Africa - Sambac). What is deplorable is that many African universities ranked way below UNAZA are now not only ranked ahead of the three major universities of the DRC (University of Kinshasa, Lubumbashi, and Kisangani) but are also placed well on the top of the list. The challenges in the Congolese higher education and university sector are enormous. The degradation of the education system, plagued by corruption and mismanagement, is among the causes.

DRC political leaders, scientists, and decision-makers recognize the value of science, technology, and innovation in boosting economic development, reducing poverty, and attaining sustainable development goals (MDGs). Despite the importance of science, technology, and innovation, research and development (R&D) has been marginalized because of limited resources that could trigger research and Innovations. As a result, higher education and universities in the RDC have failed for so long to deliver their core mission (teaching, outreach, and research) and compete efficiently at local, regional, or continental levels. The little research carried out in universities and research institutes is dictated and funded by donor organizations (Belgian Cooperation, USAID, and others).

---

[48] Hill, J. (2006). History of Christianity. Oxford: Lion Publishing Parelius, R. & Parelius, A. (1987). The Sociology of Education. New-Jersey: Prentice Hall. Wattenberg, B., & Ralph Lee Smith. (1963). The New Nations of Africa. New York: Publishing Company.

[49] Bashonga, Y. (2008). A study of Challenging in Ensuring Quality Higher Education in the Democratic Republic of the Congo. [Unpublished master's Thesis, Strayer University].

Infrastructure in education has been one of the five chantiers included in the Sino-Congolese agreement without prior conditionality on good governance and human rights. [50]

3.1.2 Distribution of Higher Education and University Institutions Across the Country

The number of higher education and universities in the DRC is still being determined. The World Bank (2005) and the Ministry of Higher Education and Universities (Enseignment Supérieur et Universitaire - MESU) provide contradicting numbers. Despite that, it is safe to argue that today, the DRC has approximately 123 universities and institutes of higher education[51]. It could have had more, but 175 institutions were deemed non-viable and closed in May 2015.

What is certain is that all the provinces have at least a higher education and university institutions. However, there is a wide variation in the number of these institutions nationwide. The well-endowed higher education and university provinces include Kinshasa, Katanga, North Kivu, and South Kivu. Kinshasa, North Kivu, and South Kivu each have more than 25 higher education institutions. Katanga has 16 to 25 higher education and university institutions; Kongo Central (11-15) and the provinces of Haut Lomami, Kisangani, and Equateur have about 5 to 10 higher education and universities. All other remaining provinces have, on average, less than five higher education institutions per province.

Notwithstanding these distributions, it is therefore vital to know that the diagnosis that several observers make of the higher education system in the DRC is alarming: it suffers in abundance from a crisis of relevance of its action (raison d'être). Therefore, it is clear that in their current management, universities and other higher institutes in the DRC, whether public, private, or community, as social

---

[50] Shirambere, P., (2020) "The Democratic Republic of the Congo-China's Deals on Construction of Roads in Exchange of Mines", Afrika Focus 33(2), doi; https://doi.org/10.21825/af.v33i2.17578

[51] https://www.4icu.org/cd/

regeneration institutions, do not significantly play the role of change, innovation, and creation. The university in the DRC has ceased to contribute to the self-reflection of society, to allow a confrontation of ideas, and to play a cultural role. Despite many reforms the government and other agents took, many negative aspects continue to plague the university environment. The current (October 2022) Minister of Higher and University Education is implementing the government's 2021-2023 action program to improve and innovate this sector. The program aims to establish education as the primary foundation in the drive for sustainable development and prosperity for Congolese society (University World News)[52]. Figure 1 below shows the distribution of higher education and universities in DRC nationwide.

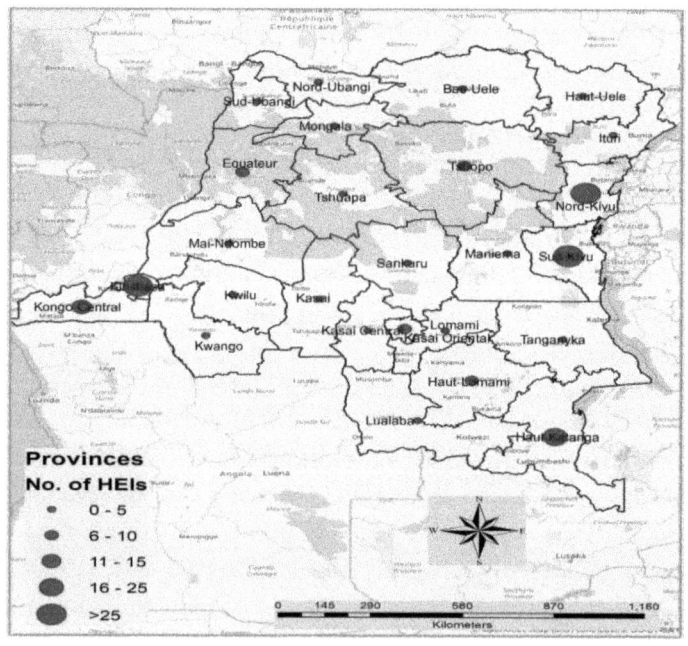

Source: Ruforum (2020): Strengthening higher education and technical education in DRC.

---

[52] University World News, African edition, September 21, 2021. https://www.universityworldnews.com/post.php?story=20210922162044456

3.1.3 Major Issues Confronting the Higher and University Education Sector in the DRC

Since 1971, when the UNAZA, the multi-campus National University of Zaire, was created, the higher and university education sector has faced significant issues that prevent it from playing its role in the development and prosperity of Congolese society. These issues are well documented in several publications.[53] Below, the present paper summarizes them, in a nutshell, to allow whoever is interested in this strategic sector to quickly understand the straitjacket blocking bold that the industry must, modicum, remove for successful, pragmatic, innovative, and vital reforms to come. These issues include

1. Unsuccessful past reforms;
2. Poor working and living conditions of teaching, administrative, technical, and other staff;
3. Political and Economic evolutions and conditions have toppled universities into ways of mistakes and anti-values, creating unsustainable universities, schools, and institutes;
4. Under-qualified teaching and administrative personnel offering inadequate education and cut-price qualifications wrestling in "discount degree canteens";
5. Asymmetrical distribution of professors and concentration of qualified teachers" in the three universities of Kinshasa, Kisangani, and Lubumbashi;
6. Quality and quantity actual deficit in producing scientific, academic publications;
7. Unfeasible student-teacher ratio by a division between research and teaching;
8. Limited funding from the government and lack of monitoring of government actions to improve colleges and universities' institutional goals;
9. Lack of private donors;

---

[53] https://en.wikipedia.org/wiki/National_University_of_Zaire

10. Poor control and monitoring of partnerships between universities and businesses.

Given these bitter observations, one ought to believe that the Sino-Congolese trade agreement, in its education and infrastructure components, would intentionally tackle and address the above insufficiencies.

3.2 The Sino-Congolese Contract: Infrastructure

The Sino-Congolese contract of 2007-8, often called the "mining contract," is based on five pillars, including Infrastructure Development, such as the construction and rehabilitation of roads, railways, hospitals, health centers, housing units, and universities.

Roughly speaking, as part of the agreement, a US$2 billion loan was intended to modernize the mining production facility. Two Chinese companies – Sinohydro and CREC (China Railway Engineering) – were expected to carry out infrastructure work valued at $6 billion, including the construction of 3500 km of paved roads, a highway, and bridges connecting the main cities of the country (Lubumbashi, Bukavu, Goma, Kisangani), as well as the construction and repair of 450 km of roads within the capital city. Additionally, the agreement included the construction or rehabilitation of 3213 km of railway, the establishment of 31 hospitals with 150 beds each, the creation of 145 health centers, the construction of 5000 units of low-cost housing, and the establishment of two universities. As noted above, the interest of this paper is essentially in the construction and rehabilitation of 2 large modern universities and two vocational training centers for building and public works in Kinshasa and Lubumbashi. However, reports indicate that little to no progress has been made on these projects.

The lack of progress has been attributed to various factors, including delays in funding, bureaucratic hurdles, and project management and oversight issues. As a result, the construction and rehabilitation of the universities have stalled, leaving the projects incomplete.

Despite the results of the reports we have read on the construction of the two universities, this study is invaluable because it aims to confirm or refute the reports alluded to by using primary data and a survey of Congolese academics, both men and women, who are sufficiently educated about the Sino-Congolese contract.

4. Theoretical Framework and Development of Hypothesis

The Socio-economic impact, the Triple Bottom Line (TBL)[54], is the conceptual or theoretical framework this study adopts to analyze the impact of constructing and rehabilitating two universities and vocational training centers in Kinshasa and Lubumbashi (RDC). This framework would assess the project's socio-economic impact, including its contribution to job creation, skills development, and overall economic growth.

In the context of this study, the Triple Bottom Line (TBL) framework suggests that when governments or organizations enter into contracts with either private or public contractors, such as the Sino-Congolese agreement, they should consider three performance dimensions: economic, environmental, and economic (financial). John Elkington proposed the TBL in 1994[55], and has since become a widely used theory of sustainability and corporate social responsibility (CSR). The three dimensions are often called "profit, planet, and people."

4.1 Economic Impacts

The economic impact of a university's construction or remodeling infrastructure is context-specific, and each university may vary. Ceteris paribus, this particular paper considers only (1) the long-term economic impact and (2) some qualitative impact metrics, although

---

[54] Sánchez del Río-Vázquez, M.-E., Rodríguez-Rad, C. J., & Revilla-Camacho, M.-Á. (2019). Relevance of social, economic, and environmental impacts on residents' satisfaction with the public administration of tourism. Sustainability, 11(22), 6380. https://doi.org/10.3390/su11226380

[55] Elkington, J. (1997). Cannibals with Forks: The Triple Bottom Line of 21st Century Business. Oxford: Capstone Publishing

some papers add direct and indirect impacts to the list as well as quantitative metrics.

Regarding long-term economic impact, it has been acknowledged that new facilities positively increase enrollment by attracting new students, both domestic and international. Enrollment with new students might increase tuition, revenue, and economic activities in the area (Kinshasa and Lubumbashi, for instance). Furthermore, new construction or remodeling, in this particular case, can improve research and innovation. Indeed, renovated research labs and facilities can enhance a university's reputation, attract grants, and foster innovation. Lastly, the long-term economic impact also emphasizes community engagement. In this matter, facilities such as theaters, sports complexes, and conference centers draw visitors, generating additional revenue and stimulating local businesses.

Concerning the qualitative factors[56], a university's construction and renovation improve the quality of life with improved facilities that enhance the overall campus experience for students, faculty, and staff. Also, it can significantly affect the overall community perception because a well-maintained campus can positively influence the community's perception of the university. Finally, one should include that the upgraded facilities can attract top researchers and foster collaboration.

4.2 Environmental Impact

Universities can balance the environmental impact of construction and renovation by making informed decisions, prioritizing sustainability, and leveraging existing resources. Kinshasa and Lubumbashi are the RDC cities facing severe environmental challenges. Any actions to tackle these issues directly or indirectly are to be undertaken. Therefore, the construction and renovation of universities and other vocational training centers mentioned in the

---

[56]Marzo-Navarro, M., Pedraja-Iglesias, M., & Vinzón, L. (2015). Sustainability indicators of rural tourism from the perspective of the residents. Tourism Geographies, 17, 586–602. https://doi.org/10.1080/14616688.2015.1051162

Sino-Congolese agreement should have addressed these environmental issues. Properly handling these ecological issues through construction and renovation projects has several benefits.

When renovating, repurposing, or upgrading universities and other vocational training centers, chances are that the agreement could turn time-worn buildings into leading-edge facilities. Another advantage is related to energy efficiency and resource conservation. Indeed, the Sino-Congolese deal had the potential to incorporate energy-efficient designs, sustainable materials, and efficient systems. Other advantages include indoor environmental quality (IEQ)[57], which argues that proper ventilation, natural lighting, and low-VOC (Volatile Organic Compounds) materials contribute to healthier indoor environments. VOCs are chemicals that can quickly evaporate into the air at room temperature. They are often found in many materials and products, such as paints, cleaning supplies, and building materials. VOCs can have short-term and long-term health effects and contribute to indoor air pollution.[58] Finally, the additional benefits of renovating buildings as described in the Sino-Congolese agreement are that they are more cost-effective, with the core and shell of the old building remaining in place, saving on initial costs.

4.3 Social-Cultural Impact

In the context of the Sino-Congolese trade agreement, the TBL's social-cultural dimension underlines the importance of considering the agreement's broader societal and cultural impacts on its infrastructure activities beyond the traditional financial measures. If the RDC government effectively manages this dimension, it can contribute to positive social change while improving its long-term sustainability and reputation. The social-cultural TBL includes[59] (1)

---

[57] https://www.usgbc.org,

[58] https://sftool.gov/learn/about/1/indoor-environmental-quality-ieq

[59] Sánchez del Río-Vázquez, M.-E., Rodríguez-Rad, C. J., & Revilla-Camacho, M.-Á. (2019). Relevance of social, economic, and environmental impacts on residents' satisfaction with the public administration of tourism. Sustainability, 11(22), 6380. https://doi.org/10.3390/su11226380

social responsibility addressing societal needs and concerns, such as poverty alleviation, education, healthcare, and community development, (2) community engagement by actively engaging with and supporting the communities in Kinshasa and Lubumbashi in particular where the two universities and training centers will be built, (3) diversity and inclusion within the Congolese workforce enhancing organizational performance and innovation, (4) ethical practices and cultural preservation and (5) Organizations operating in diverse cultural environments stakeholder engagement.

4.4 Graphical Representation of the Triple Bottom Line

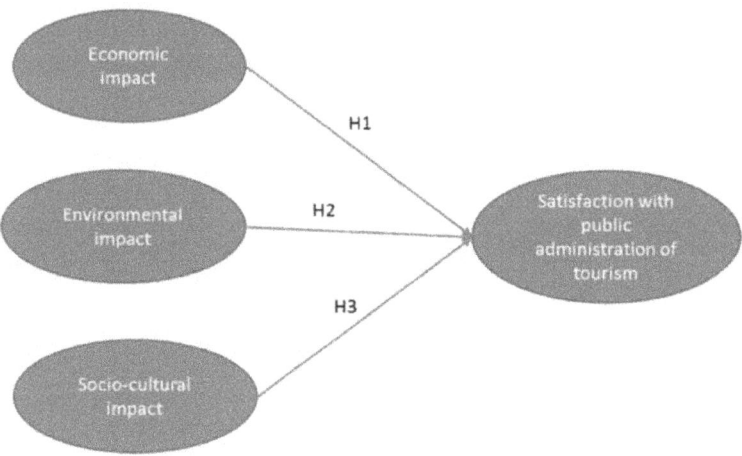

5. Methodology and Data Collection

This study uses a quantitative research method with a questionnaire as a data collection tool. The questionnaire consists of 14 questions aimed at potential college graduates in the DRC who are likely to know about the Sino-Congolese agreement. The questions focus on their awareness of the construction projects of two universities in Kinshasa and Lubumbashi and training centers and whether these constructions have been completed. Approximately 90 respondents were selected based on their potential knowledge of the Sino-Congolese agreement.

The questionnaire was distributed to the respondents chosen for the data collection procedure. The instructions for completing the questionnaire were clear, and anonymity and confidentiality of responses were maintained. Descriptive statistics were used to analyze the responses. The percentage of respondents who were aware of the construction projects and their completion status was computed. Lastly, for the validity and reliability of the statistics, the questionnaire was tested through a pilot study to ensure that respondents understood the questionnaire for what it meant and that it measured what it was intended to measure.

6. Results

This study evaluated the economic, environmental, and social impacts of building two major modern universities and two vocational training centers for construction and public on the Congolese, particularly on the population of Kinshasa and Lubumbashi under the Sino-Congolese agreement.

6.1 Descriptive Statistics

There were 90 respondents, of whom 77% were men and 33% were women. Regarding education, 84% hold a bachelor's degree, and 15% hold a master's or PhD degree. This statistic indicates our respondents' education quality; they are knowledgeable, and consequently, the quality of their responses is good. Most of the respondents, 63%, attended universities other than the RDC's three most prominent universities (Kinshasa, Lubumbashi, Kisangani). Twenty-three percent (23%) of the respondents participated at the University of Kinshasa, one of the three renowned universities in DRC. The majority of the respondents, about 54%, work either in the private (31%) or public sector (23%). The rest work for public administration (15%), primary and secondary education (8%), and higher education (8%).

The study also investigated the respondents' knowledge of the Sino-Congolese agreement. Specifically, the study asked the following question: "On a scale of 0 to 10, with 0 meaning you know absolutely nothing and ten meaning you know perfectly well, what is your level of information or knowledge about the Sino-Congolese cooperation program/agreement on the financing of the five major projects concluded in 2008 between the government of the DRC and a consortium of Chinese companies represented by the companies CREC and Sinohydro?"

The result was disturbing in light of all the propaganda about this trade agreement with the Chinese. Figure 1 shows, on the vertical axis, the number of respondents and, on the horizontal axis, their corresponding level of knowledge about the trade agreement. For instance, 23 on the vertical axis under the score of 0 on a scale of 0 to 10 indicates that 23 out of the 86 participants who responded to this question (26.74%) said they had 0 knowledge about the trade agreement. Similarly, 11 on the vertical axis under the score of 1 on a scale of 0 to 10 indicates that 11 out of the 86 participants who responded to this question (12.79%) scored one as their knowledge of the sino-agreement deal—no participants scored 8, 9 or 10.

Figure 1

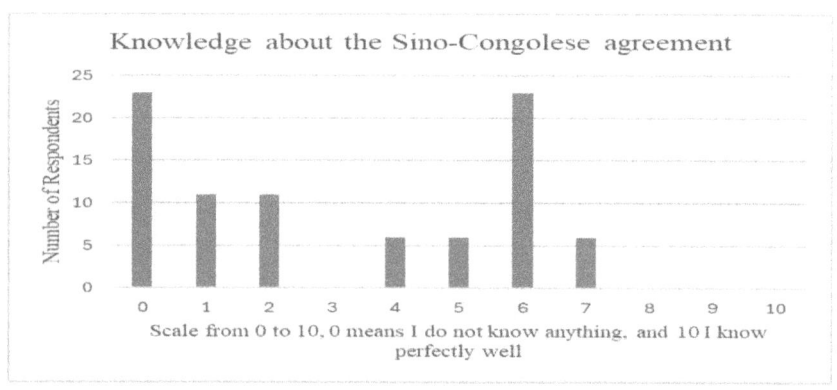

Similarly, Figure 2 below shows the number of respondents and, on the vertical axis, their corresponding level of knowledge about the construction by the Sino-Congolese trade deal of the two modern universities and training centers on the horizontal. For illustration, 23 on the vertical axis under the score of 0 on a scale of 0 to 10 indicates that 23 out of the 74 participants who responded to this question (31.08%) said they had 0 knowledge about the construction of the two universities and training centers under the Sino-Congolese trade agreement. Similarly, 45 on the vertical axis under the score of 1 on a scale of 0 to 10 indicates that 45 out of the 74 participants who responded to this question (60.81%) scored one as their knowledge of the construction in reference —no participants scored 2, 3, 4, 5, 7, 8 or 10. Nearly 92% of the participants were not informed about the construction of these two universities and training centers.

Figure 2

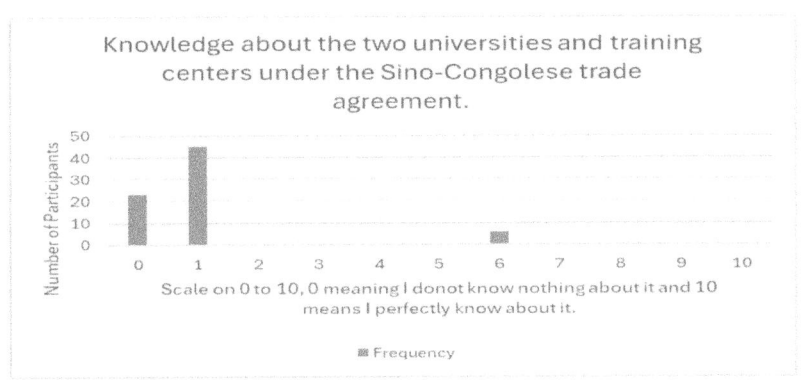

What is most shocking from both figures is the respondents' limited knowledge of the agreement and its content regarding the construction and renovation of infrastructure at higher education. Figure 1 shows that 51 out of 86 (60%) who participated in this survey scored between 0 and 4, and no one rated 8,9 or 10, implying a minimal knowledge of this agreement. Note that these are individuals supposed to be among the most educated.

Regarding Figure 2, about 92% of the respondents scored 0 or 1, indicating minimal knowledge about this Sino-Congolese agreement. Figures 3 and 4 show respondents' assessment of the progress made in constructing the two universities and the training centers, respectively. Figures 3 and 4 indicate that about 84% of the respondents needed more information about the progress in constructing two universities and training centers under the Sino-Congolese trade agreement, making it challenging to assess the agreement's economic, environmental, and social impacts.

Consequently, they could not determine if the construction had taken place. However, 14 out of 90 (16%) respondents who indicated that the two universities and the training centers had been built were unable to determine the economic, environmental, and social impacts of these constructions and renovations on the Congolese, particularly in Kinshasa and in Lubumbashi.

Figure 3

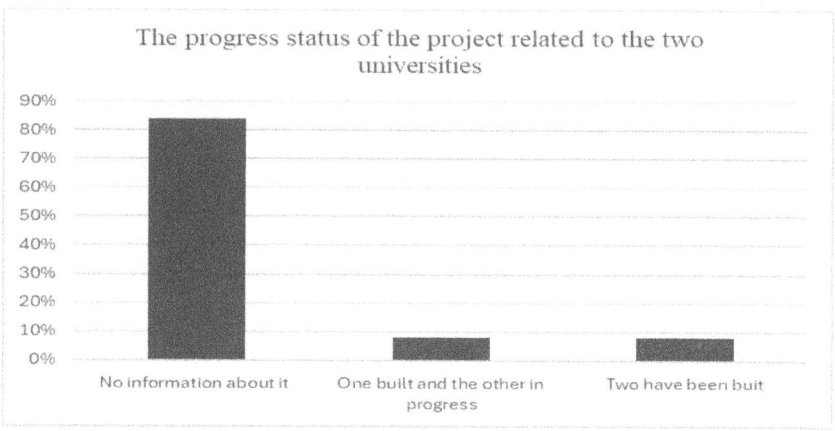

Figure 4

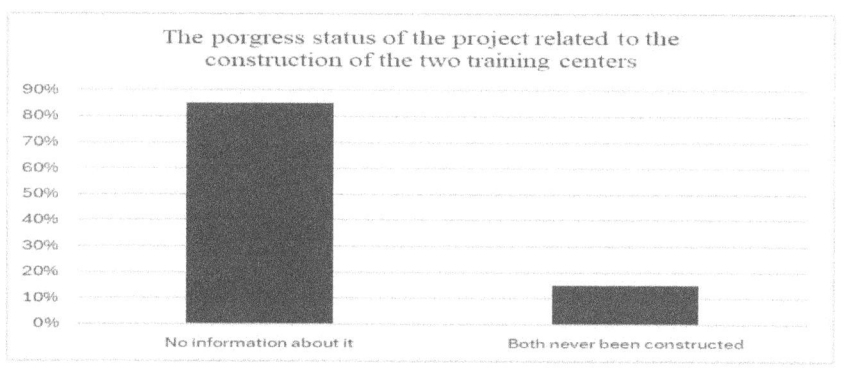

6.2 About the agreement's economic, environmental, and social impact

The goal of this paper was to assess the economic, environmental, and social impact of the construction of two universities and the renovation of training centers in Kinshasa and Lubumbashi on the Congolese in general and on the populations of Kinshasa and Lubumbashi in particular. Because so little is known about this specific subject by our respondents and also because of the substantial data gap, the study consulted other sources, such as a focus group, and interviewed some government officials at the office of the Ministry of Finance and the Ministry of Mines. Additionally, several data sources have been checked to mitigate the unreliability of statistics, and relevant qualitative information has been included to go beyond quantitative statistics.[60]

The construction of two modern universities and training centers included in the Sino-Congolese agreement was a significant component of the contract. However, the contract for these constructions and renovations was carried out differently than planned, and many consider it a fiasco. Below, the paper explains the main reasons this project failed and, more importantly, why it became challenging to assess its global impacts on the Congolese.

US millions of dollars were released by the Sino-Congolaise des Mines (Sicomines), which have been accounted for. According to Congolese officials in the focus group and those interviewed at the Finance and Mines Ministries, the problem of the trade agreement with the Chinese is more profound and not limited to the Sino-Congolese contract alone. For many, all stems from an inadequate economic model, widespread structural corruption, and an ineffective rule of law on the Congolese part that must be addressed during the subsequent renegotiation[61]. Based on the report from the Inspectorate General of Finance (IGF), a robust public institution directly under the authority of the Head of State, several other issues go beyond Sicomines and affect the entire Congolese extractive sector. The IGF posits that several investigations, including those by Congo Hold Up, posit that corruption and mismanagement within mining companies had deprived the DRC of a significant portion of its budget revenues.

---

[60] Andoni Maiza-Larrarte, Gloria Claudio-Quiroga (March 2019). The impact of Sicomines on development in the Democratic Republic of Congo, *International Affairs*, Volume 95, Issue 2, March 2019, Pages 423–446, https://doi.org/10.1093/ia/iiz001

[61] Andoni Maiza-Larrarte, Gloria Claudio-Quiroga (March 2019). The impact of Sicomines on development in the Democratic Republic of Congo, *International Affairs*, Volume 95, Issue 2, March 2019, Pages 423–446, https://doi.org/10.1093/ia/iiz001

By the way, the IGF carries out various missions to ensure the proper management of the financial operations of the Congolese state, decentralized administrative entities, public establishments, and parastatal bodies[62].

Additionally, between 2003 and 2021, a coalition called CNPAV (*Congo n'est pas a vendre* or Congo is not for sale) estimated that DRC lost 1.95 billion US dollars due to predation in the extractive sector. One can see that the country could have used that money to construct more than 8,000 kilometers of asphalt roads, more than 10,000 schools, and training centers and provide access to primary health care for 21 million people.

For the Head of the State, the IFG, and other relevant Congolese stakeholders, the successful implementation of these construction and renovation projects hinges on several key factors. Firstly, ensuring that the necessary financing is fully available is paramount. Secondly, addressing potential managerial issues such as delays, planning errors, and internal conflicts is crucial to avoid hindrances in the implementation process. Thirdly, it is essential to manage diplomatic tensions between the DRC and China effectively, as these tensions can impact the progress of these projects. Additionally, dealing with problems related to compliance with local standards, environmental regulations, and quality requirements is essential to prevent any obstacles to construction. Finally, strengthening communication gaps between project stakeholders, including the Congolese government and Chinese companies, is often overlooked but vital in preventing misunderstandings and delays.[63]

IGF[64] found that the Sicomines deal didn't guarantee fair value for Congo's minerals. Despite its flaws, the agreement offers lessons,

---

[62] Andoni Maiza-Larrarte, Gloria Claudio-Quiroga (March 2019). The impact of Sicomines on development in the Democratic Republic of Congo, *International Affairs*, Volume 95, Issue 2, March 2019, Pages 423–446, https://doi.org/10.1093/ia/iiz001

[63] Our 2023 conversation with His Excellency, Mr. Adolphe Muzito, former RDC Prime Minster from 2008-2012 and other focus group at the Finance Ministry.

[64] Our conversation with the General Inspectorate of Finance

especially in dealing with foreign nations. In the future, the DRC should reconsider such contracts, ensuring they include China supplying value-added goods and skilled workers in exchange for Congo estimating and benefiting from the economic, environmental, and social impacts, including job opportunities for its people.

In a nutshell, Congolese government officials in charge of such a deal must (1) learn to protect Congo's interest, (2) develop skills and competencies for managing contracts through small pioneer initiatives, and (3) use this failed project as a tool for improving on similar future contracts.

7. Conclusion

The paper examined the economic, environmental, and social impacts of constructing two universities and training centers within the 2008 trade agreement between China and the DRC, known as the Sino-Congolese agreement. We began by providing a context on the DRC, a country facing a significant dilemma given its poor population despite its natural wealth, including being one of the top two world producers of coltan.

The paper then addressed the degradation of the higher education sector in the DRC and the challenges it faces. The present study highlighted that, although there are many ways to achieve economic development, education is often neglected in developing countries despite being crucial for economic growth. In this context, the paper considered the Sino-Congolese trade agreement an opportunity to make higher education more competitive at the local, regional, and even continental levels.

A quantitative approach was used to conduct this study, collecting data through interviews with 90 participants. The results showed that over 80% of the respondents needed adequate information about this trade agreement, especially regarding the constructing of the two modern universities and training centers. This information gap has made it difficult to measure the consequences of the construction of the universities and training centers according to the trade agreement based on the quantitative approach. An additional source was used to understand the project better.

As the paper highlights in section 6.2, the present study advocates for (1) the necessary financing for these constructions and renovation to be fully available for implementation, (2) to avoid managerial issues such as delays, planning errors, or internal conflicts because of their potential to hinder the implementation of the constructions, (3) control diplomatic tensions between the DRC and China so that they do not affect the implementation of these projects, (4) properly deal with the problems related to compliance with local standards, environmental regulations, or quality requirements to prevent potential obstacles to the construction, (5) one often overlooked issue is strengthening the gaps in communication between project stakeholders, including the Congolese government and Chinese companies, to preventing both misunderstandings or delays.

It is vital to conduct a thorough analysis to determine why these constructions were not carried out despite the importance of the contract. Doing so can provide valuable lessons to avoid such failures in the future.

In conclusion, the Congolese authorities must take measures to inform and involve stakeholders, especially academic staff and students, in development projects such as constructing educational infrastructure. Better communication and increased participation could help maximize these projects' economic, environmental, and social benefits, thereby strengthening the education sector in the DRC and contributing to the country's overall development.

REFERENCES

Andoni Maiza-Larrarte, Gloria Claudio-Quiroga (March 2019). The impact of Sicomines on development in the Democratic Republic of Congo, *International Affairs*, Volume 95, Issue 2, March 2019, Pages 423–446, https://doi.org/10.1093/ia/iiz001

Bashonga, Y. (2008). A study of Challenging in Ensuring Quality Higher Education in the Democratic Republic of the Congo. [Unpublished master's Thesis, Strayer University].

Commodity Report 2008: Tantalum" (PDF). United States Geological Survey. Retrieved 2008 - 10 - 24

Elkington, J. (1997). Cannibals with Forks: The Triple Bottom Line of 21st Century Business. Oxford: Capstone Publishing

Hill, J. (2006). History of Christianity. Oxford: Lion Publishing

https://doi.org/10.1080/14616688.2015.1051162.

https://doi.org/10.21825/af.v33i2.17578.

https://en.wikipedia.org/wiki/National_University_of_Zaire.

https://investingnews.com/daily/resource-investing/critical-metals-investing/tantalum-investing/2013-top-tantalum-producers-rwanda-brazil-drc-canada/

https://www.4icu.org/cd/

https://www.usgbc.org,

https://www.worldbank.org/en/country/drc/overview#1

Kabaka, P.I, (2018). La Chine en RD Congo : relecture du contrat infrastructures contre minerais. Ffhal-01711338ff.

Marzo-Navarro, M., Pedraja-Iglesias, M., & Vinzón, L. (2015). Sustainability indicators of rural tourism from the perspective of the residents. Tourism Geographies, 17, 586–602.

Our 2023 conversation with His Excellency, Mr. Adolphe Muzito, former RDC Prime Minster from 2008-2012 and other focus group at the Finance Ministry.

Our conversation with the General Inspectorate of Finance

Ozturk, Ilhan, 2001. "The role of education in economic development: a theoretical perspective," MPRA Paper 9023, University Library of Munich, Germany.

Parelius, R. & Parelius, A. (1987). The Sociology of Education. New-Jersey: Prentice Hall.

Sánchez del Río-Vázquez, M.-E., Rodríguez-Rad, C. J., & Revilla-Camacho, M.-Á. (2019). Relevance of social, economic, and environmental impacts on residents' satisfaction with the public administration of tourism. Sustainability, 11(22), 6380. https://doi.org/10.3390/su11226380.

Sánchez del Río-Vázquez, M.-E., Rodríguez-Rad, C. J., & Revilla-Camacho, M.-Á. (2019). Relevance of social, economic, and environmental impacts on residents' satisfaction with the public administration of tourism. Sustainability, 11(22), 6380. https://doi.org/10.3390/su11226380

Shirambere, P., (2020) "The Democratic Republic of the Congo-China's Deals on Construction of Roads in Exchange of Mines", Afrika Focus 33(2), doi;

Stefaan, M & Sara G,. (2009). Win-win or unequal exchange. The case of the Sino-Congolese cooperation agreement. *Journal of Modern African Studies,* 47 (3), 371 - 396. doi:10.1017/Soo22278.

Stefaan, M & Sara G,. (2009). Win-Win or unequal exchange. The case of the Sino-Congolese cooperation agreement. *Journal of Modern African Studies,* 47 (3), 371 - 396. doi:10.1017/Soo22278.

The World Bank, World Development Indicators (2020). Retrieved from http://data.worldbank.org/indicator/NY.GDP.PCAP.CD

The World Bank, World Development Indicators (2021).. Retrieved from

University World News, African edition, September 21, 2021. https://www.universityworldnews.com/post.php?story=20210922162044456

Wattenberg, B., & Ralph Lee Smith. (1963). The New Nations of Africa. New York: Publishing Company.

Appendix

1.

Gender	Male	77%
	Female	33%
Level of education	Bachelor Degree and Less	84%
	PhD & Master	16%
College attended	Other Universities	62%
	University of Kinshasa	23%
	Universite Protestante du Congo	7%
	Universite Pedagogique Nationale	7%
Working sector	Private	31%
	Public	23%
	Public administration	15%
	Primary and secondary education	15%
	Higher education	8%
	Other	8%
Knowledge about the Sino-Congolese agreement	Frequency	Cumulative
0	23	23
1	11	34
2	11	45
3	0	45
4	6	51
5	6	57
6	23	80
7	6	86
8	0	86
9	0	86
10	0	86
Knowledge about two universities and two training centers	Frequency	Cumulative
0	23	23
1	45	68
2	0	68
3	0	68
4	0	68
5	0	68
6	6	74
7	0	74
.	0	74
9	0	74
10	0	74
New outlet you read about Sino-Congolese agreement	Print media	46
	Other	22
	Audiovisual (Television)	15
	Friends	7
The progress status of the project related to the construction of two (2) modern universities?"	No information about it	84%
	One built and the other in progress	8%
	Two have been built	8%
The progress status of the project related to the construction of the training centers ?"	No information about it	85%
	Both never been constructed	15%

2.

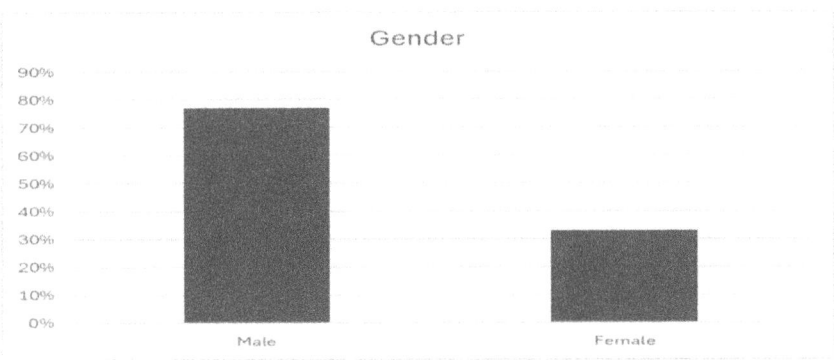

3.

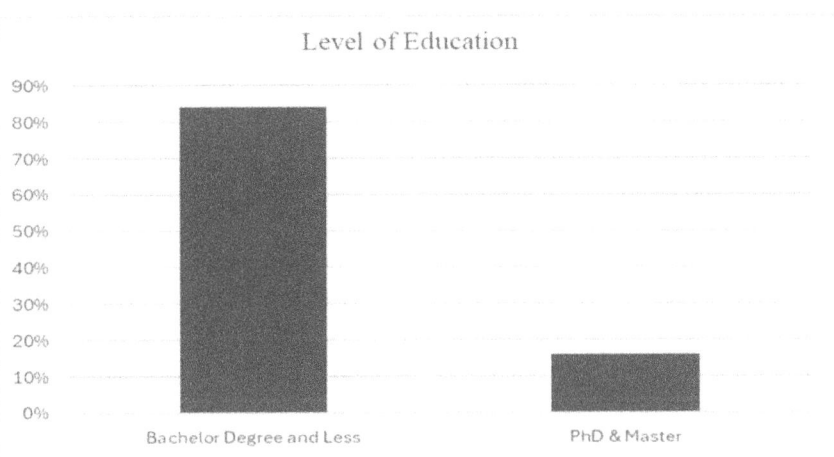

4.

5.

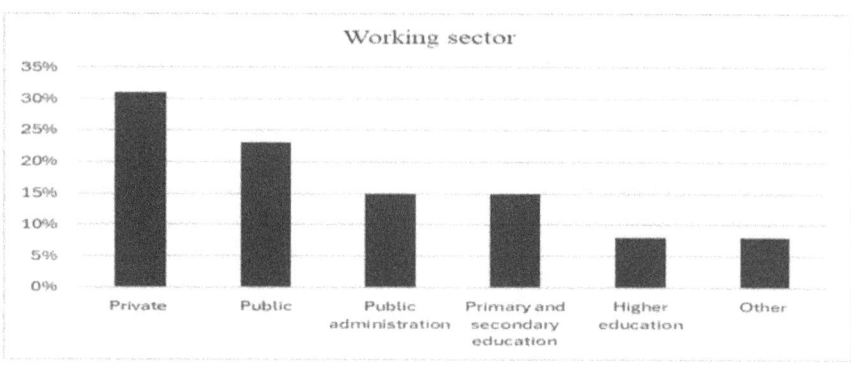

6.

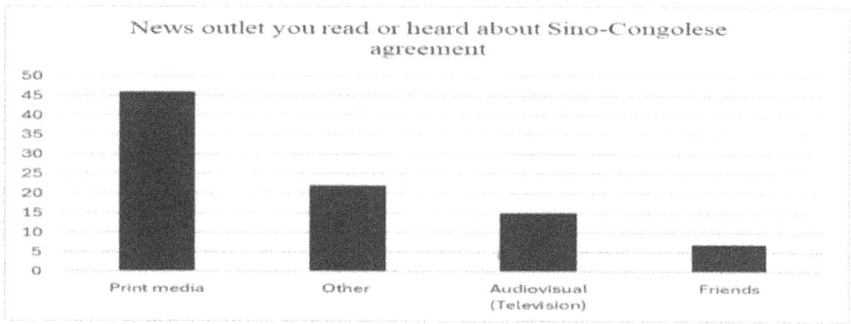

CHAPTER V

CHINA-AFRICA SCIENCE AND TECHNOLOGY COOPERATION

By

Tongele N. Tongele, PhD

1. Introduction

Today, China's presence in Africa is bold and noticeable and is interpreted in many different ways by China's allies and foes alike. For example, some believe that Beijing's outreach to *Africa* is largely driven by the desire for support on the international stage from the continent's 54 countries [1]. Others believe that China is *attracted to Africa because of its natural resources and export markets, while African leaders hope that Chinese engagement will bring* economic development [2].

In any case, it is generally recognized that modern Africa-China relations began in the late '50s and early '60s when many African countries were gaining their independence from European colonial powers [3]. This early Africa-China relationship was said to be primarily sought by China to build ideological solidarity with other underdeveloped countries to advance Chinese-style communism [4]. The relationship then developed into a full fledge partnership with the establishment in 2000 of the Forum on China-Africa Cooperation (FOCAC), a uni-multilateral partnership platform between China and 53 African states.

In theory, FOCAC creates a form of multilateralism in which all countries are equal partners, but China's interest effectively dictates 53 pairs of bilateral relationships under a single architecture [5]. As far as China is concerned [6], FOCAC, two decades later, has yielded rich fruits with respect to its initial goals of responding to the challenges emerging from economic globalization and seeking common development. FOCAC has become an important platform for collective dialogue between China and Africa and an effective mechanism for pragmatic cooperation, thus solidifying the China-Africa friendship and mutually beneficial cooperation. In his 2018 keynote speech themed "Walk Together towards Prosperity" at the opening ceremony of the high-level dialogue between Chinese and African Leaders and Business Representatives [7], President Xi Jinping of China said that "China and Africa have embarked on a distinctive path of win-win cooperation." This win-win cooperation stems from the 2006 Chinese government's African Policy Paper, which presented to the world the objectives of China's policy toward Africa and the measures to achieve them. The policy paper was divided into six parts. The fourth part was titled "Enhancing All-round Cooperation Between China and Africa" and was laid out in four sections. The third section, titled "Education, science, culture, health and social aspects," had ten titled paragraphs. The second paragraph was titled "Science and technology cooperation" and was described as follows: "Following the principles of mutual respect, complementarity, and sharing benefits, China will promote its cooperation with Africa in the fields of applied research, technological development, and transfer, speed up scientific and technological cooperation in the fields of common interest, such as bio-agriculture, solar energy utilization, geological survey, mining and research and development (R&D) of new medicines. It will continue its training programs in applied technologies for African countries, carry out demonstration programs of technical assistance, and actively help disseminate and utilize Chinese scientific and technological achievements and advanced technologies applicable in Africa." The objective sought here, in this article, is to check on the health of the "win-win" China-Africa science and technology cooperation, assess how this cooperation is being implemented, and evaluate the shared benefits in the fields of common interest as described in the policy paper.

2. Methodology

A qualitative analysis of data, facts, and information collected from reviewed works of literature on China-Africa science and technology cooperation will be conducted. The common baseline for the analysis is established by defining and briefly describing the concepts of science and technology [8-10]. This will guide the understanding of how science and technology cooperation between China and Africa is implemented and interpreted. It is hoped that this paper will provide insightful observations on the effectiveness of the cooperation, remarks on the health of China-Africa science and technology cooperation, and concluding recommendations on ways forward.

3. Science and Technology

3.1 Concept of science

Science refers to a system of acquiring and developing knowledge. This system uses observation and experimentation to describe and explain natural phenomena. The term science also refers to the organized body of knowledge people have gained using that system. Less formally, the word science often describes any systematic field of study or the knowledge gained from it.

The purpose of science is to explain the natural world and the universe through observing, thinking, and investigative practices to produce a better understanding of the portion of the natural world being examined. Scientists examine and interrogate portions of the natural world in order to construct explanations of them. In other words, science is the study of the world around us. The study generates knowledge stored in human memory and transmitted orally from person to person, or knowledge consigned in texts and books, or knowledge converted into data stored in electronic and mechanical devices.

As a human activity, science informs the fabric, the sociocultural construct, of the world people live in. In fact, understanding and gathering information that explains aspects of the natural world often leads to actions that improve living conditions.

3.2 Concept of technology

Technology is about translating knowledge, the understanding of the natural world, into practical applications, such as conceiving and designing tools or crafts, coming up with methods or techniques to solve a problem, a social problem, or creating an artistic perspective. The purpose of technology is to apply knowledge to produce something new or improve things that currently exist. Simply put, technology is a field where science is applied to create different devices and gadgets. These devices help people solve problems and do certain tasks, and overall, they make life easier and better.

3.3 Relationship between science and technology

The main connection between science and technology is that technology is the application of science [11]. Throughout history, science has paved the way for different advances in our society, and technology has been the application of scientific progress that we, as humankind, have made in the past few decades to improve living conditions. For example, from nomad hunters and gatherers, humans settled down to become farmers; they invented fire, numbering systems, and science in the heart of Africa and transformed caves into organized villages and cities [12-16]. The Western agricultural and industrial revolutions characterized by mass production have impacted and transformed our world significantly [17-18]. Mass production refers to the manufacturing of large quantities of products using efficient methods. Mass production is typically accomplished by using assembly lines, automation technology, or robotics. Manufacturers who use mass production techniques establish highly organized methods of production. The main characteristics of mass production are specialized machines, interchangeable parts, and division of labor. Being able to produce high volumes at great speed gives companies a competitive edge. Mass production has enabled countries to grow faster. However, there are also disadvantages that come with the effects of mass production. For example, by using automated technology or robotics to mass produce goods, companies may also require fewer workers.

Science provides knowledge, which is a direct source of new technological possibilities. Scientific knowledge is applied to make goods and products. Science provides a knowledge base that is essential for assessing technology and its social and environmental impact. Technology reciprocally has a great impact on science by inciting new scientific questions and helping to justify the allocation of resources and resolutions for future endeavors. Science and technology each represent a larger category of activities that are highly interdependent but distinct.

Science contributes to technology in at least six ways:

- New knowledge which serves as a direct source of ideas for new technological possibilities;
- Source of tools and techniques for more efficient engineering design and a knowledge base for evaluation of feasibility of designs;
- Research instrumentation, laboratory techniques, and analytical methods used in research that eventually find their way into design or industrial practices, often through intermediate disciplines;
- The practice of research as a source for the development and assimilation of new human skills and capabilities eventually useful for technology;
- Creation of a knowledge base that becomes increasingly important in the assessment of technology in terms of its wider social and environmental impacts;
- The knowledge base that enables more efficient strategies of applied research, development, and refinement of new technologies.

The converse impact of technology on science is of at least equal importance:

- Through providing a fertile source of novel scientific questions and thereby also helping to justify the allocation of resources needed to address these questions in an efficient and timely manner, extending the agenda of science, and

- As a source of otherwise unavailable instrumentation and techniques needed to address novel and more difficult scientific questions more efficiently.

The main connection between science and technology is that technology is the application of science as well as the engine for further advances in science. Manufacturing and the industries are the results of science and technology. Tools that help society are the result of manufacturing and industries. One such tool is the computer, a work of art that has transformed many ways of living and working in society. The impact of science, technology, and manufacturing on human lives, on society, and on the natural world cannot be overemphasized. Day-to-day life in the modern world is driven by science, technology, and manufacturing, to mention things like electricity, telephone, computers, automobiles, aircraft, and household appliances. Society cannot do without science, technology, manufacturing, and the industries the world has today [19-21].

4. Science, Technology, Africa, and the World

Geologists and paleontologists have documented facts that strongly support the opinion that science, technology, and manufacturing began in Africa [22-23] with the human species' successful conversion of natural resources into simple tools. The prehistorical discovery of the ability to control fire increased the available sources of food. The later invention of the wheel helped humans travel and control their environment. Recent technological developments in the West, including the printing press, the telephone, and the internet, have lessened physical barriers to communication and allowed human interactions on a global scale.

However, not all technology has been used for peaceful purposes in the world; the development of weapons of ever-increasing destructive power has progressed throughout history, from clubs to nuclear weapons. Unfortunately, the many destructive conflicts and wars around the world reveal the downside of the truth about science, technology, manufacturing, and industries when misused by humans [24-25].

It is often lamented how Africa, a continent that gave birth to humans, science, and technology, has fallen so behind! Will science and technology (S & T) cooperation with China make Africa rebound from its economy, which is essentially based on the export of raw materials and natural resources, to an economy driven by science and technology innovations?

5. China's Experience in International Science and Technology Cooperation

5.1 Strategy

In 1995, President Jiang Zemin pointed out that the International Science and Technology Cooperation (ISTC) justifies its existence on the basis of reciprocity and mutual interests and on its benefits to the science and technology advancement and economic development in different countries, and must play a positive role in promoting China's science and technology advancement and economic growth. Consequently, China made a conscious decision, through well-organized cooperative activities, to ensure that the international science and technology cooperation plays, and it has played, a leading role in supporting dedicated national science and technology programs in the major fields, capacity building, building of industrialization system, building of supportive environment, building science and technology infrastructure development and science and technology services. Short and long-term science and technology programs and implementing activities are planned with associated evaluation mechanisms.

5.2 Principles

Equality and reciprocal benefits, results sharing, protection of intellectual property rights, and observance of international norms are all China's principles.

5.3 Guiding policies

With safeguarding the national interest and security as the fundamental objectives, ISTC should realize its roles as a promoter, guider, supporter, and service provider to foreign affairs, economy, and science and technology, in accordance with the requirements put forward by China's national economy, social development, and science and technology activities and with the overall deployment of national economic, and science and technology development strategies. The development strategies ensure that ISTC supports China's master foreign policies domestically and helps implement strategies for rejuvenating the nation with science, education, and sustainable development. ISTC should also adopt an open strategy of "reaching out" and promoting "thriving the trade with science and technology."

5.4 Five-year plan period

China made a conscious decision to set a year planning, execution, and evaluation period for science and technology innovation capacity building, with a focus on strengthening inter-governmental cooperation with the major science and technology world powers. Hence, during ISTC, China pays more attention to the digestion, absorption, and adaptation of imported technologies and actively encourages industrial enterprises to join international science and technology cooperation and exchanges on the cutting edge of technological development. China decided to initiate, support, and promote China's high-tech industries to enter the international market, making their technical innovation activities in line with international norms and merging into international communities on China's own initiatives and objectives.

China puts effort and means to tap up the intellectual resources in ISTC in order to encourage the flow of overseas intellectual resources into China. This is the key to understanding China's achievement of the frog-leap science and technology development in the country.

5.5 China's ISTC Awards

China established its concrete mechanism for attracting and enabling the flow of science and technology from world powers to China. One of these mechanisms is the China International Science and Technology Cooperation Award (ISTC), established in 1992 to recognize and encourage foreign science and technology experts and science and technology management experts who have rendered outstanding contributions to China's international science and technology cooperation. In addition to this top national honorable award in the field of foreign science and technology affairs, other governmental agencies, such as the State Foreign Experts Administration, Ministry of Agriculture, Shanghai Municipality, and other local authorities, have also created their own international cooperation awards or friendship awards.

From 1995 to 1998, 14 foreign experts from the UK, Germany, Japan, USA, Russia, France, Singapore, etc., had been conferred with the China International S&T Cooperation Award. Among the winners are foreign nationals who have been enthusiastic about the cooperation of science and technology with China, though also including some famous people of Chinese blood, such as Tsung-dao Lee, Chen Ning Yang, and Leoh Ming Pei.

5.6 China's bilateral S&T cooperation

Another mechanism that enables and supports China's leapfrog of science and technology development is China's aggressive and systematic embankment into bilateral science and technology cooperation with world powers. After 1978, China started its massive inter-governmental cooperation and exchanges with developed nations. Up to date, there have been 152 countries or regions in the world that have established S&T cooperation and exchange ties with China, of whom 96 countries have signed with China inter-governmental S&T cooperation agreements or economic, trade, and S&T cooperation agreements. *5.6.1 Inter-governmental S&T cooperation agreements* As of March 30, 1999, China's intergovernmental S&T cooperation agreements include:

- One with 23 countries or organizations in Asia: People's Democratic Republic of Korea, Mongolia, Pakistan, Kampuchea, Philippines, Bangladesh, Thailand, Japan, Turkey, Sri Lanka, Cyprus, Iran, India, Laos, Jordan, Singapore, Malaysia, Korea, Israel, ASEAN, Indonesia and Syria;
- One with 30 countries in mid-Asia and East Europe: Czech, Romania, Hungary, Poland, Russia, Albania, Bulgaria, Yugoslavia, Uzbekistan, Estonia, Lithuania, Belarus, Ukraine, Amnesia, Moldova, Tajikistan, Georgia, Slovenia, Azerbaijan,

Croatia, Kazakhstan, Macedonia, Kirghizia, Latvia, Turkmenistan;
- One with 11 countries in Africa: Sudan, Libya, Zambia, Nigeria, Algeria, Gabon, Morocco, Egypt, Tunis, Cote d'Ivoire, South Africa;
- One with 17 countries in west Europe: France, Italy, Germany, UK, Sweden, Finland, Greece, Belgium-Luxembourg, Norway, Austria, Denmark, European Union, Spain, Ireland, Switzerland and Portugal;
- One with 14 countries in Latin America: Cuba, Mexico, Argentina, Chile, Venezuela, Brazil, Ecuador, Trinidad and Tobago, Nicaragua, Peru, Guyana, Bolivia, and Uruguay; 1 With three countries in North America and Oceania: the US, Australia and New Zealand.

5.7 China's three major bilateral S&T cooperation

China-USA

China-US S&T cooperation, together with the trade and economic cooperation between the two countries, constitute the three major pillars of the bilateral relationship between China and the US. The international S&T cooperation has played an extremely important role in promoting the China-US relationship. In 1998, former US President Clinton expressed that China-US bilateral S&T exchanges and cooperation had made one of the most successful cooperative areas between the two countries. Some projects of China-US S&T cooperation possessed major S&T and economic importance, with their results reaching the internationally advanced level. The remote sensing satellite ground station of the Chinese Academy of Sciences, Beijing electron-positron collider, China digital seismological network, and marine sediment survey, among many others, are fine examples of such cooperation achievements.

China-Germany

The S&T cooperation has long been an active area between local regions of China and Germany. Almost every state in Germany has signed its formal cooperative agreement or S&T cooperative agreement with one or a number of Chinese provinces or municipalities.

China-Russia

China-Russia S&T cooperation has become a major component of the strategic partnership between the two countries in the 21st century.

5.8 China's mastery of multi-lateral S&T cooperation

China has enjoyed an increasingly active multi-lateral S&T cooperation. China has established about 6,000 bilateral in the world, regional and global S&T cooperative programs, and several hundred bilateral or multi-lateral S&T cooperation funds. In a short period of just one year in 1999, China had become the new member of 34 international S&T organizations (5 of them are governmental organizations and 29 non-governmental). Up to 2001, the number of international S&T organizations enjoying China's membership has cumulatively reached 1010 or more.

The first Asia-Pacific Economic Cooperation (APEC) S&T ministerial meeting convened in October 1995 in Beijing laid a foundation for full-fledged S&T cooperation in the Asian and Pacific regions. Meanwhile, the first Asia-Europe S&T Ministerial Meeting sponsored by China in October 1999 kicked off the S&T cooperation between the two continents. The said two ministerial meetings made the milestones for directing international S&T cooperation and multilateral S&T cooperation to serve diplomatic activities and S&T development and enhanced the visibility of S&T cooperation in diplomatic activities [26-30].

Since then, China's disciplined, meticulous, and serious S&T engagements have strengthened and propelled China's S&T capacities to the worldwide stage of expertise and competency. China is recognized as a world leader in S&T development and embraced by other S&T world leaders through regional, bilateral, and multilateral cooperation. It is with such a rich experience in international S&T cooperation that China engages with Africa in science and technology cooperation.

6. Africa's Experience in International Science and Technology Cooperation

Until the name change from Organization of African Unity (OAU) to African Union (AU) in Lusaka, Zambia, in July 2001, African countries made attempts to organize for economic development but did not specifically envision cooperation in science and technology. Examples of such economic development organizations include the Monrovia Strategy in July 1979, the Lagos Plan of Action [1980–2000], and the Final Act of Lagos in April 1980. The adoption of the Abuja Treaty in 1994 established an African Economic Community (AEC). Among the many conferences that followed the Lagos Plan of Action was the CASTAFRICAII, organized by UNESCO/OAU/AEC, which brought together experts and 26 African ministers to develop strategies for the economic recovery of Africa.

The AU vision was to "build an integrated, prosperous and peaceful Africa, an Africa driven and managed by its own citizens and representing a dynamic force in the international arena," which, in fact, was not specifically about science and technology cooperation. It was only in June 2014 that the 23rd Ordinary Session of AU Heads of State and Government Summit adopted a 10-year Science, Technology, and Innovation Strategy for Africa (STISA-2024).

The strategy defined four mutually reinforcing pillars, which were prerequisite conditions for the strategy's success. These pillars were building and/or upgrading research infrastructures, enhancing professional and technical competencies, promoting entrepreneurship and innovation, and providing an enabling environment for science, technology, and innovation (STI) development in the African continent. Continental, regional, and national programs were to be designed, implemented, and synchronized to ensure that their strategic orientations and pillars were mutually reinforcing in order to effectively achieve the envisaged developmental impact.

Hence, the implementation of STISA-2024 was to take place at three levels. At the national level, Member States were to incorporate this strategy into their National Development Plans. At the regional level, Regional Economic Communities (RECs), regional research institutions, networks, and partners were to leverage the strategy in designing and coordinating initiatives. At the continental level, the African Union Commission (AUC), New Partnership for Africa's Development (NEPAD) Agency, and their partners were to advocate and create awareness, mobilize necessary institutional, human, and financial resources, track progress, and monitor implementation. Continental, regional, and national targets and indicators were to be defined to facilitate comparability of data and regular Monitoring and Evaluation (M&E) of the programs.

At the 31st Ordinary Session of the Assembly of African Union Heads of State and Government in Nouakchott, Mauritania, in June 2018, a decision was made to transform the NEPAD Planning and Coordination Agency into the African Union Development Agency-NEPAD (AUDA-NEPAD). The establishment of AUDA-NEPAD was part of the global reforms geared at improving the Union's impact and operational efficiency.

The mandate of AUDA-NEPA was to:

- Coordinate and execute priority regional and continental projects to promote regional integration towards the accelerated realization of Agenda 2063 and
- Strengthen the capacity of African Union Member States and regional bodies, advance knowledge-based advisory support, undertake the full range of resource mobilization, and serve as the continent's technical interface with all of Africa's development stakeholders and partners.

The new AUDA-NEPAD mandate gives the organization a wider role in terms of providing knowledge-based advisory support to AU Member States in the pursuit of their national development priorities. The core functions of the Agency are to:

- Incubate innovative programs in various fields, including technology, research and development, knowledge management, and data analytics;
- Provide technical and implementation support to RECs and Member States in the development and execution of priority projects and programs;

- Assist Member States and RECs to strengthen capacity in key areas such as food and nutrition, energy, water, infrastructure, information and communication technology and digital economy, natural resource governance, climate change, and institutional and human capital development and innovation;
- Provide advisory support in the setting up and application of norms and standards in thematic priorities of the AU to accelerate regional integration;
- Provide technical backstopping to the AU in implementing policy recommendations at the continental, regional, and national levels;
- Monitor and assess Africa's development trends and progress with the view to achieve key continental and global goals for the purpose of technical reporting;
- Undertake, apply, and disseminate research on policy development support for Member States;
- Coordinate, facilitate, and promote cooperation with Africa's strategic partners and stakeholders for effective resource mobilization;
- Coordinate and facilitate partnerships with stakeholders and African academia;
- Foster cooperation in Africa with the private sector; and
- Coordinate between AU Specialized Agencies, Organs, and other institutions to create an enabling and supportive environment for the achievement of the goals and priorities of Agenda 2063.

In short, the analysis of data, the annual reports, and the regular progress reviews constitute an important management tool for the entire system. While there are conventional mechanisms for funding Research and Development (R&D) and Innovation, the AU recognized that it was essential to establish efficient, effective, and coordinated financing mechanisms to implement the strategy. Hence, the AUC and NEPAD Agency were to mobilize and coordinate resources for technical support in developing and implementing national and regional plans and priority programs. The AU Member States and RECs were to take a lead role in mobilizing public, private, and donor resources for the coordinated implementation of national and regional programs.

The evidence speaks for itself: today, in 2024, it is noticeable that African leaders have pledged to devote more resources to the development of science and technology, an area deemed vital for economic development yet long neglected and poorly funded in many countries. Most African countries have yet to transform their political pledges into feasible programs for science-led development.

Sub-Saharan Africa contributes about 2.3 percent of the world's gross domestic product but is responsible for only 0.4 percent of global expenditure in research and development (R&D). With 13.4 percent of the world's population, the continent is home to only 1.1 percent of the world's scientific researchers. It has about one scientist or engineer per 10,000 people, compared with 20–50 in industrial nations.

Over the years, the science and technology gap between Africa and the rest of the world has grown. While other regions constantly upgrade their technologies, Africa is failing to keep up and falling behind. Some economists feel that this widening gap is partly responsible for the continent's stagnation, regression, and worsening underdevelopment in our modern time.

The most serious challenges hindering the development of science and technology in Africa include a steady decline in funding, brain drain (flight of skilled personnel to other areas), inadequate infrastructure, insufficient levels of literacy, and a shortage of women in science. Also, links between industry and science and technology institutions are the weakest in the world. As a result, research findings are often not used by local industries, particularly small and medium-sized enterprises. In fact, the AU acknowledges that the lag is not only the result of limited funding but also a lack of appreciation for the value of such investments. The "return on the investment in science and technology is not appreciated by policy makers and even African industry," the AU reports have repeatedly expressed.

To assist Africa's less industrialized countries, the UN Department of Economic and Social Affairs is currently running a project to promote emerging technologies, such as information and communication technologies, biotechnologies, nanotechnologies, and fuel technologies. Note that the UN, not the AU, is running the project. Donor agencies, not African countries, are the ones recognizing the need to renew funding for education and even determining where and what to fund, shifting between primary, secondary, or higher education in African countries. For example, the World Bank and other donors argued that investment in primary education yields higher returns to society as a whole, while tertiary education produces returns only for individual graduates. But what do African governments say and do about their primary and tertiary education?

In a 2005 report, the Commission for Africa, a 17-member panel of experts convened by the UK's then Prime Minister Tony Blair, recommended that Africa promotes science and technology through partnerships with other developing countries such as Brazil and India, international organizations such as the World Bank and donor nations. The commission called for the development of centers and networks of excellence in collaboration with institutions of higher learning in other countries. The Blair Commission recommended that the international community provide $3 billion over 10 years for the development of such African centers of excellence.

The New York-based UN Millennium Project recommended that the international community either directly support under-funded research areas in Africa or fund international teams to conduct world-class research in relevant fields in Africa. It also called on international donors to support international research networks that work closely with developing countries, such as the Consultative Group on International Agricultural Research.

However, the critical question remains unanswered: What do African leaders themselves say, determine, decide, and do with respect to science and technology development in their respective countries?

The fact is that today, in 2024, many African colleges and universities are inadequately staffed and ill-equipped. Their quality of education has declined. Most African countries struggle to maintain even clean living conditions on their university campuses, and the academic research output in the region is among the lowest in the world. While it may appear obvious that countries that neglect higher education cannot do well in science and technology, many African countries have been doing just that while talking, pledging, and pretending to support higher education in science and technology: just words. But the world keeps moving forward.

African governments need to honestly fact-check their words and promises regarding the development of science and technology on the continent. They need to come up with effective policies. All the recommendations put forth by international commissions and donor agencies will work only if they are developed with the active participation of African countries and if African countries are serious enough to incorporate these recommendations into national legislations and policies, actively plan and execute the implementation. But so far, as facts can demonstrate, African governments have remained passive or have been promoting investments that have little to nothing to do with science and technology development.

With respect to the AU's interventions and cooperation mechanisms to boost science and technology development on the continent, most of them are not adequately designed to promote African ownership, accountability, and sustainability. While many good intentions and promises and pledges have been expressed in Africa, intentions and promises are not enough to enable science and technology to become a developmental resource. It is action on the ground that will make the difference [31-35].

Voilà: it is with the habit of talking but no action; it is with meager experience, fragile background, profound ineptitude, and near-total lack of will power for disciplined, meticulous, and serious work in S&T development that Africa is engaging with China in science and technology cooperation.

7. China-Africa Cooperation

In 2006, the Chinese government issued an African Policy Paper [36], where China-Africa science and technology cooperation was described in these terms: "Following the principles of mutual respect, complementarity and sharing benefits, China will promote its cooperation with Africa in the fields of applied research, technological development and transfer, speed up scientific and technological cooperation in the fields of common interest, such as bio-agriculture, solar energy utilization, geological survey, mining and R&D of new medicines. It will continue its training programs in applied technologies for African countries, carry out demonstration programs of technical assistance, and actively help disseminate and utilize Chinese scientific and technological achievements and advanced technologies applicable in Africa."

The 8th Ministerial Conference of the Forum on China-Africa Cooperation (FOCAC) held in Dakar, Senegal, November 29-30, 2021 [37], adopted an action called *Forum on China-Africa Cooperation Dakar Action Plan (2022-2024)*. The document has this table of contents:

1. Preamble

2. Political Cooperation

2.1 High-level Visits and Dialogue

2.2 Exchanges Between Political Parties, Legislatures, Consultative Bodies and Local Governments

2.3 China, the African Union, and Africa's Sub-regional Organizations

2.4 International Cooperation

3. Economic Cooperation

3.1 Agriculture, Food Security and Food Safety

3.2 Infrastructure Development

3.3 Industrial Partnership and Production Capacity Cooperation

3.4 Investment and Economic Cooperation

3.5 Trade

3.6 Customs and Market Supervision

3.7 Digital Economy

3.8 Finance

4. Social Development Cooperation

4.1 Development Cooperation

4.2 Medical Care and Public Health

4.3 Education and Human Resources

4.4 Cooperation and Exchanges on Poverty Reduction and Rural Development

4.5 Science and Technology Cooperation and Knowledge Sharing

4.6 Cyber Security Cooperation

5. Cultural and People-to-People Exchanges

5.1 Tourism

5.2 Culture

5.3 Press and Media

5.4 Academia and Think Tanks

5.5 Sub-national and People-to-People Exchanges

5.6 Youth and Women

6. Peace and Security Cooperation

6.1 Military, Police, Counter-terrorism and Law Enforcement

6.2 Anti-corruption, Consular Affairs, Immigration and Judiciary

7. Green Development

7.1 Ecological Protection and Climate Response

7.2 Maritime Cooperation

7.3 Cooperation on Energy and Natural Resources

8. Experience Sharing on State Governance

9. FOCAC Institutional Development

In this table of contents, section 4.5 deals with science and technology cooperation and knowledge sharing between China and Africa and has the following content:

4.5.1 The two sides will enhance synergy between strategies and policies on scientific and technological innovation, jointly implement the Belt and Road Science, Technology and Innovation Cooperation Action Plan and the China-Africa Science and Technology Partnership Program 2.0, promote cooperation on technology-supported poverty reduction, and fully leverage scientific and technological innovation to underpin and guide the sustainable economic and social development of China and Africa.

4.5.2 The two sides will jointly build a multi-tiered system for scientific, technological, and people-to-people exchanges. China welcomes the participation of African scientific professionals in the "International Outstanding Young Scientists Exchange Program" and the "Innovative Talent Exchange Project." China will carry out the "Africa Young Scientists in China" Program and provide African countries with training on readily applicable technology and science management.

4.5.3 The two sides will use the China-Africa Innovation Cooperation Center in Wuhan to jointly carry out cooperation activities on technology transfer innovation and entrepreneurship. Both sides support young Chinese and Africans in sharing innovation outcomes and promoting mutual development.

4.5.4 The two sides will make full use of the China-Africa Joint Research Center and support this platform in playing a continued exemplary role in areas such as modern agriculture, biodiversity, eco-environmental protection, and public health.

4.5.5 The two sides acknowledge that in today's world, aerospace is one of the most important high-tech sectors. The two sides will enhance cooperation on space technology, promote Africa's space technology application and infrastructure development, and use the space industry to drive social development and improve people's living standards.

4.5.6 The AU and the China National Space Administration will jointly explore and release the White Paper on China-Africa Space Cooperation to identify key areas and directions for cooperation. China will use space technology to enhance cooperation with African countries in such areas as scientific and technological development, poverty and hunger elimination, promotion of social security, disaster prevention and relief, climate change, and eco-environmental protection.

4.5.7 The two sides will actively work to establish a sub-forum on China-Africa space cooperation under the FOCAC framework. Both sides will focus on supporting projects concerning satellite remote sensing, communications satellite , and space city building in an effort to drive the development of the space industry of African countries. China will set up centers for China-Africa cooperation on satellite remote sensing applications.

4.5.8 China will train specialized aerospace professionals for African countries and promote the capacity building of aerospace in African countries. The two sides will fully leverage the role of the UN-affiliated Regional Centers for Space Science and Technology Education in China, Nigeria, and Morocco, as well as African Union Space Agency headquartered in Egypt, and make good use of the Belt and Road Aerospace Innovation Alliance to promote exchanges and cooperation between Chinese and African universities, work to build a regional development center of the Belt and Road Aerospace Innovation Alliance in Africa, and contribute to the training and education of aerospace professionals in Africa.

4.5.9 The two sides support the CubeSat Middle School Student Science Project. The two sides will set up a China-Africa youth space alliance as a platform for space exchanges between Chinese and African middle school students and explore new ways of science popularization in China-Africa space cooperation so as to lay the foundation for realizing the development vision of emerging space countries in Africa.

4.5.10 The two sides will enhance communication and cooperation on platforms such as the UN Committee on the Peaceful Uses of Outer Space to jointly promote international space cooperation and global space governance that are fair and reasonable and take into account the special needs of developing countries.

4.5.11 The two sides acknowledge that nuclear technologies play an important role in economic and social development. China will continue to leverage the Chinese Government Atomic Energy Scholarship Program and existing cooperation platforms between the two sides to continue to deepen mutually beneficial cooperation between China and Africa in such areas as nuclear science research, nuclear personnel training, nuclear technology application, and nuclear power project development, and jointly tackle challenges including climate change, energy supply, food security, health, and protection of water resources.

Two important points to note: First, both the 2006 and 2021 documents are generic in nature and have no specifics or detailed plan(s) of action. Second, China is a country, and Africa is a continent of sovereign countries, each supposedly having its own priorities.

From these two points, it is understood that even if China were to engage with Africa through the African Union (AU), it's still not the platform where concrete actions of cooperation in science and technology can take place. Hence, China-Africa science and technology cooperation has no choice but to become China-Africa science and technology cooperation with each African country. Surely enough, it is through an individual memorandum of understanding (MOU) that China deals with each African country within the China-Africa science and technology cooperation framework. It is, therefore, the MOU China signs with each African country that specifies the type of project to tackle in the science and technology cooperation framework.

8. China-Africa MOUs

China has signed a number of MOUs with African countries for science and technology cooperation. A few of these MOUs that are publicly mentioned are listed here and briefly commented on.

8.1 China – Algeria

In November 2006, a few days after the China-Africa summit concluded, China's president Hu Jintao signed two separate MOUs with the leaders of Algeria and Egypt for scientific cooperation. Under the deals, the countries were to collaborate on research in various scientific and technological fields and would set up a common fund to pay for their joint scientific activities. Information technology, technology transfer, health, traditional medicine, space technology, agriculture, and peaceful use of nuclear energy were some of the areas planned for collaboration.

Later, in 2014, China and Algeria signed a science, technology, and higher education cooperation agreement. Under this China-Algeria higher education cooperation agreement, the exchange of students and university staff was to be developed, and postdoctoral training and enhanced partnerships between universities in the two countries would be developed. The agreement also included organizing seminars and symposia on major challenges facing higher education, as well as developing joint projects between research teams in Chinese and Algerian universities. China and Algeria agreed to work on structured research projects centered on social concerns and major economic common interests, as well as the development of the Chinese language in Algeria.

The agreement also included China supporting Algeria's new academy, which was to act as a collective hub to organize scientific endeavors and motivate, support, and reward excellence in scientific research. The academy would act as a think-tank that brings together multidisciplinary expertise to advise policy-makers on how to address present challenges facing Algeria and to help envision strategies for driving future development, including, crucially, critiquing science policies. The academy would focus on tasks of contributing to the progress of sciences and technologies and their applications, improving the teaching of science and technology from primary schools to universities, and providing consultative services on knowledge, technology development and transfer. The academy would also promote international collaboration, support the publication of a magazine to disseminate new results to national and international scientific communities, participate in the scientific debate on major topical issues, organize conferences, grant awards, and medals, and organize meetings between researchers and politicians to promote the interaction of science with society.

The Algeria-China cooperation plan would encourage scientific and technical exchanges and technological cooperation between companies and entrepreneurs of the two countries in energy and mineral resources research. Included in the cooperation plan and expected to be boosted by the plan were sectors such as education, industry, information technology, communications, mechanical engineering, agriculture, water conservation, and infrastructure construction.

One concretization of the plan came in December 2017, when China launched a communication satellite for Algeria named Alcomsat-1 into a preset orbit from the Xichang Satellite Launch Center in the southwestern province of Sichuan. The satellite was hailed by China and Algeria as the first cooperative project in the aerospace industry between the two countries. Alcomsat-1 was designed for a life of 15 years and would be used by Algeria for broadcast and television, emergency communication, distance education, e-governance, enterprise communication, broadband access, and satellite-based navigation [38-40].

8.2 China-Egypt

8.2.1 Agreements

The November 2006 science and technology MOU was signed by China's president Hu Jintao with the leaders of Egypt and Algeria in Beijing, China. Under the Egypt-China agreement, the countries were to collaborate on research in various scientific and technological fields and set up a common fund to pay for their joint scientific activities. Information technology, technology transfer, health, traditional medicine, space technology, agriculture, and peaceful use of nuclear energy were some of the areas planned for collaboration. Before 2006, a bilateral agreement between China and Egypt had already been in effect. The years 2002-2003 saw progress in cooperation between China and Egypt in the fields of agriculture, environmental protection, medicine, small and medium enterprise development, and enterprise incubators.

In 2016, Egypt and China inked five MOUs in the fields of education and scientific research. These MOUs were said to build upon previous ones and included a scholarship exchange program between the two countries, with China offering 100 scholarships annually to Egyptians until 2020.

In 2021, Egypt and China signed another MOU to conduct cooperation on technology incubators. This MOU was a deal signed by the Shanghai Institute of Microsystem and Information Technology (SIMIT) of the Chinese Academy of Sciences and Egypt's Electronics Research Institute (ERI). Under the deal, the Chinese science and technology innovation platform, InnoSpring incubator, would support the establishment of the technological innovation capacity of the Egyptian TARIEIC incubator through technology transfers. The two parties would jointly promote the transformation of research results into commercial product prototypes, enhancing mutual visits of personnel and sharing incubator operation and management experience. SIMIT and ERI would also cooperate in carrying out technological research and development, product marketing, and patent commercialization to jointly support the technological innovation and development of small- and medium-sized enterprises.

8.2.2 Areas of exchange activities

Applied technology of agriculture: the two sides plan to cooperate in establishing a pilot shrimp production project and a training center. Introducing Chinese bamboo to Egypt has entered into the consultation stage.

Area of environmental protection: cooperation in introducing purification of drinking water and sewage water treatment technology from China.

Area of pharmaceutical study: in cooperation with the Egyptian counterpart, Shanghai Dongbao Company started producing insulin, and it was reported that the product gained a market occupying ratio of 50% in Egypt. The Ministry of Health of Egypt agreed to approve the cooperation production of another nine medicines with the Chinese side.

Satellite-lab cooperation: The Egyptian National Authority of Remote Sensing and Space Flight under the Ministry of Scientific Research paid a technical exchange visit with the assistance of the Ambassador Foundation of the Embassy of China in Egypt.

Cooperation in Science Park: Shenzhen High Tech Park and Mubarak City for Scientific and Technology Applications identified four cooperation projects. The four projects got financial support from the Department of Science and Technology of Shenzhen Municipal Government in 2003.

Small and medium enterprise development: the Research Institute of Advanced Manufacturing Technology under the Xi'an Communication University strengthened its cooperation with Egypt's Tabbin Institute for Metallurgical Studies. Two Egyptian trainees were assigned to participate in the training course on rapid prototyping manufacturing in Shanghai.

Cooperation in enterprise incubator: project of building an international Enterprise Incubator in Egypt. China will share its experience and achievements in scientific development with Egyptian counterparts and stimulate innovation-driven development with Egypt.

Chinese Ministry of Science and Technology (MOST) agreed to establish a Chinese-Egyptian Research Fund (CERF) to support joint application-oriented research projects. With the aim of promoting bilateral research cooperation between the two countries in areas of mutual interest, grants are to be provided to give researchers - including young scientists - an opportunity to address new areas of scientific research. The two countries agreed to launch jointly funded research projects and call for project proposals in the areas of new energy, water, agriculture & food, and health. The two sides also reached multiple consensuses on how to further cooperate in the short-term exchange of visits, joint labs, science parks & incubators, and the engagement of Egyptian researchers in the Talented Young Scientist Program [41-44].

8.3 China-Kenya

In 2028, Kenya and China signed a memorandum of understanding (MOU) to promote cooperation in the areas of science, research, and innovation.

Under the MOU, the Ministry of Education, Science and Technology of Kenya and the Chinese Academy of Sciences will support a variety of science, technology, innovation, and higher education cooperative activities in the areas of ecosystem and environment protection, biodiversity conservation and sustainable development, agriculture, health, the development and demonstration of adaptable technologies via the Sino-Africa Joint Research Center (SAJOREC). The SAJOREC is a talent cultivation and scientific research institute aided by the Chinese government and serves as an outreach with around 20 projects for academic institutions in Kenya. Additional projects to be developed under the framework of SAJOREC included the joint development of research and development centers for modern agriculture and traditional medicines, as well as a ground-based satellite data-receiving station. SAJOREC would also partner with Kenya's Jomo Kenyatta University of Agriculture and Technology and the Chinese Academy of Sciences to focus on research in sustainable natural resource conservation, biomedicines for universal health, and modern agricultural techniques. In short, the Sino-Kenya cooperation was to develop an ecosystem necessary to foster cutting-edge research and innovation that would go to full commercialization [44-47].

8.4 China – Morocco

In 2017, Morocco and the Chinese government signed an initial MOU, which was evaluated at $10 billion, to build a new industrial and technology hub near the northern city of Tangiers. The project was to be financed by the Chinese group Haite 002023.SZ, BMCE's Bank of Africa, and the Moroccan government. The $10 billion investment would be made over a 10-year period for multiple industrial zones specializing in sectors including aeronautics, automobiles, telecommunications, renewable energy, and transport equipment.

China's relations with Morocco remain pragmatic, about expanding trade and investment, and cover multiple areas, mainly in the commercial realm. These ties have allowed China to increase its presence and achieve its wider geopolitical objectives. China's relatively successful engagement in recent decades is due to its shift away from international relations with the developing world based on ideology (the approach it took in 1949–79) to those based primarily on commercial deals (since the economic reforms introduced under Deng Xiaoping), which has made it more attractive to Morocco. Hence, Morocco views China as a potential source of means to fix its infrastructure gaps, increase foreign investment, expand trade, and reduce poverty and other socio-economic challenges. This shared interest in developing relations with China coincides with Beijing's own new approach toward the Arab world [48-50].

8.5 China-Nigeria

On 12 April 2016, President Xi Jinping held talks with Nigerian President Muhammadu Buhari. After the talks, Mr. Wang Zhigang, Vice Minister of Science and Technology of China, and Dr. Christopher Ogbonnaya Onu, Minister of Science and Technology of Nigeria, signed an Intergovernmental MOU on Science and Technology Cooperation under the witness of the two heads of state. According to the agreement, the two sides will set up a joint committee to promote various forms of cooperation in science, technology, and innovation between governmental departments, research institutions, universities, and businesses, including supporting joint pilot and research programs, facilitating the exchange of visits between scientists and research personnel, organizing thematic seminars and exhibitions and conducting technical training. The signing of the agreement has laid the foundation for the two countries to plan and promote the relevant cooperation within the framework of the China-Africa Science and Technology Partnership. China's education aid to Nigeria encompasses higher education and vocational training, Chinese language instruction, and school construction [51-52].

8.6 China-South Africa

8.6.1 Agreement

The science and technology cooperation agreement between South Africa and China was signed during the first session of the joint commission meeting on scientific and technological cooperation, held in Pretoria in March 1999.

8.6.2 Visits and exchanges

A South African science and technology delegation visited China in August 2000 to finalize the first call for research and development proposals. The first call for project proposals was completed in March 2000, and the second in March 2001. Areas covered in the two calls included new materials, information and communication technology, laser technology, and environmental management and technologies. In October 2000, a South African task team on indigenous knowledge systems visited China to study its policy and strategic development frameworks and determine best practices for developing indigenous knowledge programs in South Africa.

Reciprocally, Chinese biotechnology experts visited South Africa in August 2001, and in June 2002, the Chinese visited South Africa to promote agricultural development in both countries. The Chinese Deputy Minister for Science and Technology led a delegation to South Africa in March 2003 to hold the second joint commission meeting, where progress on bilateral relations and projects supported up to that time was reviewed.

The South African Department of Science and Technology went to China in September 2004 as part of the state visit to China by the then-Deputy President Zuma to develop a framework for cooperation among experts from the two countries. That same year, China was the biggest exhibitor at the International Science, Innovation, and Technology Exhibition in South Africa.

The former South African Minister of Science and Technology, Mr Mosibudi Mangena, visited China with a technical delegation in September 2005. A provincial delegation from Guangdong reciprocated with a visit to South Africa later that same year on a fact-finding mission.

In March 2006, a delegation from the Beijing Academy of Science visited South Africa and participated in the annual Sasol Science Festival in Grahamstown. In April 2006, the Chinese Vice-Minister of Science and Technology visited South Africa to promote bilateral cooperation on science and technology. In November 2006, a small South African delegation visited China to elevate science and technology cooperation between the two countries ahead of the visit by President Mbeki.

In 2008, South Africa and China celebrated their 10-year anniversary of diplomatic relations. The South African Department of Science and Technology and the Chinese Ministry of Science and Technology participated by holding seminars on paleontology and on projects that were supported between 1998 and 2008. A book with a list of at least seventeen projects supported since the start of the relationship was published.

8.6.3 Collaboration between South African and Chinese institutions

The China Africa Engineering Association was established in October 1997 to promote the exchange of information and expertise between Chinese and South African engineers. This partnership has grown considerably, with the Chinese placing an expert at the Tshwane University of Technology (South Africa). The University has accepted a number of Chinese students in various science and technology programs.

South Africa and China are both members of the International Standards Organizations. The South Africa Bureau of Standards collaborates with China on rotating machines, mechanical engineering, rubber and plastics, textiles, and electrical motors and cables.

The South African Council for Geosciences has a bilateral agreement with the Chinese Academy of Geological Sciences, which includes exchanges in maps and publications, as well as bilateral cooperation on analyses of subparts per million of gold, platinum, and palladium.

Mintek, South Africa's national mineral research organization, and BachTech of Australia have sold gold bioleaching technology to Laizhou Gold Metallurgy in Shangdon Province, China. Mintek appointed Gold Yard International Exchange Service to promote its products in China.

The provincial Department of Agriculture in Limpopo (South Africa) signed a memorandum of understanding with China in December 2004. That Department hosted a Chinese delegation in May 2005, and a South African delegation visited China in October 2005. The partnership is aimed at sharing expertise in the use of technology to mitigate drought-related challenges that farmers in Limpopo face.

8.6.4 Science and Technology Forum

At the second joint commission meeting, which was held in Pretoria in 2003, it was agreed that the Science and Technology Forum would be established during the next meeting. The third joint commission meeting took place on 20 September 2005, and ten (10) research projects were supported. The Forum took the form of a seminar. Experts from both countries were invited to make presentations on transport technology, nanotechnology, and new materials, biotechnology (including agro-processing and the Spark Program, which is a Chinese government-driven program aimed at promoting the development of the rural economy through science and technology), and information and communication technologies. The presentations and the ensuing discussions were aimed at identifying possible areas for further collaboration.

8.6.5 Joint science and technology initiatives and projects

South African and Chinese researchers have been working together on projects. Since the establishment of the Science and Technology Forum, the South African Department of Science and Technology and the Chinese Ministry of Science and Technology have been funding joint research projects selected after open calls for proposals. Forty-six joint research projects and initiatives were funded in the areas of biotechnology, advanced manufacturing, information and communication technology (ICT), palaeosciences, health (traditional medicines), transport technology, and mineral resources, among others. The Chinese have also been supportive of a pilot telemedicine project being run by the Medical Research Council.

Over the past few years, South African and Chinese research teams have tapped into each other's strategic strengths to maximize benefits for the two countries. China is keen to extend its support of projects supported through the South African National Research Foundation. Most of the research projects have contributed to human capital development through exchange programs, the training of young scientists, publications in science journals, and academic papers presented at science forums and conferences.

To strengthen and create longer-term bilateral research and development cooperative relationships with the People's Republic of China, the South African Department of Science and Technology is participating in the Shanghai World Expo this year. The Expo will be used to promote South African science, technology, and innovation objectives, such as marketing South Africa as a preferred destination for research, development, and innovation. It is also aimed at showcasing South Africa's advancements and achievements in science, technology, and innovation (as contributors to building a modern economy) [53-57].

8.7 China – South Sudan

In 2012, China signed onto South Sudan's plan to build five new university campuses with $2.5 billion in oil-backed loans from China to boost education in South Sudan. Despite South Sudan netting billions of dollars in oil revenues between 2005 and 2011, the government has struggled and continues to struggle to build up state institutions and provide basic services. South Sudan decided to move its five public universities to new, modern campuses with Chinese loans. The project was due to start in 2017 but was said to be delayed because South Sudan closed off its oil output in a dispute with Khartoum over how much it should pay to export crude through pipelines in Sudanese territory.

In December 2021, South Sudan and China launched the second phase of the China-Aided Technical Cooperation Project in Education for capacity building for local teachers and also the printing of more textbooks for learners. The second phase of the project was to be funded with a grant of nearly 20 million U.S. dollars from the Chinese government and would also include the compilation and printing of primary school textbooks for the subjects of English, Mathematics, and Science, the capacity building of teachers and educational management personnel. Additionally, the deal includes the development and supply of textbook usage evaluation systems, the supply of teaching equipment, and the carrying out of Chinese language programs in South Sudan public schools. The education project was going to be carried out by the Shanghai Educational Publishing House, a leading educational press in China. South Sudan government said that the implementation of the second phase of the China-Aided Technical Cooperation Project has already begun, in terms of the review of curriculum material (already underway) and the teaching of Chinese language already taking place at Juba Day Secondary School. Chinese ambassador to South Sudan, Hua, disclosed that China has supported the construction of a number of primary and secondary schools in South Sudan, trained over 5,000 professionals in various sectors, and provided hundreds of scholarships for South Sudan students to study in China. The Chinese envoy revealed that more than a million textbooks in English, science, and mathematics subjects were shipped to Juba, benefiting more than 150,000 South Sudanese teachers and students. In addition, he noted that over 200 South Sudanese teachers attended capacity-building training in China [58-59].

8.8 China – Tunisia

In 2006, Tunisia signed a scientific cooperation deal with China in a bid to promote science development and technology transfer. The deal was to pave the way for scientific cooperation between research institutes, scientific societies, and technology organizations from each country. The deal was to encourage the exchange of knowledge and expertise in the areas of desertification, management of arid lands, the peaceful use of nuclear energy, sea technologies, and new technologies in the textile sector. Tunisia and China recognized that both countries experience drought, high temperatures, and salinity, which puts serious constraints on crop production and adverse socio-economic impacts. Hence, the two countries agreed to cooperate on the production of environmental stress-resistant plants using genetic engineering technology to benefit both countries.

On a visit to China in October 2008, Tunisia's minister for public health, Ridha Kechrid, said he hoped there would be increased cooperation between the two countries in the medical sector in the future, including developing traditional Chinese medicine. Tunisia has also called upon Chinese expertise to build a solar power plant (the plan was to develop at least 835 megawatts of solar power plants by 2030). In July 2019, the Tunisian authorities signed a memorandum of understanding with Chinese corporations with expertise in renewables to develop solar energy and to continue importing equipment and products from China [60-61].

8.9 Remarks on China-Africa MOUs

This short survey of China-Africa MOUs with individual African countries provides important details and insight into the content of China-Africa science and technology cooperation, thus providing a baseline for appreciating and evaluating the cooperation termed as win-win cooperation by China and Africa.

9. The Health of the China-Africa Science and Technology Cooperation

One observation from the MOUs survey is the frequent use of expressions such as "China will assist," "China will build," "China will help," "China will train," "China aid," "loan from China," "grant from China," "scholarship to…China," etc. These terms clearly show that the China-Africa science and technology cooperation is mostly perceived by African countries and often articulated by China as an economic assistance rather than a "win-win" scientific cooperation. Both China and Africa seem to align their articulation (China) and perception (Africa) in defining the win-win S&T cooperation as a cooperation where China assists Africa.

On the China side, the articulation flows from the January 15, 1964, Chinese Government's Eight Principles for Economic Aid and Technical Assistance to Other Countries [63], expressed by Chinese Premier Zhou Enlai as outlined during his state visit to Ghana reported in the paragraph below, where expressions and words that highlight the assistance component inherent to the principles are italicized (by the author).

When *providing economic aid and technical assistance* to other countries, the Chinese Government shall act in strict compliance with the following eight principles:

- The Chinese Government always bases itself on the principle of equality and mutual benefit in *providing aid* to other countries. It never regards such aid as a kind of unilateral alms but as something mutual.
- In *providing aid* to other countries, the Chinese Government strictly respects the sovereignty of the recipient countries and never attaches any conditions or asks for any privileges.
- China *provides economic aid* in the form of interest-free or low-interest loans and extends the repayment time limit when necessary so as to lighten the burden of the recipient countries as much as possible.
- In *providing aid* to other countries, the purpose of the Chinese Government is not to make the recipient countries dependent on China but to help them embark step by step on the road of self-reliance and independent economic development.
- The *Chinese government tries its best to help the recipient countries build projects that require less investment while yielding quicker results so that the recipient governments can* increase their income and accumulate capital.
- The *Chinese government provides the best quality equipment and materials for* its own manufacture at international market prices. If the *equipment and materials provided by the Chinese Government* are not up to the agreed specifications and quality, the Chinese Government undertakes to replace them.

- In *giving any particular technical assistance*, the Chinese Government will see to it that the personnel of the recipient country fully master such technique.
- The *experts dispatched by China to help* in construction in the recipient countries will have the same standard of living as the experts of the recipient country. The Chinese experts are not allowed to make any special demands or enjoy any special amenities.

The "China will provide..." articulation was also well present when China's Ministry of Science and Technology launched the China-Africa Science and Technology Partnership on November 24, 2009 [64]. It was announced that technological cooperation will be enhanced in areas such as water management and conservation, sanitation, crop breeding, health, and renewable energy. One hundred joint research partnerships will be created, and *100 African scientists at the postdoctoral level will have the opportunity to conduct research at China's technology parks, research institutes, and private enterprises*. Chinese scientists and engineers will also travel to African countries *to provide technical guidance*, and in order to increase the research capacities of African countries, *China will also donate laboratory equipment*.

On the Africa side, most African countries seem to be more interested in, or rather seem to understand, their S & T cooperation with China in terms of economic and technical assistance to be provided by China – under more generous agreement terms than the West. Hence, the S & T cooperation agreements sought are believed to make China's development financing grants and loans available to African countries. In practice, African countries have viewed and interpreted their S &T cooperation with China as joint economic relations and development cooperation relations, through which development financing and technical cooperation are provided by China in support of their development agenda, including funding their education systems.

As presented above, the articulation by China and the perception by African countries of the S&T cooperation through the MOUs and agreements clearly show that the main objectives of the China-Africa S&T cooperation are not being achieved.

There are, however, mutual benefits from these MOUs and agreements, but not in terms of science and technology "win-win" cooperation that is supposed to be at the heart of the China-Africa S&T cooperation.

Here are some of these benefits for China.

- A first noticeable benefit for China that covertly results from these S&T MOUs and agreements is the flow of minerals and natural resources from Africa to China to fulfill China's growing demand for raw materials in support of its manufacturing expansion. This has little to nothing to do with the core objectives of China-Africa science and technology cooperation.
- A second noticeable benefit for China is the rapid expansion of the export of manufactured goods from China to Africa. This, too, has little to nothing to do with the core objectives of China-Africa science and technology cooperation.
- A third noticeable benefit for China is the overwhelming favorable economic partner status China enjoys in African countries, relegating Western countries that occupied that position behind China. That, too, has little to nothing to do with the core objectives of China-Africa science and technology cooperation.

African countries, through China-Africa S&T cooperation, are also receiving benefits that have little to do with the core objectives of China-Africa science and technology cooperation.

- A first noticeable benefit for African countries is a variety of grants and loans from China under S&T cooperation MOU often diverted to pay for China's works to build roads and buildings (basic infrastructures) in recipient countries. Infrastructures are great, but that's not really the fulfillment of the core objectives of China-Africa science and technology cooperation.

- A second noticeable benefit for African countries that touch on the objectives of China-Africa S & T cooperation is China building and equipping schools, training teachers, offering scholarships to students to study in Chinese Universities, funding joint research projects undertaken by Chinese and African researchers, both in China and in Africa. Still, China assists, helps, and provides, and Africa receives and is thankful.

From the benefits point of view, can it be said that the China-Africa S&TC is a cooperation? Yes, it looks like it. But is it a "win-win" cooperation? One could say it is because of the benefits gained by both sides. But it really looks more like one-sided assistance where the donor is China, and the receiver is Africa. Is it a S&T cooperation? Clearly, no, it is not, as explained above.

Hence, it can be stated that the health of China-Africa S & T Cooperation is frail and fragile. The development of China-Africa S & T cooperation seems to be side-tracked and heading in the wrong direction. This cooperation mode dominated by one-sided assistance has to gradually give way to a new mode of joint investment, cooperative for research and development (R & D) in science and technology, with results shared and disseminated in the wider science and technology community worldwide. Otherwise, Africa will remain the recipient of aid and exporter of raw materials under all sorts of agreements and MOUs, even when labeled as S&T cooperation.

10. Africa Needs Skilled Science and Technology Professionals, not Economic Assistance

This cannot be overemphasized: African countries need to catch up in socio-economic transformation by developing skilled professionals in applied sciences, engineering, and technology fields. The greatest asset of Africa is its youth. Africa is a continent of young people who are eager to learn and build their future. Therefore, African governments must put forth relevant infrastructures, ways, and means at national levels to motivate and support their millions of youth to acquire, master, and develop science and technology in order to integrate themselves faster into an increasingly innovative and technological workforce, and address the continent's challenges through scientific and technical research and innovation. Africa seeking aid and assistance will not get this job done.

Specifically, African countries must establish viable science, technology, and innovation policies and substantially increase their research and development (R&D) budget. This has to translate, at the national level, by partnering with local private capital to establish technology and innovation hubs and incubators to develop an environment for R&D and technology-led entrepreneurship so that millions of youth can conceive and apply novel and scientific solutions to various challenges facing Africa, including climate change, food security, health, and energy. African governments must become serious and make conscious and consequential decisions to invest in increasing the number of scientists and engineers trained to transform local natural resources into products to satisfy local needs. Teaching science and technology must be applied to the local environment and reality, not memorizing textbooks, so that African graduates in scientific disciplines can become transformers of the African society rather than seekers of jobs that usually do not exist, and therefore, they become condemned to unemployment with their diplomas in hands. This is because their diplomas do not reflect creative and innovative abilities, skills, and competencies developed during their schooling but rather a testimony to having memorized principles and theories well and reproduced them well on papers to pass the exams. However, memorized knowledge vanishes quickly after graduation, and the graduate remains without any real skills, abilities, or competencies to become a problem solver or business creator.

The engagement with China has boosted revenue from natural resources for many African countries. African countries should take advantage of the growing revenue to conceive and launch a paradigm shift that equips a new generation with the skills to transform raw commodities into higher-value products that can satisfy local needs, compete in global markets, and sustain additional foreign direct investment and job creation. Most importantly, a fundamental shift is necessary to orient the continent toward value-added production and manufacturing, enhancements through technology, and innovation in order to find local solutions to local problems. Unfortunately, as shown by facts, most of the revenue is squandered in corrupt practices and self-destructive behavior through greed that disenfranchises the youth and wars that decimate millions of talented youth who would otherwise become scientists and engineers to transform Africa into a developed continent.

Heavy investment in infrastructures (road and belt) is a hallmark of China on the continent of Africa, sometimes inaccurately labeled as an achievement from S&T cooperation. This has, of course, helped alleviate the suffering due to poor infrastructure, which is a major limit to Africa's development. Unfortunately, in most cases, African governments are happy to pay for China's work with minerals and natural resources without realizing that this practice continues and reinforces Africa's mineral and plantation economies.

African leaders should have ambition and vision to make their countries big players in the global economy, and this does not happen with banana or mineral exports. It will surely happen when millions of African youth are trained in science, technology, engineering, and math to become innovative entrepreneurs. Africa must lead in doing that with its own resources and means; only then will cooperation with China and other countries boost an effort that is first local and national.

The mentality of African countries to badmouth the West for not helping them develop and to believe that they can do nothing themselves, continue with the practice of corruption and mismanagement, and China will do the magic of developing the continent is absolutely irrational. It will not and will never happen. Africa must help itself first, and any outside assistance and cooperation should be supplemental in boosting the African effort to help itself. Any misunderstanding of this will only lead the continent of Africa into a hell of poverty and strife.

African governments must and should learn from their past history of being dominated and exploited. From the colonial period to modern times, the continent has been treated largely as a supplier of raw materials [65-66]. It is beyond reason to see African governments stick to being suppliers of bananas and natural resources, with little attention given to shifting the paradigm to science and technology innovation, mature trade, and diplomatic relations. Given its past history of being dominated and exploited, one would think that Africa would renew its vision and adopt a new approach to its relations with the outside world, including China. One would think that African governments today would be bold and decisive in creating a new generation of technical and entrepreneurial universities to develop ecologically-sound technologies, which is of common interest to Africa, China, and the industrialized world, which are all struggling with the effect of pollutions they generate, (pollutions) endangering our planet earth. Africa's developing ecologically sound technologies will undoubtedly win the world respect and recognition, as well as unsolicited outside investment. Unfortunately, African governments seem to be enthusiastically signing MOUs with China, hoping that China will do what they must do themselves.

Truth must be faced by and spoken to by African governments. The near-total lack of progress in S&T and the appetite for aid in Africa have side-tracked the intent of China-Africa S&T cooperation, and the relationship is moving not toward an equal partnership but rather toward China assisting Africa. China-Africa S&T cooperation does not seem to be building a relationship in which partners obtain mutual benefit through a joint funding system conducive to mutual respect and great results. It is often said that science is a common wealth of humankind. It is therefore believed that in this 21st century and in the centuries to come, international S&T cooperation ought to play a more active role in diffusing S&T accomplishments, promoting world peace, and advancing human civilization. However, African countries cannot wait idly for handouts and hope to share their accomplishments in the S&T. As things go, African countries are not participating actively, not contributing viably, not mastering the language and the meaning of the achievements, and therefore, will be passed by and kept as providers of raw materials – a role African countries and governments seem to happily like to play and be praised for it.

11. Looking to the Future: Corrective Actions Required

This paper has shown that the China-Africa S&T cooperation may not be boldly achieving its objectives or growing in the direction of producing great results. Although African countries receive economic assistance from the S&T cooperation, economic assistance is not the core outcome sought in S&T cooperation. The main objective that ought to be pursued is for African S&T research to gain a foothold in the global science and technology chain through cooperation with China and one day become an active contributor to the advancement of S&T to benefit humankind. It's therefore critical for Africa to reassess and reevaluate the S&T relationship with China, to correct what needs to be corrected, to redirect and reshape what needs to be adjusted, so that the China-Africa S&T cooperation does not hit a dead end, but finds ways to develop into full-fledged, vibrant and productive cooperation for the good of humanity. The following actions are suggested [67-69].

11.1 Thorough review of the current situation

African countries must review the state of science and technology in their countries. How is science taught in schools? How much consideration is given to science, technology, engineering, and mathematics in schools (STEM)? Is science applied to socioeconomic problems? Is science taking on the challenges of industrial application? Are there policies that clearly define the roles of science and technology in the development of the country? What is the quality of scientists produced in the country in terms of their work and productivity, and how do they apply science to help solve problems in society? What reforms need to be carried out for science, technology, and innovation to create a better future?

11.2 Reassessment of the basic policy on cooperation

What are the country's policies on cooperation? Is the country developing rapidly and increasing its economic output? Are the country's markets growing enough to accommodate win-win partnerships and cooperation? With respect to science and technology cooperation, does the country have a large enough qualified workforce to inject into joint science and technology research so that it can achieve big?

11.3 Review of the framework for the cooperation

How do we define a framework for cooperation? When an agreement is signed on science and technology cooperation, what fields of S&T are to be covered and why? Is it better to sign an MOU for each individual field of science/technology than an MOU that covers multiple fields? How is the country prepared to enter a relationship/agreement in which both parties obtain mutual benefit through a joint funding system in which the country funds its institutions and the partner also funds its own institutions? Does the country have in place a mechanism to measure the benefit, success, or failure of a joint activity?

11.4 Reassessment of the categories emphasized in the cooperation

What are the fields of high priority that must be focused on by the government as a whole? Does each agency and institution have its own priority fields? What are they? Are there measures of caution regarding cooperation with other countries in some fields? What fields of science and technology have a direct impact on military programs? How are these fields dealt with regarding cooperation with other countries?

11.5 Identifying specific examples of success and failure as a baseline for renewal

What science and technology cooperation is underway in the country? In what fields? What are the results of joint research in those fields? What are the examples of success? What are the examples of failures? Has a failure analysis been performed to determine the causes of the failure? How are corrective actions designed and implemented? How is the implementation assessed?

11.6 Establishing mechanisms for regular assessment of cooperation implementation

Several models for international science and technology cooperation exist and are publically available. Some of the elements found in the different assessment mechanisms include objectives, evaluation, assessment cycle, and management.

11.6.1 Objectives

Key objectives of the cooperation include expected short, medium, and long-term results. Expected results are parameters for determining the extent to which the cooperation has been successful, whether it can be improved, whether it should continue, and whether there are more cost-effective alternatives. This is achieved through the use of systematic research methods that provide relevant, objective, and credible evidence on the effectiveness of cooperation.

11.6.2 Evaluation

The heart of the evaluation is the information that addresses three basic cooperation issues: *cooperation relevance* (whether the cooperation continues to be consistent with organizational and government-wide priorities and to be an appropriate response to an ongoing need); *cooperation success* (whether the initiative has met its objectives and is producing the intended outcomes); and *cost-effectiveness* (whether the cooperation incorporates the most efficient design and delivery alternatives).

11.6.3 Assessment cycle

The assessment cycle can be bi-annually, annually, every two years, every three years, or every five years. The cycle selected depends on the overall period of the cooperation, the priority level for the expected outcome, and the urgency of needs to be met.

11.6.4 Management

The heart of management is proper data collection. Performance data are data collected when the cooperation is being implemented. This serves ongoing management needs and establishes a results-information base, which, along with data from whatever additional research is necessary, feeds the in-depth evaluation study at some time in the future.

12. Conclusion

China-African S&T cooperation is reviewed and analyzed based on the guiding principles (China policy paper), the Forum on China-Africa Cooperation Dakar Action Plan (2022-2024), the MOUs and agreements, the implementation, and some of the results. The health of China-African S&T cooperation is determined to be frail and fragile. The cooperation is found to be side-tracked from its core objectives and may be heading in the wrong direction. In spite of the benefits that both China and African countries derive from the S&T cooperation, the real objectives are not being achieved.

China is expanding its in-road in Africa and is expected to expand and deepen connections in the coming years, given the region's strategic significance and lack of clear vision from its leaders, which is a void China is filling by providing assistance and leadership. African governments seem to be thirsty for assistance, grants, and loans of all sorts, including those under S&T cooperation agreements. However, there should be some caution on their part regarding the burden of debt and its risks.

The need for African countries to review and reassess the implementation of their S&T cooperation MOUs and agreements with China is urgent. This will lead to corrective actions to reroute the cooperation to achieve its core objectives. It is the responsibility of African countries to reassess themselves and their priorities so that they can work with China to find win-win modalities of engagement that produce great results in terms of innovations that lead to entrepreneurship, prosperity, and stability in Africa. This will lay the groundwork for productive and mutually beneficial cooperation for years to come, promising a bright future for China and its African partners. This partnership and collaboration will speed up the effort and work to be done by each African country to develop science and technology at the national level and to develop a vibrant intra-African collaboration in science and technology. Without viable science and technology development at national and continental levels, cooperation MOUs and agreements will be ineffective. China–Africa collaboration will grow in a win-win modality not because China is emerging as a leading global research hub in the world, but it will only be because African countries are determined and put means where their mouths are in order to boost science and technology development on their soil.

At minimum and at last, if nothing else, China-Africa S & T cooperation could and should become a source of inspiration and a model for African countries to emulate how China transformed itself from a poor developing nation into an economic giant today. African countries can learn from China's science and technology and other experiences and adapt some of the lessons learned to their realities [70].

- *A nation that was once colonized can rise to become a superpower*

China has a history of being colonized, as the USA once was. Colonization can make a nation lose its pride, dignity, identity, and self-belief, but China has managed to regain all of these and even overtake its former colonizers to become the world's second-largest economy today. Colonization and slavery robbed Africa and took away its pride, dignity, identity, and self-belief. Africa can learn from China that a nation can go through such a dehumanizing experience and still regain what was lost and rise again. In Chinese universities, Chinese history classes are compulsory for all students. The same happens in American universities. The same has to happen in African universities. Africa, knowing its history, will be able to connect with its roots and regain a sense of pride. Only when Africa has changed from the colonial mindset and regained her pride, dignity, identity, and self-belief can it attain greatness.

- *A nation must create its own economic and political system guided by its national interests*

China realized that it required stability to develop. Without the political stability that comes from having a consistent government, China would not have been able to develop the way it has and as quickly as it has.

Africa is allover without consistency or determination. Africa has tried to be communist, socialist, and capitalist over time and has failed. It is stability and consistency that matters, and Africa countries can learn to be pragmatic and do whatever is necessary to serve and protect their national interests. Therefore, each African country must develop political and economic systems that ensure that national interests, such as food security, good quality healthcare, education for all, and access to opportunity for all, are met: bold and consistent actions, not just words.

- *A nation must always have clear programs that are bold and have vision*

Throughout China's history, there have been bold programs with vision, such as the "Great Leap Forward" (19541964), "Cultural Revolution" (1966-76), "Open Door Policy" (1978), and the "Go Abroad Policy" (2000). These programs had clear objectives even though the intended results in some cases were not always fully achieved. However, China has always had a clear, bold, and intentional program. The programs are created by the Chinese for Chinese and not by the International Monetary Fund (IMF) or World Bank.

African nations need clear programs that are bold and have vision. Africa knows its plight better than anyone else and has the human resources to implement the programs effectively. Why are African governments laying back to let their economic policies be crafted by foreigners who use aid packages and loans from international institutions to implement the policies? African nations must ask themselves what they want to achieve – the vision – and craft clear programs for achieving that vision.

- *A nation must train its youth to develop skills that serve national interests*

In China, each year, university admissions for various disciplines are allocated in proportion to what skills the country requires most at that point in time. If China needs more engineers, then there will be more university admissions for engineering than other disciplines.

Africa has a young population; some estimates show that 60% of Africa's total population is between the ages of 15 and 25. Africa's population continues to grow younger, and the trend does not seem to change anytime soon. In fact, some estimates say that by 2025, about 85% of Africa's population will consist of young people.

Therefore, African nations must be deliberate in training their youth so that they can contribute meaningfully to national development. This may mean that African nations have to change their schools' curricula to be biased towards the skills the nations require. Vocational skills training should also be in line with the needs of the nation to ensure employment and entrepreneurship after completion of school. African countries must gear their education systems to equip the millions of African youth to become job creators and problem solvers as opposed to the current situation where millions of youth are unemployed with diplomas in their hands, neglected, disenfranchised, and ready to join armed groups and terror activities to survive.

- *A nation must be proud of its cultural heritage so it can have a strong national identity*

China has turned traditional holidays that were celebrated by its ancestors centuries ago, such as the Spring Festival and the Dragon Boat Festival, into public holidays and has maintained its language and most of its customs, therefore establishing a strong national identity.

African countries can do the same. In fact, Africa is rich with many fascinating myths, traditions, and customs that make the continent a well of cultures. These can be used to instill pride in youth, thereby promoting a strong national identity.

- *A nation's State Owned Enterprises (SOEs) can be key drivers of the economy*

The key drivers of China's economy are state-owned enterprises (SOEs). The 2011 Global Fortune 500 list, which lists the largest companies in the world, had three Chinese SOEs in the top 10, namely Sinopec Group, China National Petroleum, and State Grid. In the same year, Global Fortune's 500 most profitable companies on the world list had two Chinese state-owned banks in the top 10, namely the Industrial Commercial Bank of China (ICBC) and China Construction Bank. Chinese SOEs are estimated to account for about half of the country's industrial output, therefore contributing significantly to China's $8 trillion Gross Domestic Product (GDP) and more than $3 trillion cash reserves.

African nations have state-owned banks, companies, and enterprises. Unfortunately, governing leaders are directly involved in these companies' activities and pocket most of the revenues. This has to stop. African governing leaders must rather stick to just regulating the environment for the private sector to run state-owned enterprises and drive the economy. In some cases, African state-owned enterprises fail because they are neglected and lack skills and technology. In other cases, they fail because incompetent people (friends and families of the president and ministers) are nominated in key positions to run the SOEs.

Furthermore, African nations cannot continue to rely on tax revenue and insignificant mining royalties to generate the needed funds to develop their countries. China's example shows that if African SOEs are commercialized (they remain state-owned but run like private corporations), they can generate profits for national development. If the right talents with the right mindset are appointed to run state-own enterprises, as China and other countries have done with their SOEs, then efficiency and profitability will become the new culture in African countries.

African nations must give greater value to SOEs because of the huge positive impact they can have on the economy and the citizens, as China has demonstrated. If managed well and focused on strategic sectors, SOEs can become key drivers of African economies. It is illogical and criminal for a nation to give control of its natural resources to others and to allow them to benefit more from those resources than its own citizens.

- *A nation must be quick and decisive in policy implementation*

In 2008, while the rest of the world was busy debating how to deal with the world financial crisis, China was busy implementing its economic stimulus plan of increasing public investment in infrastructure, lowering taxes, etc. Almost every major road was being repaired, new buildings were being constructed, and existing ones were being renovated or repainted. Almost everywhere you went, there was some construction activity going on.

The quick and decisive implementation of policies by China is a great contributor to the country's success. Simply put, when the Chinese government decides on what to do, they go ahead and do it. This is a characteristic that African nations can learn from.

African nations should focus on getting the most qualified and competent people to work in government. In addition to living salaries and good working conditions, African nations must emphasize patriotism and pride in serving their nation, which are great reasons the most qualified and competent Africans should seek to work in their governments. African nations must stop the culture of corruption and theft in government and emphasize discipline and excellence.

- *A nation must be proud of and promote its own brands*

In China, the Chinese search engine Baidu is bigger than Google. Instead of YouTube, there is Youku. Instead of eBay, there is Taobao. Instead of Facebook, there is RenRen. Instead of Twitter, there is Weibo. China has blocked YouTube, Facebook, and Twitter and has promoted its own Chinese alternatives. The Chinese have pride in their good local brands and always make a conscious decision to support them whenever possible.

African nations must make their citizens more economically conscious. Each dollar spent can have a positive or negative effect on the economy, and since most African economies are small, every dollar counts even more.

Where there are African alternatives, Africans should support African brands because they are more likely to benefit Africans. But Africa must produce. African countries must train and educate scientists and engineers who create enterprises and businesses and produce so that things can produced in Africa to meet the needs of Africans. Then, Africans will consume in Africa and trade within Africa, and the continent will be in a better position to determine its economic destiny.

- *A nation must have the courage to make decisions that are in the best interest of its people regardless of criticism*

China has been criticized in some circles for various positions it has taken, but this has not stopped China from doing what it feels is in the best interest of its people. China is criticized for not being a multiparty democracy and instead choosing to remain as a one-party state. However, China believes that it is good for its people, so it sticks to it.

China initiated the "Go Abroad" policy in 1999 to spread its footprint around the world because it was good for the Chinese. Today, Chinese companies are investing abroad and either acquiring or partnering with foreign companies and making big money. In fact, the Chinese are in Africa to further their interests, and if African nations allow themselves to be exploited by the Chinese, then the fault is theirs. The Chinese are doing what is in the best interest of their people, and so it is up to African nations to do what is in the best interest of their people. Does it cross Africa's mind to think of how it should use China to further its own interests? No, not at all. African governing leaders are rather seeking commissions and kickbacks for personal gains while allowing their countries to be pillaged and their people to further slip into deep poverty and misery.

- *A nation that exploits its competitive advantage can become globally competitive*

China has taken technology from Europe and cheap raw materials from Africa and combined them with its relatively cheap and efficient labor to manufacture and export finished goods to the world. From high-quality goods typically found in the US and Europe to the cheap goods typically found in Africa, China makes something for everyone because it has capitalized on its strengths to be globally competitive.

Africa has fertile soils, abundant water resources, and a favorable climate for agriculture. Africa also has abundant mineral wealth and a young population. The African Union estimates that 65% of Africa's slightly over 1 billion populations is under the age of 35. These are strengths of Africa.

Does it cross Africa's mind to think of how to capitalize on its competitive advantages? Currently, most African nations export unprocessed agricultural produce and minerals. Processing and beneficiation are being done in other countries, therefore providing jobs and higher profits in those countries. In some cases, the finished products are being sold back to the same African nations at higher prices.

Africa can make agriculture a key driver of its economy by being involved in the entire value chain. This would mean that instead of exporting just cotton, you export fabric. Instead of just timber, you export furniture and fittings. Instead of just cocoa, you export coffee or chocolate. This will create jobs for the youth of Africa, and more importantly, poverty will be reduced.

Some will argue that African nations do not have the capital, skills, and technology. Neither did China initially, but by focusing their scarce resources on key areas and transferring the needed skills and technology from those who had them, they did it. There is no reason why Africa cannot do the same and better if not for its leaders' ineptitude, incompetence, and their politics of survival that ruin the continent.

On a final note, Africa's future is brighter than Africa currently thinks. There is nothing that China has done that African nations cannot do or even surpass. Africans only need to start by believing in themselves and having the right mindset, and they, too, can achieve great things. Short and long-term science and technology programs and implementing activities need to be planned with associated evaluation mechanisms, and Africa will make it. Through China-Africa S&T cooperation, Africa can learn lessons from China get inspired, and the African people will do great things by themselves for themselves and for the world.

REFERENCES

[1] Thierry Pairault, China's Presence in Africa Is at Heart Political, The Diplomat, August 11, 2021. https://thediplomat.com/2021/08/

[2] Larry Hanauer and Lyle J. Morris, China in Africa: Implications of a Deepening Relationship. Source: https://www.trand.org/pubs/research_briefs/RB9760.html

[3] China Policy in Focus (n.d.), "The History of Sino-Africa relations," Retrieved from The History of Sino-Africa Relations - China Policy in Focus (google.com).

[4] SAIIA (2015), "China-Africa Factsheet," Retrieved from China-Africa-Factsheet.pdf (saiia.org.za).

[5] Shirley Ze Yu (2022), "What is FOCAC? Three history stages in the China-Africa relationship," Retrieved from What is FOCAC? Three stages in the new China-Africa relationship | Africa at LSE.

[6] State Council Information Office of the PRC (2021), "China and Africa in the New Era: A Partnership of Equals," Retrieved from China and Africa in the New Era: A Partnership of Equals (fmprc.gov.cn).

[7] Xinhua (2018), "Xi: China, Africa on a distinctive path of win-win cooperation," Retrieved from Xi: China, Africa on distinctive path of win-win cooperation | Nation | China Daily (chinadailyhk.com).

[8] Robert E. Snow, Core Concepts for Science and Technology Literacy, Bulletin of Science, Technology and Society, Volume 7, Issue 3-4, 1987, pp.720-729 (https://doi.org/10.1177/0270467687007003).

[9] https://smartwritingservice.com

[10] https://ukessays.com

[11] Harvey Brooks, The relationship between science and technology, Research Policy, vol. 23. (1994): 477-486 (John F. Kennedy School of Government, Harvard University, 79 J.F.K. Street, Cambridge, MA 02138, USA (PII: 0048-7333(94)01001-3. (belfercenter.org)).

[12] Sally Archibald, et al., Evolution of human-driven fire regimes in Africa, PANAS, December 19, 2011, Vol.109, No. 3, pp. 847-852. https://doi.org/10.1073/pnas.1118648109.

[13] Marco Werman and Rhitu Chatterjee, Evidence of Early Use of Fire Found in South Africa Cave, The World, April 2, 2012. Source: https://theworld.org/stories/2012-04-02/evidence-.

[14] Thierry Zomahoun, Africa: The Cradle Of Mathematical Sciences, WSCJ San Francisco.2017. Source: wcj2017.org/session/Africa

[15] Ancient African Mathematics. Source: www.taneter.org/math.html

[16] Torrance Stephens, How we know math was created in Africa, rollingout, July 14, 2021. Source: https://rollingout.com/2021/07/14/how-.

[17] Indeed Editorial Team, Mass Production : Definition, Advantages and Disadvantages, February 21, 2022. Source: https://www.indeed.com/career-advise/career-development/mass-production.

[18] MasterClass, Mass Production Pros and Cons: How Assembly Lines Work, February 16, 2022. Source: https://www.masterclass.com/articles/mass-production.

[19] J. Gonzalez (editor), Science, Technology and Society: A Philosophical Perspective, Netbiblo, 2005 (Science, technology and society: a philosophical perspective (core.ac.uk)).

[20] DJ Wardynski, How Society and Technology Become Partners in Changing Our Lives, Brainspire, October 24, 2019. Source: https://www.brainspire.com/technology and ...

[21] James Adams, The Contribution of Science and Technology to Production, The Reporter, No.1, March 2006. Source: https://www.nber.org/reporter/2006number1/contribution-...

[22] Francesco d'Errico, Christopher S.Henshilwood, Additional evidence for bone technology in the southern African Middle Stone Age, Journal of Human Evolution, Volume 52, Issue 2, February 2007, Pages 142-163.

[23] Matthew L. Sisk and John J. Shea, The African Origin of Complex Projectile Technology: An Analysis Using Tip Cross-Sectional Area and Perimeter, International Journal of Evolutionary Biology, Volume 2011, Received 15 September 2010; Accepted 31 January 2011, (doi:10.4061/2011/968012).

[24] Andrew R. J. Yeaman, The Misuse of Technology, TechTrends, Washington, Vol.48, Issue 5, (Sep/Oct 2004): 14 -16, 83.

[25] Nadine Gurr, Benjamin Cole, New Face of Terrorism: Threats from Weapons of Mass Destruction, I.B. Tauris & Co. Ltd, United Kingdom, 2000.

[26] Denis F. Simon, China's International Science and Technology Trends and the US-China Relationship, Open Access, 29 September 2021 (https://link.springer.com/chapter/10.1007/978-981-16-5391-9_23).

[27] Li Linxu, China's Sci-tech Circle of Friends Expanding. Source: Science and Technology Daily |2021-12-30 10:21:46|

[28] Yukihide Hayashi, Science and Technology Cooperation between China and Leading Nations. Source: https://www.jst.go.jp/crds/pdf/en/CN20160127_EN.pdf

[29] Cong Cao, *China's 15-year science and technology plan*, Physics Today 59, 12, 38 (2006); https://doi.org/10.1063/1.2435680.

[30] Yutao Sun & Cong Cao, *Planning for science: China's "grand experiment" and global implications*, Humanities and Social Sciences Communications, Volume 8, No. 215 (2021).

[31] Gumisai Mutume, *Africa aims for a scientific revolution: More funding needed for research institutes and universities.* Source: https://www.un.org/africarenewal/magazine/october-2007.

[32] Adedokun J. Olusegun, and al., *Development and Position of Africa in Science and Technology Today.* Source: American International Journal of Science and Engineering Research, August 2019, 2(2):60-68. DOI:10.46545/aijser.v2i2.103.

[33] https://www.nepad.org/who-we-are...

[34] Michael J. Kahn, *The Status of Science, Technology and Innovation in Africa. Source: Science, Technology and Society*, March 27, 2022, Volume 27, Issue 3. Source: https://doi.org/10.1177/09717218221107854.

[35] Mugabe, J., O., (2011), *Science, Technology and Innovation in Africa's Regional Integration: From Rhetoric to Practice.* Source: ACODE Policy Research Series, No. 44, 2011. Kampala.

[36] *China's African Policy*, January 2006. Source: Chinese Government Issues African Policy Paper (china-embassy.gov.cn).

[37] The 8th Ministerial Conference of the Forum on China-Africa Cooperation (focac.org). www.focac.org/focacdakar/eng/

[38] John Calabrese, Sino-Algerian Relations: On a Path to Realizing Their Full Potential? Source: https://www.mei.edu/publications (October 31, 2017).

[39] *China, Algeria to enhance cooperation in aerospace field.* Source: Xinhua (China, Algeria to enhance cooperation in aerospace field (www.gov.cn), Apr 3, 2018).

[40] *China launches communication satellite for Algeria.* Source: Xinhua (China launches communication satellite for Algeria (www.gov.cn), Dec 11, 2017).

[41] *China, Egypt ink cooperation deal on technology incubators.* Source: Xinhua | English.news.cn (xinhuanet.com).

[42] *New Progress Achieved in Sino-Egyptian Scientific and Technological Cooperation.* Source: mfa.gov.cn.

[43] 7th China-Egypt S&T JCM Held. Source: Ministry of Science and Technology of the People's Republic of China (most.gov.cn) August 15th, 2016.

[44] Fourth Call for Joint Chinese- Egyptian Research Proposals Through the "Chinese-Egyptian Research Fund" (CERF). Source: Egypt-China Co-Fund-Call 4_2020.pdf.

[45] Kenneth King, *China's cooperation in education and training with Kenya: A different model?* Source: International Journal of Educational Development, volume 30, Issue 5, September 2010, pages 488-496. https://www.sciencedirect.com/science/article/abs/pii/S0738059310000362.

[46] Xinhua: *Kenya, China sign MOU to promote cooperation in science, innovation.* Source: www.xinhuanet.com/english/2018-12/13/c_137672299.htm

[47] Globalbiz, *Agricultural cooperation with China to improve food security in Kenya.* Source: https://news.cgtn.com/news/2022-07-12.

[48] Reuters Staff, Morocco signs preliminary financing agreement for $10 billion tech city. Source: https://www.reuters.com/article/us (March 20, 2017).

[49] Global Times, China, Morocco's Joint BRI implementation plan injects new energy into Global South cooperation framework. Source: https://www.globaltimes.cn/page/202201/1246500.shtml (Janvier 20, 2022).

[50] Yahia H. Zoubir, Expanding Sino-Maghreb Relations: Morocco and Tunisia. Source: https://www.chathamhouse.org/2020/02

[51] *China and Nigeria Sign an MOU on S&T Cooperation.* Source: P020210828551423507640.pdf (china-consulate.org); China's Ministry of Science and Technology, 20 April 2016.

[52] E E Chidiebere and Wang Hui, *China-Nigeria Cooperation In Education And Training: A Comparative Analysis*, North American Academic Research, Volume 1, Issue 7; 2018, 1(7) 144-165.

[53] *South Africa and China launch cooperation agreements on science and technology.* Source: https://www.dst.gov.za.

[54] *China, South Africa Sign Protocol on Scientific Cooperation.* Source: www.china.org.cn/english/2003/Mar/58131.htm.

[55] *South Africa's Science and Technology Relations with China.* Source: South African Government, www.gov.za

[56] Monique Vanek, *South Africa, China to Revamp 10-Year Strategic Cooperation Plan.* Source: https://www.bloomberg.com, (28 September 2020).

[57] *China-South Africa Educational Cooperation Mutually Beneficial.* Source: www.stdaily.com/English/Opinion/2022-01/06/content_1244430.shtml.

[58] *South Sudan, China launch 2nd phase of education cooperation.* Source: Xinhua| 2021-12-06 23:54:35|Editor: huaxia.

[59] Wagdy Sawhel, *US$2.5 billion Chinese loan to upgrade universities (South Sudan).* Source: https://www.universityworldnews.com/post.php?story=2012092816345196.

[60] Wagdy Sawahel, Tunisia signs science cooperation deal with China. Source: https://www.scidev.net/global/news. 30 October 2006.

[61] *Tunisian -Chinese Scientific, Technological Cooperation Agreement Signed in Tunis.* Source: https://allafrica.com/stories/200610260637.html.

[62] Yahia H. Zoubir, *Expanding Sino–Maghreb Relations: Morocco and Tunisia.* Source: https://www.chathamhouse.org/sites/default/files/CHHJ7839-SinoMaghreb-Relations-WEB.pdf.

[63] *The Chinese Government's Eight Principles for Economic Aid and Technical Assistance to Other Countries*, January 15, 1964. Source: Wilson Center, Digital Archive. https://digitalarchive.wilsoncenter.org/document/chinese-...

[64] Jing Zhang, Calestous Juma, *Exploring the Sino-African Relationship: Both Sides Have Something to Offer*, February 2, 2008. Source: Harvard Kennedy School Belfer Center for Science and International Affairs. https://www.belfercenter.org/publication/exploring sino-african...

[65] Ewout Frankema, *How Africa's colonial history affects its development*, World Economic Forum, July 15, 2015. Source: hppts://www.weforum.org/agenda/2015/07/how-

[66] Lee Wengraf, *Legacies of colonialism in Africa: Imperialism, dependence, and development*, International Social Review, Issue # 103. Source: https://isreview.org/issue/102/lecacies-.

[67] Chunfeng Liu et al., *The evaluation model of international science and technology cooperation based on set pair analysis*, Journal of Interdisciplinary Mathematics, 21 May 2014. https://doi.org/10.1080/09720502.2014.881151.

[68] Catherine P. Ailes, *Cooperation in Science and Technology: An Evaluation Of The U.S.-Soviet Agreement*, eBook published on 16 July 2019. https://doi.org/10.4324/9780429035982.

[69] Eliezer Geisler, *The Metrics of Science and Technology*, Quorum Books, London, 2000.

[70] News African, Xi Jinping in Africa: *10 Lessons from China that can transform Africa*, NewAfrica, 23/07/2018. Source: https://newafricanmagazine.com/17158/. Original book: *Ten Lessons from China that can transform Africa*, Copyright © 2014 Manyika Kangai.

CHAPTER VI

SCIENCE AND TECHNOLOGY IN AFRICA: FROM COOPERATION TO REVOLUTION

by

Tongele N. Tongele, PhD

1. Introduction

This paper is based on the findings in the article "China-Africa Science and Technology Cooperation" [1]. The article determined that the China-Africa Science and Technology Cooperation (S&TC) was rooted in the Chinese government-issued African Policy Paper (2006), as well as the 8th Ministerial Conference of the Forum on China-Africa Cooperation (FOCAC) held in Dakar, Senegal, November 29-30, 2021, which adopted an action called *Forum on China-Africa Cooperation Dakar Action Plan (2022-2024)*. Section 4.5 of the Forum on China-Africa Cooperation Dakar Action Plan (2022-2024) deals with science and technology cooperation and knowledge sharing between China and Africa and describes in eleven (11) points what the two sides will do in terms of science and technology cooperation.

The African Policy Paper, the Forum on China-Africa Cooperation Dakar Action Plan (2022-2024), the multiple Agreements and Memoranda of Understanding (MOUs) between China and African countries to implement the "win-win" science and technology cooperation (S&TC), as well as publications on some results of such cooperation were analyzed in the referenced article. It was found that science and technology objectives were not being achieved, but other mutual benefits were being accomplished, and these mutual benefits were not central to the China-Africa S&TC.

The benefits for China included:

- The flow of minerals and natural resources from Africa to China to fulfill China's growing demand for raw materials in support of its manufacturing expansion;
- The rapid expansion of export of manufactured goods from China to Africa and
- The overwhelming favorable economic partner status China enjoys in African countries, Relegating Western countries that occupied that position behind China.

These benefits have little to nothing to do with the core objectives of China-Africa science and technology cooperation.

Conversely, African countries also received benefits, which included:

- A variety of grants and loans from China under S&TC MOUs are often diverted to pay for China's works to build roads and buildings (basic infrastructures) in recipient countries. Infrastructures are great, but that's not really the fulfillment of the objectives of China-Africa S&TC.
- China is doing the work of building and equipping schools, training teachers, offering scholarships to students to study in Chinese Universities, and funding joint research projects undertaken by Chinese and African researchers both in China and in Africa. Although this benefit touches on the objectives of China-Africa S&TC, it is still China assisting, helping, providing, and Africa receiving and being thankful, which is not the intended and expected win-win outcome of equal partners in cooperation.

It is based on these findings that this paper intends to present how African nations can recalibrate the S&TC not only with China but with industrialized nations and make S&TC a real tool for the industrial revolution that enhances people's productivity to improve living conditions in villages, towns, and cities throughout Africa.

2. Recalibrating S&TC

S&TC is not and should not be lip service. It should not be or become a "sexy" topic for international trips and meetings that conclude with handshakes, lavish dinners, and receptions. S&TC is and must be about producing outcomes in terms of technological research, discoveries, and innovations in fields such as biotechnology and bio-agriculture, solar energy utilization, geological and mining research, medicines, artificial intelligence and machine learning, semiconductor and microprocessor, advanced computing, robotics, advanced material and manufacturing, aerospace and hypersonics, etc. S&TC is and must be a serious business with tangible and intangible results that are applied to improving the living conditions of real people in villages, towns, and cities [2].

This is further justified by the fact that most African countries lack basic technologies to manufacture commodities for basic needs. Consequently, poverty all over the continent does not seem to shock leaders of the continent. Most African countries are far behind in science and technology research and innovations, far from technology frontiers [3-5]. The hope for an economic catch-up requires the development and accumulation of knowledge and innovation capacities, hence moving closer to the technology frontiers.

The path to catching up in socioeconomic transformation is by developing skilled professionals in the sciences, engineering, and technology fields [6]. The greatest asset of Africa is its youth. Africa is a continent of young people who are eager to learn and build their future. Therefore, African governments must put forth relevant policies, infrastructures, ways, and means to motivate and support their millions of youth to acquire, master, and develop science and technology to make things happen for themselves and their communities. Africa, consumed with cooperation for seeking aid and assistance, will only fall behind farther and farther while the rest of the world moves fast pace ahead with scientific and technological research and innovations.

African countries must make conscious policy decisions to establish national mechanisms and systems to sustain applied science and technology and promote research and development (R&D) in science and technology fields that build local capacities to get things done. African governments must set aside a budget for science and technology research and innovation and their application in solving the myriad of problems each country faces on the continent, especially uplifting people out of poverty. African governments must create sociopolitical environments that support and promote individuals' creativity and entrepreneurship, which will constitute strong private sectors. Governments can then partner with such private sectors to establish technology and innovation hubs and incubators and to boost the development of more R&D and technology-led entrepreneurship. Hence, millions of empowered and technology-savvy youth will conceive and apply novel scientific and technology-based solutions to various challenges facing the continent, including climate change, food security, health, energy, etc. [7-8].

African governments must seriously recalibrate their science and technology cooperation with China and other nations by making conscious and consequential decisions to invest in increasing the number of scientists and engineers trained to transform local natural resources into products to satisfy local needs. Teaching science and technology must be applied to the local environment and reality, and not just memorizing textbooks, so that African graduates in scientific disciplines can become transformers of the African society rather than seekers of jobs that usually do not exist, and therefore (African graduates become) condemned to unemployment with their diplomas in hands. The high youth unemployment in Africa is due to the fact that graduates hold diplomas that do not reflect creative and innovative abilities, skills, and competencies developed during their schooling but rather a testimony to having memorized principles and theories well and reproduced them well on paper to pass the exams. However, memorized knowledge vanishes quickly after graduation, and the graduates remain without any real skills, abilities, or competencies that would make them problem solvers or business creators. What is being advocated here is no less than an African industrial revolution.

3. Applied S&T for an Industrial Revolution

Applied science and technology (S&T) is the road to the industrial and manufacturing revolution. African nations remarkably excel in the export of natural resources and raw materials to industrialized nations. The mining sector that dominates the export provides little direct employment in the countries and regions where extractions take place. Additionally, factors such as corruption and weaker institutions lead to spending less on education, and nearly nothing is spent on science and technology research and innovation. Consequently, the majority of the population, especially the youth, does not possess the skills and competencies to be productive and create wealth. Hence, poverty and unemployment have become prevalent on the continent of Africa. It can change, and it has to change.

The change needed consists of developing tools and means to produce cleanly and sustainably to meet local, national, and regional needs. No one else but Africans is to develop these tools and means on the continent through science, technology, engineering, and mathematics (STEM) education and training for an industrial revolution on the continent, something that is not foreign to Africa. In fact, it is often wrongly believed that humanity has known four industrial revolutions that began in Great Britain around the second half of the 18th century with mechanization, the extraction of coal, and the invention of the steam engine. This is inaccurate. Humanity has known five industrial revolutions, the first of which took place in Africa with the invention of fire [9].

The invention and control of fire in Africa changed the course of human evolution, allowing our ancestors to stay warm, cook food, ward off predators, and venture into harsh climates. It also had important social and behavioral implications, encouraging groups of people to gather together and stay up late in the night [10]. This first industrial revolution is incredibly significant in terms of the permanent change it brought to humanity. It is recognized as the root, the incubator, the mother of all industrial revolutions, or the proto-industrial revolution, which began in Africa hundreds of thousands of years ago. It is there, on the continent of Africa, that the first humans, Africans, ancestors of humanity, began the long arc of transformation of nature to help make lives easier and, at the same time, try to perfect this effort of transformation and bring it to the next level [11].

Between the proto-industrial revolution and the second half of the 18th century, many things happened in terms of human migrations, conquest, and the transformation of nature, which culminated in what is commonly known as the first of the last four industrial revolutions [12-13], briefly described below.

3.1 The first Industrial Revolution: Coal in 1765

What is considered the first industrial revolution is the transformation of our economy from agriculture to industry. Processes became mechanized, and products were manufactured for the first time. During this period, the discovery of coal and its mass extraction, as well as the development of the steam engine and metal forging, completely changed the way goods were produced and exchanged. Inventions such as spinning machines and looms to make fabric were making their appearance. Canal transportation began replacing wagons and mules to move around these goods.

3.2 The second Industrial Revolution: Gas in 1870

As the first industrial revolution was driven by coal, the second revolved around the discovery of electricity, gas, and oil. The invention of the combustion engine went hand-in-hand with these fuel sources. Both steel- and chemically-based products entered the market during this time. Developments in communication technology got a jump start with the telegraph and, later, the telephone. Transportation grew by leaps and bounds with the invention of the plane and car. Mechanical production grew in speed through the advent of mass production.

3.3 The third Industrial Revolution: Electronics and Nuclear in 1969

After another hundred years, nuclear energy and electronics enter the landscape. Nuclear power began in Europe, grew in both Great Britain and the United States, went into remission for years, and grew in Asia. The third revolution brought forth the rise of electronics, telecommunications, and, of course, computers. The third industrial revolution opened the doors to space expeditions, research, and biotechnology through new technologies.

3.4 The fourth Industrial Revolution: Internet and Renewable Energy in 2000

As we continue moving through the fourth industrial revolution, we see a shift to renewable energy, such as solar, wind, and geothermal. However, the momentum comes not from the shift in energy but from the acceleration of digital technology. The internet and the digital world mean a real-time connection within more and more components of a production line, both inside and outside facility walls. As the development of the Industrial Internet of Things, cloud technology, and artificial intelligence continues, a virtual world will merge with the physical world. Predictive maintenance and real-time data will lead to smarter business decisions and work order solutions for a myriad of companies around the world.

4. Technology Drives Industrial Revolutions

Whether it was mechanical inventions or new ways of doing old things, industrial revolutions are powered by technological innovations. At the very start, people thought and conceived ideas that they applied to make tools and solve practical problems in day-to-day life. Technology and manufacturing were born. People have always felt the need to improve efficiency, come up with new techniques for doing things and solving problems, and create new products and services. Hence, the sense of taking technology to the next level began with the proto-industrial revolution and continued all the way to the 18th century, the first industrial revolution, and has continued all the way to the present day.

Key inventions and innovations have always shaped the way humanity evolves. Human activities in terms of productivity and economy were and are affected by changing technologies. The following are some key areas of technological forces driving changes for the last four industrial revolutions [14].

4.1 Agriculture

The proto-industrial revolution was characterized by subsistence farming. Several factors came together in the 18th century to bring about a substantial increase in agricultural productivity. These included new types of equipment, crop rotation, and land use, soil health, development of new crop varieties, and animal husbandry. The result was a sustained increase in yields, capable of feeding a rapidly growing population with improved nutrition. The combination of factors also brought about a shift toward large-scale commercial farming, a trend that continued into the 19th century and later. Poorer peasants had a harder time making ends meet through traditional subsistence farming. The enclosure movement, which converted common-use pasture land into private property, contributed to this trend toward market-oriented agriculture. A great many rural workers and families were forced by circumstance to migrate to the cities to become industrial laborers.

4.2 Energy

Deforestation in England had led to a shortage of wood for lumber and fuel starting in the 16th century. The country's transition to coal as a principal energy source was significant and even revolutionary. The mining and distribution of coal set in motion some of the dynamics that led to Britain's industrialization. The coal-fired steam engine was, in many respects, the decisive technology of the first Industrial Revolution. The steam engine turned the wheels of mechanized factory production. Its emergence freed manufacturers from the need to locate their factories on or near sources of water power. Large enterprises began to concentrate in rapidly growing industrial cities.

4.3 Metallurgy

Britain's wood shortage necessitated a switch from wood charcoal to coke, a coal product, in the smelting process. The substitute fuel eventually proved highly beneficial for iron production. Experimentation led to some other advances in metallurgical methods during the 18th century. For example, a certain type of furnace that separated the coal and kept it from contaminating the metal and a process of "puddling" or stirring the molten iron both made it possible to produce larger amounts of wrought iron. Wrought iron is more malleable than cast iron and, therefore, more suitable for fabricating machinery and other heavy industrial applications.

4.4 Textiles

The production of fabrics, especially cotton, was fundamental to Britain's economic development between 1750 and 1850. Those are the years historians commonly use to bracket the first Industrial Revolution. In this period, the organization of cotton production shifted from a small-scale cottage industry, in which rural families performed spinning and weaving tasks in their homes, to a large, mechanized, factory-based industry. The boom in productivity began with a few technical devices, including the spinning jenny, spinning mule, and power loom. First human, then water, and finally steam power was applied to operate power looms, carding machines, and other specialized equipment. Another well-known innovation was the cotton gin, which was invented in the United States in 1793. This device spurred an increase in cotton cultivation and export from U.S. slave states, a key British supplier.

4.5 Chemicals

This industry arose partly in response to the demand for improved bleaching solutions for cotton and other manufactured textiles. Other chemical research was motivated by the quest for artificial dyes, explosives, solvents, fertilizers, and medicines, including pharmaceuticals. In the second half of the 19th century, Germany became the world's leader in industrial chemistry.

4.6 Transportation

Concurrent with the increased output of agricultural produce and manufactured goods arose the need for more efficient means of delivering these products to market. The first efforts toward this end in Europe involved constructing improved overland roads. Canals were dug in both Europe and North America to create maritime corridors between existing waterways. Steam engines were recognized as useful in locomotion, resulting in the emergence of the steamboat in the early 19th century. High-pressure steam engines also powered railroad locomotives, which operated in Britain after 1825. Railways spread rapidly across Europe and North America, extending to Asia in the latter half of the 19th century. Railroads became one of the world's leading industries as they expanded the frontiers of industrial society. Then came commercial airplanes, which allowed people to travel larger distances in shorter amounts of time.

4.7 Remarks on technology and the industrial revolution

From the proto-industrial revolution to the fourth industrial revolution, it is technological Innovation that drives industrial revolution. The invention of the fire jump-started the original Industrial Revolution, steam propelled the first Industrial Revolution, electricity powered the second, preliminary automation and machinery engineered the third, and the internet, supercomputing, and artificial intelligence are shaping the fourth Industrial Revolution.

With technological innovations, new jobs and new and better ways of doing things are created, which in turn improve aspects of life in society. The invention of fire, the discovery and use of new basic materials, chiefly iron and steel, the discovery and use of new energy sources, including fuels and motive power, such as coal, the steam engine, electricity, petroleum, and the internal-combustion engine led to the invention and development of new machines and the automation. All these boosted innovations and developments in transportation and communication, including the steam locomotive, steamship, automobile, airplane, telegraph, radio, and the internet. These technological changes revolutionized the industry and made possible the transformation of natural resources into consumable commodities and the mass production of manufactured goods.

5. Science and Technology in Africa

5.1 From proto to the first industrial revolution

Starting with the original industrial revolution to the first industrial revolution (second half of the 18th century), the continent of Africa was the principal locus of technology development that drove changes on planet earth [15]. Using multiple sources, Isaac Samuel and others [16-18] explained in detail the development of science and technology in pre-colonial Africa, which is summarized below.

The emergence and spread of classical agricultural and metal-using technologies were revolutionary for the people throughout the continent. Technologies of domesticating food production emerged later primarily because African populations were able to support themselves by foraging plants, hunting, and fishing. Ecological changes, such as the drying of the Sahara in the north of Africa, were major factors that contributed to the shifts towards new technologies like farming and animal husbandry, while contact with the outside world encouraged iron-making. The smelting of iron existed in West Africa among the Nok culture of Nigeria as early as the sixth century B.C., and between the years 1400-1600, iron technology is believed to have facilitated the growth of significant centralized political communities in western Sudan and along the Guinea coast of Western Africa. Ironcraft was strongly pursued as it was associated with weaponry and led to extensive agriculture systems and more efficient hunting and warfare practices that helped build large urban centers.

Scripted mathematics was developed in Egypt and was found to include division, multiplication, and geometric formulas to calculate the area and volume of shapes. The Yoruba people in present-day Nigeria developed their own numeration system based on units of 20, which required subtraction to identify different numbers. Documentary evidence also suggests that scholars throughout the Nigerian kingdoms were highly skilled in the science of magic squares and were consulting Coptic Solar Calendars to develop agricultural science, which included charts dealing with agronomic activities, the right time to harvest, the time of germination, and which insects appear during different seasons. It is reported that the Namoratunga megalithic site in northwestern Kenya, built around 300 B.C., has 19 aligned basalt pillars purposely built to be oriented towards particular stars and constellations, suggesting that a complex calendar system based on astronomical and agricultural knowledge was in use throughout the region.

Another craft that was developed from the proto-industrial revolution to the first industrial revolution on the continent of Africa was various types of boat building, which included the building of canoes, small reed-based vessels, dhows, and sailing boats, and grander structures that had cabins and cooking facilities. Some of the canoes used by the Mali and Songhai peoples were between 25 and 30 meters in length and were capable of carrying more than 100 men. Although most of these boats were built to be used in inland waters, the people who lived along the Guinea coast used canoes and dhows to fish several miles out at sea and to trade longer distances along the coastline.

Africa has a rich history of science and technology, which, unfortunately, has been largely neglected by academia. Few of the hundreds of manuscripts of a scientific nature from west and eastern Africa have been studied, and there have hardly been any studies on African architecture and engineering on Africa's ancient ruins beyond cursory observations and mentions by archeologists. Discourses on African technologies and sciences, such as metallurgy, should move beyond debates on its genesis and instead explore the extent of the production and use of metals in past African societies and early industries. African medical manuscripts should also be studied to complement modern medical practices. Africa's scientific and technological legacy offers us not just a peek into the African past but also a foundation on which modern innovations and studies in science, technology, engineering, and mathematics (STEM) can be situated better within the African context.

5.2 Slavery and colonialism destroyed science and technology in Africa

5.2.1 Slavery

Despite the early developments of science and technology on the continent of Africa, European and Arab shifts from trade to slavery and colonialism interfered with and obstructed the social and economic relationships that Indigenous technologies needed to advance. Contemporaneous to the first industrial revolution, Europe's rise to riches was built on the blood, sweat, toil, and death of enslaved people. Europeans enslaved millions of men and women on the African continent during their colonization of the Americas. Those who survived the transatlantic voyage were forced to labor on sugar, tobacco, cotton, and coffee plantations in the Caribbean and in North and South America. In the process, Europeans accumulated vast wealth, either from the slave trade itself, from plantation production, or from the wider triangular trade between Europe, Africa, and the Americas. Growth in Europe took off during the century when the slave trade and overseas slavery in European colonies reached their greatest scale [19].

Before 1820, four times as many people were brought westward across the Atlantic from Africa than from Europe, with the Africans coming in chains to do the brutal and unremunerated labor that made Europe's colonies so immensely profitable [20].

Slavery was indispensable to the European development of the New World. It is inconceivable that European colonists could have settled and developed North and South America and the Caribbean without slave labor. Moreover, slave labor did produce the major consumer goods that were the basis of world trade during the eighteenth and early nineteenth centuries: coffee, cotton, rum, sugar, and tobacco. In fact, in the pre-Civil War United States, slavery played a critical role in economic development. One crop, slave-grown cotton, provided over half of all US export earnings. By 1840, the South grew 60 percent of the world's cotton and provided some 70 percent of the cotton consumed by the British textile industry. Thus, slavery paid for a substantial share of the capital, iron, and manufactured goods that laid the basis for American economic growth. In addition, precisely because the South specialized in cotton production, the North developed a variety of businesses that provided services for the slave South, including textile factories, a meat processing industry, insurance companies, shippers, and cotton brokers. In short, the slave economy of the southern states had ripple effects throughout the entire United States' economy, with plenty of merchants in New York City, Boston, and elsewhere helping to organize the trade of slave-grown agricultural commodities—and enjoying plenty of riches as a result [21-23].

5.2.2 Colonialism

The imposition of colonialism on Africa altered its history forever. The devastating impact of colonialism on African modes of thought, patterns of cultural development, and ways of life, forever impacted by the change in political structure brought about by colonialism, is summarized below [24-25].

Prior to the "Scramble for Africa," or the official partition of Africa by the major European nations, African economies were advancing in every area, particularly in the area of trade. The aim of colonialism is to exploit the physical, human, and economic resources of an area to benefit the colonizing nation. European powers pursued this goal by encouraging the development of a cash crop agriculture system and by building a trade network linking the total economic output of a region to the demands of the colonizing state. The development of colonialism and the partition of Africa by the European colonial powers arrested the natural development of the African economic system. Africa, prior to colonialism, was not economically isolated from the rest of the world. Indeed, African states had engaged in international trade from the time of the pharaohs of ancient Egypt, and west Africa specifically had developed extensive international trading systems during the eras of Ghana, Mali, and Songhai. These huge empires relied heavily on domestic and international trades as well as the development of local industries that manufactured crafts, tools, and commodities of all sorts.

The economic goals of colonialism were simple: to provide maximum economic benefit to the colonizing power at the lowest possible price. As the effects of the Berlin Conference, which established the "rules" of the partition game, became clear, those areas of Africa which had previously been developing significant trade and economies of their own were brought under the control of European economic policies. To the British, French, and Germans, the primary colonizing nations, the individual needs of their colonial subjects were not important. Instead, the desire to "vertically integrate" the colonies of Europe by controlling production from start to finish became the overriding goal of colonial agents.

Prior to partition, African states and empires, although dependent on international trade, exercised significant control over their economic development. These nations could produce what goods they desired, some for export and some for internal consumption. However, colonialism forced these nations to produce solely for the export market, thereby keeping prices low for their European consumers. Colonialism was not just about economic subjugation but about the ability to wrest control of the local economy from African rulers. Improving the production methods or strengthening the economy was not important. Furthermore, colonial powers instituted trade controls that limited colonial imports to those from the colonizing power and restricted exports to that same market. This reduced the freedom of choice in marketing goods that were previously available to commodity producers. Taking this power away under the guise of colonial development made traditional rulers weaker because their power base was destroyed. Since Africans were not allowed to improve their methods or to market their goods freely, they were forced into the colonial system. By insisting on the development of certain crops, Europeans undermined the existing economic power structure and made Africa totally reliant upon Europe for their economic destiny. Driven by outside forces, the local farmer was no longer able to decide for himself what crops to grow or what resources to cultivate. Instead, the decision was made for him in a predetermined market.

Colonialism lasted in Africa for only a period of about eighty years. During that time, colonial governments built a substantial infrastructure, introduced a cash crop system of agriculture, and changed the traditional standards of wealth and status. Education reforms were introduced, and in many areas, modern state systems were implemented. The infrastructure that was developed was designed to exploit the natural resources of the colonies. Also, the technological and industrial development that had been occurring in Africa was stalled by the imposition of colonialism. Prior to the partition of Africa, local production provided Africans with a wide variety of consumer goods. The policies of colonialism forced the demise of African industry and created a reliance on imported goods from Europe. Had native industry been encouraged and cultivated by the colonizing powers, Africa would probably be in a much better economic and technological position today.

5.2.3 The DR Congo exploitation and the demise of local industries

In the 1870s, Belgium, one of Europe's smallest countries at the time, decided that it, too, urgently needed to get into the business of exploiting Africa and its wealth. This set the country's leader, King Leopold II, on what at first seemed like a quixotic quest to find a foreign land that could power his country's growth, whether through unequal trade relations or an imperial takeover. This search inspired dreams of Belgian control over China and the Philippines, among other places, before finally leading him to the heavily forested heart of Africa. There, disguising his true ambitions behind a screen of anti-slavery rhetoric and humanitarianism—claiming to want to suppress the trading of Africans into slavery in the Indian Ocean—Leopold maneuvered Europe's big powers to grant him the rights to the territory that would later become the Congo, a country approximately 88 times the size of tiny Belgium and as vast as all Western Europe. The below summary of the DR Congo's exploitation and the demise of local industries comes from multiple sources [26-32].

Leopold's posturing against slavery did not prevent him from taking over this territorial bonanza as his private property, under the cruelly ironic name of the Congo Free State, and imposing a regime of forced labor for the purpose of harvesting hundreds of thousands of pounds of ivory as well as one of the successor commodities to sugar in Europe's drive toward industrialization and wealth: rubber. In the pursuit of rubber production, Leopold's Congolese subjects were ferociously overworked and mistreated. Female villagers were routinely held hostage, for example, to force men to cull rubber from wild trees in the dense forest, and those who did not meet their production quota frequently had a hand publicly amputated as punishment. In the space of three decades at the end of the 19th century, the Congo went from being one of the places in the world least explored by outsiders to one of the most brutally exploited. Local manufacturing and production for local needs were systematically destroyed, and severe punishment for cutting hands or heads was inflicted on any dissenting people.

In the Congo Free State, colonists brutalized the local population into producing rubber, for which the spread of automobiles and the development of rubber tires created a growing international market. Rubber sales made a fortune for Leopold, who built several buildings in Brussels and Ostend to honor himself and his country. To enforce the rubber quotas, the army, the *Force Publique*, cut off the limbs of the natives as a matter of policy. Rubber revenue went directly to King Leopold II, who paid the Free State for the high costs of exploitation. Because of the human rights abuses suffered under King Leopold II's rule, Congo rubber was eventually nicknamed "red rubber" in reference to the blood of the Africans killed during production.

In time, this produced an international scandal that required Leopold to surrender personal control of the Congo to the Belgian state, but as many as 10 million inhabitants of the territory were killed outright or driven to early deaths by the dire conditions that prevailed during and immediately after his rule. The Belgian state ruled the Congo very differently but also catastrophically, extracting enormous wealth from its colony while investing little.

Even today, some Belgians deny this history or try to downplay it, saying they created many roads in the colony as well as schools and hospitals. What they decline to acknowledge in making specious arguments like these is that the limited construction that was done was carried out not through investment but again through the forced labor of Africans, and almost none of Belgium's colonial subjects in the Congo were even provided secondary education.

The Belgian Congo was a source of profitable investment by private Western corporations following World War I. The region built large plantations that grew rubber, cacao, coffee, oil palms, cotton, and raised livestock. Other commodities that were harvested included zinc, cobalt, tin, copper, diamonds, gold, and uranium. While the brutalities of the Leopold reign were diminished, severe labor conditions continued through much of the 20th century. The mines and plantations were worked by African laborers who served as indentured servants. Congolese workers were required to work contracts that spanned from four to seven years. The infrastructure of the Congo was developed by forced labor, and roads and railroads were for the sole purpose of evacuating Congo's resources and wealth to Belgium.

There were hardly any initiatives put in place to promote the economic development of sectors important to the welfare of the native people. Economic developments were directly tied to the exploitation of the land. Railroads and other forms of transportation were developed to increase profits for the Belgian government. Plantations and large mining operations were formed, and native people occupied the labor pool. Congo rubber, copper, gold and diamond, tin and zinc, titanium, cobalt, lithium, and coltan have powered all the last four industrial revolutions outside the DR Congo itself.

Today, this history is of more than passing interest. The Democratic Republic of the Congo, as the successor state to the Belgian Congo, is one of the poorest countries and weakest governments in the world. Horrific misery, total disintegration of the basic infrastructures, no viable local industries and manufacturing, productivity zero, chaotic natural resources exploitation for export, corruption, and unending violence and armed conflicts.

Smartphones, computers, and electric vehicles may be emblems of the modern world, but their rechargeable batteries are frequently powered by cobalt mined by workers laboring in slave-like conditions in the Democratic Republic of Congo. Cobalt is used in the manufacture of almost all lithium-ion rechargeable batteries used in the world today. Imagine an entire population of people who cannot survive without scrounging in hazardous conditions for a dollar or two a day. There is no alternative there. The mines have taken over everything. Hundreds of thousands of people have been displaced because their villages were just bulldozed over to make place for large mining concessions. So you have people with no alternative, no other source of income, no livelihood. Now, add to that the menace in many cases of armed forces pressuring people to dig, parents having to make a painful decision, 'Do I send my child to school or do we eat today?' And if they choose the latter, that means bringing all their kids into these toxic pits to dig just to earn that extra fifty cents or a dollar a day, that could mean the difference between eating or not. So, in the 21st century, this is modern-day slavery. It's not chattel slavery from the 18th century, where you can buy and trade people and own title over a person's property. But the level of degradation, the level of exploitation, is on par with old-world slavery.

Putting this agonizing giant, the Democratic Republic of the Congo, on a strong footing technologically, economically, and politically would radically improve the prospects of large surrounding regions and help boost the trajectory of the continent as a whole, with huge benefits for the world.

5.3 Remarks on science and technology in Africa

Unlike European and Asian civilizations, many local industries throughout the African continent never had a chance to mature in time as communities were dealing with the European and Arab slave trade and colonialism. Because by nature imperialism is fortuitous, transferring to the metropolitan states the wealth of the (conquered) nations, thereby undermining them through capital and human exploitation, colonialism and contemporary neocolonialism pillaged African works of art and ruined African industries. Indeed, the historical and current technological underdevelopment of the continent of Africa cannot be explained without reference to European imperialism, economic domination, and exploitation. The imperialist domination and underdevelopment of Africa is a continuing process that affects all aspects of life on the continent. Thus, it can be further argued that even successive governments in various African nations have either deliberately or inadvertently contributed to the decline of indigenous technologies by importing all forms of foreign technology as imposed by imperialism without inputs from locals on the ground. Over time, preferences for foreign technologies have contributed to a culture of inferiority, where foreign imports are seen as superior over locally made products [33].

Have slavery and colonialism locked Africa into a perverse path of underdevelopment with no way out? It depends, in large measure, on African countries' public policies. If African governments continue with business as usual, focused on exporting raw materials and spending the revenue on consumables but not on developing technical and technological capacities, then success is unlikely. If African governments invest in the health and education of the next generations embrace and promote policies that target and favor their own manufacturing industries, then success is likely.

What the continent needs is political commitment and the audacity to implement the right policies, even in the face of strong external opposition. If African governments are serious, brave, committed, and determined for bold and creative policies and actions, then an African leapfrog for an African industrial revolution is not only possible but feasible in the short term. This is because, in the old days, countries developed incrementally; they gradually built up on the back of networks that supplied people with electricity, phones, roads, health and educational services. But today, the availability of information online means Africans can be as up-to-date about new developments and access data in the public domain via the internet as their counterparts in the industrialized nations [34]. African countries can make it to the industrial revolution, for where there is a will, there is a way. But do African countries and African governments have the will?

6. Path to Industrial Revolution

6.1 The roots

Africa must reconnect with its roots in science and technology. These roots are not past. They permeate through informal youth inventions and creativities all over the continent. African nations only need to stop neglecting and ignoring these talents in favor of quick export of raw materials for cash. Instead of using the cash to set up or stimulate education, technical schools, and local manufacturing industries, African countries—with a few exceptions—waste money on non-productive expenditures. Furthermore, corruption and mismanagement divert funds meant for important projects that never get off the ground. These projects include education, building and maintaining health and transportation infrastructures, promoting manufacturing, and establishing basic social services that improve livelihoods in villages, towns, and cities.

African countries must reconnect with and get inspiration from their history when flourishing science and technologies, manufacturing, and industries were developed but then destroyed by slavery and colonialism. Then, national strategies for education and skills development should be adopted, focusing not only on youth but also on adult workers, informal economy workers, and neglected yet talented youth and people in rural villages and towns.

What needs to change in the current African culture is its extraversion to shift into the continent's narrative that values and promotes local technology, emphasizing the significant scientific and ecological insights of various African societies.

6.2 Conscious policy decision making

The China-Africa S&TC experiment has been off target but has elements African nations can use to jumpstart their national science and technology applied to national development. African nations can adopt and adapt the following elements from China's strategy for their own national industrial revolution.

Frist, China made a conscious decision, through well-organized cooperative activities, to ensure that the international science and technology cooperation plays, and it has played, a leading role in supporting dedicated national science and technology programs in the major fields, capacity building, building of industrialization system, building of supportive environment, building science and technology infrastructure development and science and technology services. Short and long-term science and technology programs and implementing activities are planned with associated evaluation mechanisms.

Second, China made a conscious decision to set a five-year planning, execution, and evaluation period for science and technology innovation capacity building, with a focus on strengthening inter-governmental cooperation with the major science and technology world powers. Hence, during ISTC, China pays more attention to the digestion, absorption, and adaptation of imported technologies and actively encourages industrial enterprises to join international science and technology cooperation and exchanges on the cutting edge of technological development. China decided to initiate, support, and promote China's high-tech industries to enter the international market, making their technical innovation activities in line with international norms and merging into international communities on China's own initiatives and objectives.

Third, China puts effort and means to tap up the intellectual resources in the international science and technology community in order to encourage the flow of overseas intellectual resources into China. This is the key to understanding China's achievement of the frog-leap science and technology development in the country.

African countries can do the same, and none of these elements is burdensome or too expensive or require extraterrestrial ingenuity beyond the capacity of African countries. African countries are and should be able to make conscious policy decisions similar to what China has done.

6.3 Policy for an industrial revolution

6.3.1 The concept

Starting with the policy concept, this section will provide more details on elements for effective policies to stimulate science, technology, and industrialization [35-37]. The Industrial Revolution, referred to as the change from hand and home production to machine and factory production, implies learning (education and apprenticeship), manpower and skill development, and manufacturing or technology-based entrepreneurship that are shaped and unified by effective policies.

Policy is a deliberate system of guidelines to guide decisions and achieve rational outcomes. A policy is a statement of intent and is implemented as a procedure or protocol. Effective policies answer questions about what needs to be done (such as directions, limits, principles, and decision-making guidance) and why to do it. Policy is a guide to thinking and action; policy guides every thought process and activity undertaken in a society. Policy is like a creed, a guide, and a mandate that everyone must uphold, and it is a language everyone must speak. By so doing, it promotes unity and oneness. At this point, everyone would understand that although they have diverse cultures and tongues, they are one through the attainment of this creed.

The policy must be translated into programs that transform individuals into active creators who are learned and productive. Hence, it is important to formulate policies that articulate and promote personal growth, economic development, performance enhancement, and industrialization. Therefore, policies must stipulate in programmable plans the need to acquire and develop knowledge that translates into skills to improve manufacturing or technology-based entrepreneurship. Policy decisions must be reflected in resource allocations.

6.3.2 Bold funded industrial policy

Bold-funded industrial policy refers to government efforts to shape the economy by targeting specific industries, firms, or economic activities. This is achieved through a range of tools such as subsidies, tax incentives, infrastructure development, protective regulations, and research and development support.

When implementing industrial policy as part of their growth strategy, countries are often faced with competing objectives, such as securing sustainable economic growth, maintaining financial and fiscal stability, and establishing national priorities.

An example of a bold funded industrial policy is the CHIPS and Science Act (CHIPS Act), a law enacted by the United Government that allocated billions of dollars to drive American competitiveness in semiconductor manufacturing, making American supply chains more resilient, boosting and protecting key technologies, and thus supporting national security of the United States. The funding opportunity supports projects involving the construction, expansion, or modernization of commercial facilities in the United States for semiconductor materials and manufacturing equipment. These projects (will) produce the equipment, chemicals, gases, and other materials that are critical to manufacturing semiconductors in America. Such government funding helps companies increase economic resilience, create new pathways to good jobs, and boost emerging technology innovation in local communities [38-39].

The Chinese government made bold funded industrial policy its mode of governance for a long time, making innovation a top priority in its economic planning through a number of high-profile initiatives, such as "Made in China 2025," a plan announced in 2015 to upgrade and modernize China's manufacturing in 10 key sectors through extensive government assistance in order to make China a major global player in these sectors [40].

Why wouldn't African countries and governments enact bold-funded policies that support developing and executing programs to encourage domestic manufacturing, investing in research and development, and supporting workforce development?

6.4 Elements of a bold industrial policy

6.4.1 Learning and apprenticeship

Programs for acquiring knowledge and know-how are of priority. Learning begins from the novices' position and progresses to the experts' position. This, in turn, creates relatively permanent changes in knowledge, skills, and other behaviors. When a person starts an apprenticeship program, he or she usually begins from the minimum level under the guidance of an expert. At the end of the first year of learning, the learning-person is promoted to the second level, having learned the things scheduled for the first level. The growth achieved this way is sustainable. The learning person builds up capabilities or competence, i.e., the ability to do things. The ability to do things increases with learning. The build-up of competence continues as long as the learning person continues to learn. Hence, performance enhancement is continuous, sustainable, and effective. Learning and acquiring knowledge, skills, and capabilities and applying these in solving problems, including production, are the basis for achieving manufacturing, industrialization, and sustainable economic growth.

Apprenticeship is training to generate expertise or skills needed to perform a particular job or series of jobs. Training prepares people for work and develops life-skills in a working situation. The work skills are of three types: technical, interpersonal, human, and conceptual skills. These skills are obtained through learning and training. That is, from "learning-by-doing" and "learning-by-adapting" to "learning-by-design" and "learning-by-improved design" and then to "learning-by-setting-up a complete production system."

People do not learn by-letting experts do everything for them. If so, they will continually be slaves to the expert who knows, and the learner will lack the opportunity to become an expert. Learning, apprenticeship, and training develop skills for work and production that make things happen and create goods that improve living conditions and quality of life.

6.4.2 Soft and basic skills development

Bold policy must establish Skills Development Funds to promote the opportunity for the trained to apply the acquired knowledge and skills to produce goods and services. Manpower designated citizens empowered with the necessary skills required to get jobs done. Skills range from soft skills and basic artisan skills to advanced technical skills.

Soft skills

Soft skills build character; they help develop the character traits of a person, and they help define their personality. Everyone needs soft skills to prepare them and maintain a healthy working attitude. Soft skills can be learned at any age, but the nature of these skills suggests that they are best learned at a very young age because they are foundational. Soft skills build the competence and confidence of the labor force, giving room for more achievements.

Soft skills range from learning diverse languages to presentation skills, drawing skills, writing skills, reading skills, music skills, ethics and etiquette, etc. These skills improve creativity. This skill will enable the workforce to create sustainable enterprises and visionary companies. Soft skills are critical for the foundational setting of the workforce. They can provide great energy and cohesion for the members of the workforce.

Acquired knowledge is to be applied in productive activities to increase the total performance and value of goods produced and services provided within a year. The use of this knowledge improves the effectiveness of the production, i.e., being able to produce quality amounts of goods and services, etc.

Basic artisan skills

An artisan is a craftsman, someone who does skilled work, making things with his hands manually. The artisan skills range from woodland crafts, building crafts, field crafts, workshop crafts, textile crafts, and domestic crafts.

- Woodland crafts

This includes coppices, hurdle makers, rake makers, fork makers, besom makers, handle makers, hoop markers, ladder makers, crib makers, broaches and peg makers, clog sole cutters, charcoal burners, oak basket makers, stick and staff makers, field gate makers, willow basket makers, and net makers.

- Building crafts

The builders include stone masons, plumbers, decorators, bridge builders, French polishers, and sign writers.

- Farmers

This includes hedge layers, stile makers, well diggers, peat cutters, gardeners, horticulturists, tree surgeons, foresters, farmers, shepherds, shearers, bee keepers, millers, fishermen, orchardists, and veterinarians.

- Workshop crafts

This includes chair makers, iron founders, blacksmiths, wheelwrights, coopers, coppersmiths, tinsmiths, wood turners, coach builders, boat builders, boiler makers, boiler men, soap makers, gunsmiths, clay pipe makers, and tool makers.

- Textile craft

This includes spinners, weavers, dryers, silk growers, tailors, seamstresses, milliners, hatter, lace makers, button makers, mat and rug makers, crochet workers, tatting and macramé workers, knitters, quilters, smock workers, embroiderers, leather workers, and felt makers.

- Domestic craft

Fish smokers, bacon curers, dish wash makers, insecticide makers, butter makers, cheese makers, brewers, cider makers, winemakers, distillers, herbalists, ice cream makers, bakers, barrister and coffee roasters, osteopaths, naturopaths, storytellers, teacher, naturalists, historians, jesters, actors, administrators, philosophers, laborers, poets, writers, midwives, publicans, booksellers, Liberians, movie makers, public speakers, etc.

6.4.3 Advanced technical skills

Education and training are both essential tools for developing advanced technical skills. Here, education refers to formal education, which emphasizes the acquisition of theoretical knowledge and the development of basic mental capabilities and general knowledge. Formal education refers to institutionalized instructions or courses of study designed to make the learning persons, or students, experience the type of curriculum that is capable of providing essential learning needs. Education equips the individual with the ability to think and reason. It is an essential instrument for effecting economic and technological change, as well as changes in ideas and personality. The essence of education is in developing critical thinkers and enhancing performance.

The higher the university education completion rate, the higher the share of knowledge that intensive service industries receive. The Knowledge Intensive Service Industry provides consumers with knowledge-based services that rely mainly on high technology, expertise, information, and experience. The service process includes knowledge production, knowledge dissemination, and knowledge use.

The knowledge-intensive service Industry is supported mainly by science, engineering, technology, and other industries.

Innovation is possible if there are people who can perform research that generates new ways of thinking and new knowledge, who can apply their knowledge and skills, and who can adapt to change. Therefore, the workforce must aim to attain a high level of theoretical knowledge, especially science and engineering graduates. Simultaneously, s/he must receive complementary training and skills based on their age and educational attainment. A workforce should be encouraged to pursue a university degree alongside complementary training/skills. Education helps to build the technical, interpersonal, human, and conceptual skills of the workforce.

African nations need to encourage, support, and give opportunities to science and engineering graduates to input the theories they acquire in universities into their artisan/craft activities like blacksmithing, wood-works, textiles/tailoring, construction works, and factory floor work settings and all other places where skill acquisition opportunities abound. This is how countries can improve performance and produce youths who can develop independent thoughts to solve everyday problems. These youths shall evolve to become Industrialization Vanguards (IVs). Their Productivity increases as they develop manpower capability and are employed in productive activities. This, in turn, creates more room for employment through expansion, and as they continually involve themselves in productive activities, inventions/innovations sprout out, and these inventions/innovations form the basis for new knowledge.

Industrialization is not about erecting structures. It is about developing competencies and improving performance for doing uncountable things. It is about ensuring a large percentage of resources is geared towards manpower development, employment creation, increasing productivity, promoting inventions and innovations, and increasing the learning rate of the citizens.

Education generates advanced skills recognized as the underpinnings of innovations. The supporting environment includes but is not limited to the availability and utilization of libraries, educational centers, information technology centers, scientific research and publications, etc. The integration of all these into government policies goes a long way in determining the kind of industries, level of industrialization, performance, and growth prospects in the country.

6.5 Advanced skills and industrialization

Advanced skills are necessary for the mechanization or automation of artisan skills, and the production of other advanced products not possible by craftsmen alone. Advanced skills include qualitative analytical forecasting skills, military training, leadership skills, teamwork and management skills, policy formulation and advocacy skills, wafer fabrication, Integrated Circuit Design, biotech, making petrochemicals, fine chemicals, pharmaceutical, automotive machines, and cybernetics, aerospace, computer-aided design tools, and other precision engineering components.

Advanced skills involve a lot of research and development and are important to bring about innovation. Innovation improves and increases productivity, spurring industrialization and economic development. Advanced skill is a must-have collection of activities for advanced-level students. The advanced training of workers is carried out through individual and team training, both on the job and in a variety of short courses. Such training is offered by institutes for improving the skills of managerial personnel and specialists. Advanced training does not usually require taking time off from work.

Therefore, an "expert manpower" is one who has attained proper education and has been trained to an advanced professional technological level, integrating both theory and practice to improve productivity and promote industrialization.

6.6 Technology-based entrepreneurship

Technological entrepreneurship aims to create new products, design new production methods, discover new sources of raw materials, open new markets, and develop new forms of organizations through innovative skills. The performance measurement for these entrepreneurs includes but is not limited to, the number and rate of innovations, the development of new market products, new raw materials, new production processes, and new science and technology organizations.

6.6.1 Public enterprises

China is home to 109 corporations listed on the Fortune Global 500 - but only 15% of those are privately owned. Recognizing the inefficient management of government corporations that may result from excessive bureaucracy, China embarked on targeted reforms.

In 2003, China established the State-owned Asset Supervision and Administration Commission (SASAC) to implement the government's 'zhuada fangxiao' (grasp the big, release the small) policy, which has greatly reduced the number of SOEs through privatization, asset sales, and mergers and acquisitions. SASAC is currently concentrating on restructuring the remaining SOEs into modern profit-oriented corporations. Practically, all of the entities overseen by SASAC are structured as corporations and legally separate from the government with their own boards of directors, effectively delegating more authority to the executives. But, the Chinese government is determined to support SOEs and is committed to making them bigger, stronger, and more efficient [41]. The result is that China's state-owned industries are striving and producing results.

The government of the United States owns national laboratories that are Federally Funded Research and Development Centers (FFRDCs). For over 80 years, the National Laboratories have been on the leading edge of American technology and innovation, seeking solutions to some of the most pressing challenges in energy, science, national security, and environmental stewardship. The laboratories have conducted research to make fossil-based energy resources cleaner at lower costs, created new materials that advance energy storage, generation, and efficiency, and enhanced the safety, security, and effectiveness of U.S. nuclear systems and equipment. These contributions and many more are made possible by the scientists, engineers, technicians, professionals, educators, and others who make up the National Laboratory System. The Laboratories support scientists and engineers from academia, government, and industry with access to specialized equipment, world-class research facilities, and skilled technical staff. Together, they are working to solve some of the world's greatest scientific challenges [42].

African countries and governments who came to political power after independence failed to manage and grow industrial enterprises inherited from the colonial systems and, additionally, have not been able to create prosperous industrial enterprises of their own. It is time for African countries and governments to take things seriously and use the state leverage to boost science, technology, and manufacturing in Africa.

6.6.2 Private enterprises

Regarding the private sector businesses, the Forbes Business Council [43] stated that as enough tiny droplets of water slowly fill a bucket, the growth of small businesses fills the U.S. economy. Big corporations might get a lot of attention when it comes to creating jobs, but small businesses employ more people and are more resilient when times get tough. Before coming up with something innovative that propelled them into growth, all big businesses once started out small. Not only are small businesses driving the U.S. economy, but they also keep the American dream alive. Small businesses employ nearly half of the entire American workforce and represent 43.5% of America's Gross Domestic Product (GDP).

Small and medium-sized businesses (SMEs) are the lifeblood of Africa's economy. They are responsible for more than 80% of the continent's employment and 50% of the GDP. However, small businesses are buried in the informal economy, contributing between 25 and 65 percent of GDP and accounting for between 30 and 90 percent of total nonagricultural employment. On the continent, the informal economy differs from country to country but includes, among others, household enterprises that have some production at market value but are not registered, underground production where productive activities are performed by registered firms but may be concealed from the authorities to avoid compliance with regulations or the payment of taxes, or are simply perceived as illegal. The informal economy exists to varying degrees in all African countries, providing livelihoods and incomes for millions of people.

African SMEs face two significant financing challenges: accessibility and affordability. Accessibility refers to the ability of SMEs to access finance. SMEs in Africa are frequently informal—meaning they are not formally registered as businesses—and this makes it difficult for them to access financing. Moreover, even those that are formally registered still frequently suffer from a lack of accessibility. This is a significant issue because, without sufficient working capital, firms are unable to invest and grow. Affordability refers to the cost of capital or how much it costs for a firm to take out a loan or receive an investment. The total loan cost comprises not just the cost of the original loan but also the interest charged and transaction costs, like fees for lawyers to perfect collateral. This is a serious challenge in Africa because local interest rates from banks are often in the double digits, sometimes higher than 20–25 percent. Alternative finance providers, such as microfinance institutions or digital lenders, can charge even higher rates, as much as 40–50 percent. High interest rates deter SMEs from even trying to apply for financing. This lack of affordable financing seriously hinders SMEs in Africa.

Blended finance is one approach to providing SMEs with access to the capital needed to grow. Blended finance is defined as "the strategic use of development finance and philanthropic funds to mobilize private capital flows to emerging and frontier markets." Blended finance seeks to "de-risk" potential investments in such a way that private sector actors will feel comfortable investing alongside or on top. Blended finance is one of the primary ways that official finance can "crowd in" or catalyze private investment from institutions that have a lower risk tolerance or seek a higher rate of return [44].

6.6.3 Public-private partnerships

Public-private partnerships involve collaboration between a government agency and a private-sector company that can be used to finance, build, and operate projects, as explained below [45]. These partnerships work well when private-sector technology and innovation combine with public-sector incentives to complete work on time and within budget. Financing comes partly from the private sector but requires payments from the public sector and/or users over the project's lifetime. The private partner participates in designing, completing, implementing, and funding the project, while the public partner focuses on defining and monitoring compliance with the objectives. Risks are distributed between the public and private partners through a process of negotiation, ideally, though not always according to the ability of each to assess, control, and cope with them.

Partnerships between private companies and governments provide advantages to both parties. Private-sector technology and innovation, for example, can help improve the operational efficiency of providing public services. The public sector, for its part, provides incentives for the private sector to deliver projects on time and within budget. In addition, creating economic diversification makes the country more competitive in facilitating its infrastructure base and boosting associated construction, equipment, support services, and other businesses.

6.7 Remarks on the path to industrial revolution

Science generates technology, technology drives manufacturing, and manufacturing produces goods and services. That's the path to the industrial revolution.

Limited knowledge and the ability of people to innovate are the greatest challenges facing industrial processes in developing nations. Failure to continuously strengthen and increase people's knowledge base results in a declining ability of people to produce goods and services to meet their basic needs. Knowledge and innovation increase productivity, which generates wealth, and wealth reduces poverty and improves living conditions.

African countries are slow in science, technology, and industrialization. This is in part because of past slavery and colonialism, but it is in most part the result of the copy and paste policy syndrome from industrialized nations by African nations, without bold funded policies tailored to capacities development in the African countries. Simply put, the two major challenges to African rapid industrialization are namely (1) limited knowledge and knowledge acquisition processes and (2) poor policy formulation and implementation.

Historically, a large majority of Africans were denied the benefits of science, technology, and industrial revolution. Many of them were cheap slaves and contractual servants, thus robbing them of their uniqueness, self-esteem, poise, and confidence. Despite the change in state of affairs with African countries gaining a greater measure of freedom and independence, many Africans are still struggling with their uniqueness and their sense of self-worth. Many Western nations that progressed and developed through the Industrial Revolution have reinforced (by attitude, policies, and legislation) the notion that African nations do not possess the potential to develop the skills, intelligence, and sophistication necessary to equal that of industrialized nations.

The African nations are still led to look to the industrially developed nations for their measure of standard, quality, and excellence. This, in turn, breeds a sense of disrespect and suspicion for their own products and a denial of the great potential that lies dormant in African nations everywhere on the continent. There is still the notion that the presence of a foreign element is necessary for the maintenance of excellence and quality. This is not true! African nations are great; they possess the intelligence for transformation, and the sooner African nations realize this truth and believe in their ability to stimulate the industrialization process on their own, the sooner the journey to industrialization will begin.

African countries may speed things up by adopting the whole government approach, a synergy meaning working together to promote interaction of national institutions to speed up the realization of projects, minimize mistakes and delays, and amplify the results for the good of the country. This can be exemplified in public-private partnerships, government agencies, institutions of learning, and working practitioners network and communicate, bouncing around ideas to synergistically develop and/or refine innovative concepts and processes for efficient performance.

7. Conclusion

African nations post-independence have engaged in science and technology cooperation with China and other industrialized nations. Across the continent, industrialization is arguably the most talked about subject among policymakers. Industrialization has been a campaign promise across the African continent, with its acknowledged ability to bring about prosperity, new jobs, and better incomes for all. Yet the continent is less industrialized today than it was four decades ago.

Meeting the challenge of industrialization will require new thinking both in Africa and among its development partners. But the urgency for new thinking falls squarely upon African countries because it is on the continent of Africa that chronic underdevelopment condemns millions or hundreds of millions of people to live in poverty, with illnesses, and poor political and economic prospects. It is on the continent of Africa that long-term goals of economic and human development are undermined by scarce, unreliable, or unaffordable supplies of vital resources such as food, water, and energy. Africa must engage in new thinking regarding its industrialization and do it now and quickly.

This new thinking must realize that there is no copy-and-paste path to industrialization. It is rather a journey of ingenuity, creativity, and innovation that requires knowledge development and acquisition of basic and advanced skills for designing and producing goods and services.

African countries must stop their decline and backward drifting to stabilize themselves, then redirect their thinking through bold policies for skills development and capacity building, ambitious development projects, and corruption-free management of policies and project funds.

One objective to aggressively pursue is the shift from donor-driven investment to locally-driven investment. This shift needs to go hand in hand with the promotion of local industries and manufacturing, stimulating the private sector, and aggressively promoting public-private partnerships, which can be used as a tool for promoting the formation of industrial clusters.

The critical role of infrastructure can never be overemphasized. Infrastructure deficiencies are a significant barrier to industrial development. This includes the lack of power as the greatest constraint, followed by transportation. Infrastructures like roads and railroads that do not need sophisticated technologies for maintenance and rehabilitation give African nations an opportunity to test their new thinking of exclusively using local capacities and resources to do the job.

Whether Africa is able to translate science and technology cooperation into an industrial revolution will ultimately depend on the policies and public actions undertaken by African governments to strengthen, mobilize, and motivate private citizens to create, innovate, and to do actions that transform lives and societies. Less cheap and loud talks but more actions, as described above, will ensure that science and technology cooperation leads to an industrial revolution on the continent of Africa.

REFERENCES

[1] Tongele N. Tongele (2024), *China-Africa Science and Technology Cooperation*, chapter V in this book.

[2] Tongele N. Tongele (2016), *Rise and Shine: Resilient People and Immense Resources in the Shadow of Death*, Green Ivy Publishing, Illinois, USA.

[3] Bhaskar Chakravorti and Ravi Shankar Chaturvedi (2019), " Research: How Technology Could Promote Growth in 6 African Countries," *Harvard Business Review*,. Retrieved from *Research: How Technology Could Promote Growth in 6 African Countries (hbr.org)*.

[4] Louise Fox and Landry Signé (2022), "From subsistence to disruptive innovation: Africa, the Fourth Industrial Revolution, and the future of jobs," Brookings Institution. Retrieved from: *4IR-and-Jobs_March-2022_Final.docx.pdf (brookings.edu)*.

[5] Louise Fox and Landry Signé (2022), "Emerging technologies and the future of work in Africa," Brookings Institution. Retrieved from: *Emerging technologies and the future of work in Africa | Brookings*.

[6] Sampson Kofi Adotey and Serdia Holcombe (2022), "3 Ways tech and innovation can push Africa to the next level of economic growth," World Economic Forum. Retrieved from: *3 ways technology can boost economic growth in Africa | World Economic Forum (weforum.org)*.

[7] Padmashree Gehl Sampath and Padmashree Gehl (2014), "Industrial development for Africa, technology and the role of the state," *African Journal of Science, Technology, Innovation and Development*, Vol. 6, No. 5. Published Online: *https://hdl.handle.net/10520/EJC165722*.

[8] Joseph Amankwah-Amoah (2019), "Technology revolution, sustainability, and development in Africa: Overview, emerging issues,

and challenges." First published online: *https://doi.org/10.1002/sd.1950*.

[9] John A.J. Gowlett and Richard W. Wrangham (2013), "Earliest fire in Africa: towards the convergence of archaeological evidence and the cooking hypothesis." Published online: *https://doi.org/10.1080/0067270X.2012.756754*.

[10] Jennie Cohen (2023), "Human Ancestors Tamed Fire Earlier than Thought." Retrieved from: *Https://www.history.com/news/huan-ancestors-tamed-fire-earlier-than-thought*.

[11] Jessica Thompson, David Wright, and Sarah Ivory (2021), "Early humans used fire to permanently change the landscape." Retrieved from: *Early humans used fire to permanently change the landscape | PBS NewsHour*.

[12] IED Team (2019), "A Brief History of The 4 Industrial Revolutions that Shaped the World". Published online: *https://ied.eu/project-updates/the-4-industrial-revolutions/*.

[13] Britannica (2024), "Industrial Revolutions." Written and fact-checked by The Editions of *Encyclopaedia Britannica*.

[14] https://education.nationalgeographic.org/resource/industrial-revolution-and-technology/.

[15] POST (2020), "Technological Development in Pre-Colonial Africa." Retrieved from: *Technological Developments in Pre-Colonial Africa « The Confucian Weekly Bulletin (wordpress.com)*.

[16] Isaac Samuel (2021), " Science and technology in African history; Astronomy, Mathematics, Medicine and Metallurgy in pre-colonial Africa." Retrieved from: *https://www.africanhistoryextra.com/p/science-and-technology-in-aftircan*.

[17] Isaac Samuel (2021), "Monumentality, Power and functionalism in Pre-colonial African architecture; a select look at 17 African monuments from 5 regional architectural styles." Retrieved from: *https://www.africanhistoryextra.com/p/monumentality-power-and-functionality*.

[18] Isaac Samuel (2021), "War and peace in ancient and medieval Africa: The Arms, Amour and Fortifications of African armies and military systems from antiquity until the 19th century." Retrieved from: *Https://www.africanhistoryextra.com/p/war-and-peace-in-ancient-and-medieval.*

[19] Stephan Heblich, Stephen Redding, Hans-Joachim Voth, "Slavery and the British Industrial Revolution." Retrieved from: *https://cepr.org/voxeu/columns/slavery-and-british-indstrial-revolution.*

[20] Howard W. French, "Confronting Belgium's Colonial Legacy: Belgium's King Philippe is visiting Congo this week, but the country still has much to do to make amends." Retrieved from: *https://foreignpolicy.com/2022/06/06/belgium-congo-colonialism-leopold-ii-commodities/.*

[21] Steven Mintz (n.d.), "Historical Context: Facts about the Slave Trade and Slavery," Posted on *The Gilder Lehrman Institute of American History*. Retrieved from: *Historical Context: Facts about the Slave Trade and Slavery | Gilder Lehrman Institute of American History.*

[22] Dina Gerdeman (2017), " The Clear Connection Between Slavery And American Capitalism." Retrieved from: *The Clear Connection Between Slavery And American Capitalism (forbes.com).*

[23] Britannica (2023), "Slave Trade." Written and fact checked by The Editions of *Encyclopaedia Britannica.*

[24] Joshua Dwayne Settles (1998), "The Impact of Colonialism on African Economic Development," *Chancellor's Honors Program Projects.* https://trace.tennessee.edu/utk_chanhonoproj/182.

[25] Stephen Ocheni and Basil C. Nwankwo (2012), "Analysis of Colonialism and Its Impact in Africa," *Cross-Cultural Communication*, Vol. 8, No. 3, 2012, pp. 46-54. DOI:10.3968/j.ccc.1923670020120803.1189.

[26] Adam Hochschild (1998), *King Leopold's Ghost: A Story of Greed, Terror and Heroism in Colonial Africa*, New York, Houghton Mifflin Company.

[27] Tongele N. Tongele (1997), *From Congo to Zaire to Congo: Challenges and Prospects for the 21st Century*, Sacramento, Transnational Print Services.

[28] Siddharth Kara (2023), *Cobalt Red: How the Blood of the Congo Powers Our Lives*, Kindle Edition.

[29] Ralph E. Birchard (1940), "Copper in the Katanga Region of the Belgian Congo", *JSTOR, Economic Geography*, Vol. 16, No. 4 (Oct. 1940), pp. 429-436 (8 pages).

[30] Claude Van England (1984), "ZAIRE: An African nation rich in natural resources but plagued by political instability and economic stagnation," *The Christian Science Monitor*, 6 November 6, 1984.

[31] M.S.Prasad (1989), "Production of copper and cobalt at Gecamines, Zaire," *Minerals Engineering* (ScienceDirect), Volume 2, Issue 4, 1989, Pages 521-541.

[32] Dashveenjit Kaur (2021), "The future of electric vehicle with cobalt-free batteries," *Tech Wire Asia*, 6 Avril 2021.

[33] Karibu Kinyanjui (1993), "Culture, technology and sustainable development in Africa," *Asian Perspective*, Vol.17, No.2 (Fall-Winter 1993), Published by The Johns Hopkins University Press.

[34] Masimba Tafirenyika (2016), " Why has Africa failed to industrialize? Experts call for bold and creative policies," Africa Renewal: August-November 2016.

[35] Chimezirim Young and Ayo Oyewale (2021), "Africa's Journey to Industrialization." DOI: 10.5772/intechopen.94372. https://www.intechopen.com/chapters/74048.

[36] William N. Dunn (2016), *Public Policy Analysis*, Fifth Edition, Routledge, London and New York.

[37] H.K. Colebatch (2009), *Policy*, Third Edition, Open University Press, New York.

[38] Ruchir Agarwal (2023), "Industrial Policy and the Growth Strategy Trilemma," International Monetary Fund. https://www.imf.org/en/Publications/fandd/issues/Analytical-Series/industrial-policy-and-...

[39] Ian Thomas (2023), "How the CHIPS Act is aiming to restore a U.S. lead position in semiconductors," Published by CNBC. https://www.cnbc.com/2023/10/17/how-the-chips-act-...

[40] REPORT (2019), "China's Economic Rise: History, Trends, Challenges, and Implications for the United States,". https://www.everycrsreport.com/reports/RL33534.html.

[41] Amir Guluzade (2019), "The role of China's state-owned companies explained." Retrieved from: *Explained, the role of China's state-owned companies | World Economic Forum (weforum.org)*.

[42] The National Laboratories | U.S. Powerhouses of Science and Technology (nationallabs.org).

[43] Martin Rowinski (2022), "How Small Businesses Drive The American Economy," Published online: https://www.forbes.com/sites/forbesbusinesscouncil/2022/03/25/how-small-business-...

[44] Daniel F. Runde, Conor M. Savoyand, and Janina Staguhn (2021), "Supporting Small and Medium Enterprises in Sub-Saharan Africa through Blended Finance," Published by Center for Strategic & International Studies. https://www.csis.org/analysis/supporting-small-and-...

[45] THE INVESTOPEDIA TEAM (2022), "Public-Private Partnerships (PPPs): Definition, How They Work, and Examples," Published by Investopedia. https://www.investopedia.com/term/p/public-private-...

CHAPTER VII

AFRICA: FROM DEFICIT TO STRENGTH-BASED COOPERATION

By

Ndasi Zialo, PhD

1. Introduction

Africa-China cooperation is better understood in the larger context of economic and trade relations between Africa and Asia. Since the independence of African and Asian countries from Western colonialism in the sixties, more than 1 billion people have been lifted worldwide out of extreme poverty since the 1990s, largely due to developments in East Asia—and in China in particular. While trade relations between Africa and Asia have burgeoned, they remain lopsided; Africa is primarily a source of raw commodities, and Asia is an exporter of finished products (Brookings, 2022). Africa's development answers lie in providing the space for private citizens and private sectors to flourish. This will allow Africa to go from a deficit to a strength-based cooperation with the outside world, including China.

2. Africa and Asia at the Point of Decolonization

East Asia seemed to have very few advantages over Africa at the point of decolonization. Traditional East Asian societies were often characterized by ethnic disunity, frail institutions, limited governance outside of the capital, weak democracy, subsistence agriculture, fragmentary external trade linkages, and acute social stratification—conditions prevalent in many African states. Both Africa and Asia shared a history of commodity and colonial exploitation, where the conquerors were sharply divided from the conquered by race, though there was a tendency on the part of the colonizers to favor some local groups over others. But Asia has grown, while Africa is left behind: why?

Figure 1 (Brookings, 2022) shows that in 1960, the average GDP per capita of the world was just $445. At $134, sub-Saharan Africa's GDP per capita was 30 percent of the world's average. East Asia and the Pacific's GDP per capita was slightly higher, at $151. However, the relative GDP per capita of these two regions has diverged sharply since then. Now, East Asia and the Pacific's GDP per capita is almost equivalent to the global average ($11,345), while sub-Saharan Africa remains at 15 percent of that number.

Figure 1. Regional GDP per capita relative to the world's GDP per capita

At independence, both African and Asian (East Asian) countries were at similar developmental levels (Figure 1). Both African and Asian countries attempted centrally planned economic development, which was proven not to be so good of a development model. However, very quickly, Asian countries adopted a different set of developmental techniques that sustained their rise because they quickly understood that the key to development lay in government empowering private citizens and private sectors and investing in diversified economies and job creation. However, African countries remained government-owned companies, mismanaging revenues from raw materials exportation. Or mismanagement leads to dilapidation of resources and failure. Hence, Figure 1 shows a consistent rise in East Asian countries versus a consistent decline in

African countries. The explanation for this difference, the secret sauce for the Asian rise, which is explained below, is in citizens' empowerment to build businesses and innovate.

3. Citizens Empowerment: Key to Development and Strong Cooperation

Empowerment theory is defined as a rationale or conceptual framework that helps to explain or predict phenomena in the world (Creswell, 2018). It serves as a knowledge base upon which researchers build the foundation of their studies. The empowerment theory (ET) was selected as a framework for this study. The theory of empowerment is relatively new, but the concept of empowerment is old. It was first used in the Declaration of Independence of the United States in the 17th century to empower the American people against any tyrannical oppression (Rigaud, 2020).

In the 19th century, Abraham Maslow used the concept of self-actualization, which is similar to the concept of empowerment in his famous hierarchy of needs, to motivate marginalized individuals to meet their basic needs. Kurt Levin, an American psychologist, used the concept of empowerment in a group setting for social activism with a group of marginalized people. Paulo Freire, a Brazilian scholar, used the concept of critical consciousness to empower disadvantaged people. It was Barbara Solomon, an American scholar, who used the concept of empowerment as a framework for the first time in her work with marginalized African American communities. She argued that the time has come for social workers to stop dictating actions that clients must take and start focusing on clients making their own decisions by allowing them to carry out those decisions (Rigaud, 2020). Julian Rappaport introduced the theory of empowerment in the field of social psychology. This was a total paradigm shift from the traditional deficit approach of helping process to a new strengths-based practice orientation.

Table 1

Comparison of Empowerment Processes and Empowerment Outcomes Across Levels of Analysis

Level of analysis	Process (empowering)	Outcome (empowered)
Individual	Learning decision-making skills	Sense of control
	Managing resources	Critical awareness
	Working with others	Participatory behaviors
Organizational	Opportunity to participate in decision-making	Effectively compete for resources
	Shared responsibilities	Networking with other organizations
	Shared leadership	Policy influence
Community	Access to resources	Organizational coalition
	Open government structure	Pluralistic leadership
	Tolerance for diversity	Residents' participatory skills

Source: Adapted from Research Gate
https://www.researchgate.net/publication/232549776

There are many models of empowerment theory, as shown in Table 1, but Bayes (2015) has identified several of them, including the social, psychological, spiritual, organizational, and structural modalities (Bayes, 2015). Shearer (2021) has added the health empowerment model to the list. These modalities of Empowerment theory may be used in different settings. The empowerment theory is defined as a mechanism by which individuals, groups, and communities gain control over their lives (Perkins & Zimmerman, 1995; Rappaport, 1984). It is a multilevel theory with two theoretical constructs that include empowerment processes and empowerment outcomes that work simultaneously to empower people.

Perkins and Zimmerman (1995) provided an operational definition of the theory of empowerment as an intentional, ongoing process through which people lacking access to an equal share of valued resources gain greater access to and take control over those resources. It suggests that the empowerment theory is a multilevel framework by which behaviors, actions, or activities are empowering, and the outcomes of such processes result in a level of empowerment for individuals, organizations, and communities (Zimmerman, 2000). The empowering processes refer to efforts, strategies, or attempts to gain control and obtain needed services. On the other hand, empowered outcomes refer to the results of these efforts to have greater control or access to needed services.

The empowerment processes are empowering if they help people develop perceived control, skills, or behaviors to become capable of making their own decisions and solving their own problems. Zimmerman (2000) stated that empowered individuals are expected to demonstrate the capacity for personal control, critical awareness of the sociopolitical environment, and behaviors necessary to exert control over their life situations.

Citizen empowerment can be described as empowerment at the individual level of analysis, including beliefs about one's competence, efforts to exert control, and an understanding of the sociopolitical environment. Citizens have the ability or capacity to exert control over their life situations and the ability to understand the culture and sociopolitical environment in which they live. The empowerment mechanisms of citizens are about experiences, efforts, and capacities to make decisions or solve problems independently, build businesses, and flourish.

Table 2

Analytical Model Adapted from Zimmerman's (2000) Psychological Empowerment at Individual Level of Analysis

Level of analysis (predictor variable = CBMHS)	Empowering processes (moderator variable = ACM)	Empowered outcomes (outcome variable = QOL)
Intrapersonal (self-efficacy)	Emotion-focused coping	Psychological well-being
Stigmatization: self-stigma and social stigma	Reframing: meditation, acceptance, forgiveness	Sense of control, confidence, reduced stress
Interactional (critical awareness)	Social support: Trust, tolerance for diversity, formal and informal support	Socioemotional well-being
Racial discrimination: linguistic, employment, and financial discrimination		Mastery of language, culture, networking with others, equal opportunity
Behavioral (perceived control).	Problem-focused coping	Physical well-being
Lack of resources: lack of culturally specific mental health services	Planning: active coping, venting, actions, and activities	Greater access to culturally specific resources, achieved goals, and shared responsibilities.

Note. Depiction of adaptation coping mechanisms as empowering processes and quality of life as empowered outcome.

Citizen empowerment is an intrinsic human rights goal with implications for health, well-being, and quality of life (Richardson, 2018). African governments are to empower their citizens to become aware of their own talents and abilities in sociopolitical and administrative intricacies in order to develop necessary business and development strategies. Table 2 is a modified original table of psychological empowerment theory that summarizes the empowerment processes and empowerment outcomes at individual levels of analysis. These empowerment processes are applicable to citizens in a community or in a nation.

At this individual level of analysis, the intrapersonal component refers to self-efficacy, perceived control, competence, or belief in one's own capacity to change the environment in which one lives. This component may help citizens to become the architects of their own destiny, capable of building their lives by themselves through their creativities and innovations. The interactional component refers to a critical awareness of the environment, a transaction between individuals and their social environment. This can help citizens to master their sociopolitical culture, know the causal agents of their crisis situations, and become aware of resources available they can use to solve their problems. The behavioral component refers to the specific actions that one takes to exert control or influence on the environment in which one lives. This can help citizens to use adaptation coping mechanisms to navigate sociopolitical and cultural obstacles in order to improve their quality of life.

In sum, the empowerment mechanisms include individual competencies, proactive behaviors, and access to resources for self-empowerment. These empowerment mechanisms are positive strategies governments can utilize to instill patriotism in citizens. Empowered citizens focus on skills and education, on understanding the nature of business, and on the role of government in helping with the empowerment process. Empowered citizens understand themselves as being at the center of the government's actions and ready to act with and on behalf of the government. As a consequence, a relationship of trust is established between empowered citizens and their government. Citizens can lean on their government, and the government can lean on its citizens to cooperate with the outside world from a position of strength.

The deficit approach needs not to be described because that's what characterizes Africa at the moment. There are an increasing number of stories in Africa where there is a government that destroys citizens' entrepreneurial efforts and works across Africa. These stories are, unfortunately, of predatory government interference. Most African businesses that succeed are supremely practiced at circumventing government obstacles rather than relying on the government to catalyze and nurture good ideas, and must routinely find ways to work around governmental inefficient infrastructures. Any stride ahead the continent of Africa may be making is largely because of the power of individual entrepreneurship and not the efficiency of governments. It is in that context of deficit, underpowered citizens that Africa undertakes cooperation with China and the outside world.

4. Recommendation

Table 3. Road to rising to position of strength

Africa should do the following	Africa should NOT do the following
Listen to citizens and business people	Focus on natural resources alone for export
Make administration bureaucracy efficient	Focus on commodities alone
Invest in education and skills development	Take trading for development
Import ideas and talents, and learn to mastery	Infrastructures without strategy and purpose
Endlessly stimulate and improve productivity	Import everything and produce nothing
Attach a laser-like focus on job creation	Ignore the environment for the next generation
Instill the basics: political and macro stability	Use authoritarianism as a political solution

Table 3 contains a summary of what African nations and governments should and should not do to empower their citizens and rise to the position of strength for cooperation with China and the outside world.

African leadership style, policy, and governance must focus on citizen's capacity and skill development. Extracting and exporting natural resources and mismanaging or stealing the money for leaders' personal enrichment puts Africa in a position of deficit. Africa's economic successes will only result from its citizens' economic successes. African governments must invest in education, science, and technology for their citizens. They must ensure that administrative bureaucracies are responsive to citizens' needs and are less corrupt. They must enforce the rule of laws, make attractive policies for business investment, make local productivity a high priority, invest in infrastructures, and raise agriculture outputs as an initial spur to growth.

5. Conclusion

The concept of citizen empowerment is presented as the best way for Africa to cooperate with the outside world, including China, from the position of strength. It has been shown that Africa is currently cooperating from a deficit position. In fact, from the point of view of Empowerment theory, African citizens are identified as resilient populations who survive government traumatic, chaotic, and oppressive events in their homes, cities, and businesses and have developed some adaptation mechanisms to cope with life adversities originating from their own governments. In spite of government barriers and obstacles, African citizens achieve business successes based on their inner energy and determination to live a decent life, obtain a good education, get good jobs, own property and goods, and maintain peaceful relationships with others in the country. This longing of citizens is exactly what African governments need to support, enhance, and promote in order to be in a strong position to cooperate with China and the outside world.

REFERENCES

Bayes, J. (2015). *Empowerment: Understanding the theory behind empowerment*, Duramis Publications, Bryan, TX.

Brookings (2022), Africa's external relations: reinventing and pursuing new partnerships (Chapter 6). Retrieved from: *https://www.brookings.edu/articles/africas-external-relations-reinventing-and-pursuing-new-partnerships/*

Creswell, J. W. (2018). *Research design: Qualitative, quantitative, and mixed methods Approaches,* (3rd ed.), Sage

Perkins, D. D. & Zimmerman, M. A. (1995). Empowerment theory, research, and application, *American Journal of Community Psychology*, 23(5), 1-12.

Rappaport, J. (1984), Studies in empowerment: Introduction to the issue, prevention in human services, *Journal of Prevention & Intervention in the Community,* 3, 1-7. https://doi.org/10.1300/j293v03n02_02

Richardson, R. A. (2018). Measuring women's empowerment: A critical review of current practices and recommendations for researchers, *Social Indicators Research,* 137, 539-557. https://doi.org/10.1007/s11205-017-1622-4

Rigaud, J. (2020). The theory of empowerment: A critical analysis with the theory evaluation scale, *Journal of Human Behavior in the Social Environment,* 30 (2), 138-157. https://doi.org/10.1080/10911359.2019.1660294

Shearer, N. B. C. (2019). Health empowerment theory as a guide for practice. *Geriatric Nurse,* 30(2), 1-9. https://doi.org/10.10161/gerinurse2009.02.003

Solomon, B. B. (1976). *Black empowerment. Social work in oppressed communities,* Columbia University Press, New York, NY.

Zimmerman, M. A. (2000). *Empowerment Theory: Psychological, organizational, and community levels of analysis,* Handbook of Community Psychology, Plenum Publishers, Newark, York, NY. https://doi.org/10.1007/978-1-4615-4193-6-2.

CHAPTER VIII

QUO VADIS AFRICA?
RETHINKING GEOPOLITICS IN THE AGE OF HEIGHTENED RIVALRY BETWEEN CHINA AND THE WEST

by

Mutombo Nkulu-N'Sengha, PhD

Introduction

"The old world is dying and the new world struggles to be born; in this interregnum a great variety of monsters and morbid symptoms appear." Antonio Gramsci made this statement in 1930 in his "Prison notes" about the crisis in the first half of the 20th century. Nowadays, in the first half of the 21st century, Gramsci's observation eerily reverberates in our tumultuous time of transition from the old world order established in the wake of the second world war to a new one yet to be born. From Pax Romana to Pax Hispanica, and from Pax Gallica to Pax Britannica, the chaotic nature of transition has always been a traumatic experience as the British statesman Horace Walpole (1717 –1797) pointed out in the 18th century, after Britain lost its American colonies: "Woe to Britain, we are now reduced to a miserable little country like Sardinia or Denmark."[65] What would become of Europe, the US, China or Russia without their "spheres of influence" or without their access to African natural resources and those of other foreign nations?

For the observers of geopolitics in world history, if, in broad strokes, the 16th century was the "Spanish Century" (Siglo de Oro),

---

[65] Cited by Joseph Nye on global power in the 21st century, the full lecture at Central European University
https://www.youtube.com/watch?v=uAb8Z_14aQI

the 17th the Dutch century or Dutch Golden Age (*Gouden Eeuw*), the 18th the French Century, the 19th the British Century and the 20th the American century, the 21st century is progressively becoming the "Asian century," and more specifically the "Chinese Century." Speaking in 2020 to a group of German diplomats, Josep Borrell, the EU's foreign affairs chief, declared that "the end of an American-led system and the arrival of an Asian century are now happening in front of our eyes," [66]adding that, for Europeans, the "pressure to choose sides is growing," i.e. to choose between China and the US. In 2022, in his address at the Brussels Indo-Pacific Forum, Borrell gave some specifics on the importance of the rising Asian century: "In many ways, the Indo-Pacific region is where the future of our planet and of history will be decided. The region holds the arteries of the global economy: one-third of the global maritime trade - by volume - goes through the South China Sea, and 40% of the EU's trade passes through the Taiwan Strait. The Indo-Pacific creates 60% of global Gross Domestic Product (GDP). It is the second largest destination for EU exports, and home to four out of the top ten EU trading partners…The EU is the top partner for Foreign Direct Investment (FDI) for the Indo-Pacific region: total FDI in the region was €1 trillion in 2020"[67]

This shift of the geopolitical "center of gravity" from Westernization to Easternization is bound to affect Africa drastically and dramatically.

The aim of this study is to articulate a reflection on the impact on Africa of the current process of transition between the dwindling old "Unipolar" World Order shaped by the West - now about 12% of world population - over the last five centuries and the rising

---

[66] Josep Borrell, Opening remarks to the annual German Ambassadors' Conference (25.05.2020) https://www.eeas.europa.eu/eeas/opening-remarks-annual-german-ambassadors%E2%80%99-conference_und_en

[67] https://www.eeas.europa.eu/eeas/indo-pacific-opening-speech-high-representativevice-president-josep-borrell-brussels-indo-pacific_en

Multipolarity shaped by the Global Majority which is led by China, Russia, and their Global South's BRICS organization. Among the four leading economies in the world, three are now BRICS members. Today China reigns supreme with about 19% of world's GDP (in PPP), followed by the US (16%), India (7.9%) and Russia (3.55%). In 2006, the 5 founding members of the BRICS accounted for 22% of world's GDP (in PPP). However, in 2024 they accounted for 32% (and 36% with the new joiners) superseding the G-7 which accounts now for about 30%. According to the IMF, the U.S. dollar's dominance has eroded from over 70% of global reserves in 2000, to 59% in 2024. Moreover, in 2020, a publication by the Harvard Business Review reminded us that "over the past two decades, China has become a major global lender, with outstanding claims now exceeding more than 5% of global GDP. In 2017, the world owed China more than $5 trillion in total (more than 6% of world's GDP), including the $1 trillion of US Treasury debt purchased by China's Central Bank. China also became the world's largest official creditor, lending money to more than 150 countries around the globe and surpassing traditional official lenders such as the World Bank and the IMF, or all the OECD creditor governments combined."[68]

The fact that the rising BRICS has recently surpassed the GDP of the G-7 while China has become the number one world economy according to purchasing power parity measurement is a significant telltale of the geopolitical tectonic shift in front of our very eyes. While the West still wields global power, it can no longer dominate and control the whole world the way it used to, a fact recently acknowledged by the new US Secretary of State Marco Rubio who, in an astonishing volte-face contrary to the established consensus among neo-cons and neo-liberals declared *urbi et orbi* on January 30, 2025:

---

[68] Sebastian Horn, Carmen M. Reinhart and Christoph Trebesch, How Much Money Does the World Owe China? in *Harvard Business Review* (February 26, 2020): https://hbr.org/2020/02/how-much-money-does-the-world-owe-china

"At the end of the Cold War, because we were the only power in the world, we assumed this responsibility of becoming the global government in many cases…It's not normal for the world to simply have a unipolar power. That was an anomaly. It was a product of the end of the Cold War, but eventually you were going to reach back to a point where you had a multipolar world, multi-great powers in different parts of the planet. We face that now with China and to some extent Russia, and then you have rogue states like Iran and North Korea you have to deal with."[69]

We now live in a brave new world shaped by the "Global scramble for Africa" and run by a geopolitical "Wizard of OZ." Like the inhabitants of the phantasmagorical "Land of Oz", Africans find themselves in the bewildering situation where the Wicked Witch of the West, the Wicked Witch of the East, the Wicked Witch of the North and the Wicked Witch of the South league together to conquer the Land of Oz and divide it amongst themselves.

We currently witness the acceleration of the new scramble for African strategic minerals, in a period where not only China and the US, but also the UK, the EU, Russia, India, Turkey, Iran, Saudi Arabia and UAE, among others, are engaged in a ferocious competition for the control of African natural resources deemed indispensable to the new industrial revolution of our time. The long experience of Africa's interaction with foreign powers has proven that "when two elephants fight the grass suffers." Can Africa overcome the "Ten Plagues of Egypt" that besiege it in this new geopolitical landscape? From a geopolitical standpoint Africa is part of that famous "Heartland," of which Mackinder, at the outset of the 20th century, said: "who controls the heartland controls the World." This "Afro-Eurasia" is the largest landmass continuum on earth and contains the vast majority of raw

---

[69] https://www.state.gov/secretary-marco-rubio-with-megyn-kelly-of-the-megyn-kelly-show/

materials and energetic resources indispensable to modern economies and the power of nations. For world powers the control of this landmass is a matter of life and death.

At a time when Europe promotes what French President Emmanuel Macron calls "strategic autonomy" to free itself from the overbearing power of the US, at a time when the EU and the US itself promote the "de-risking" technological and economic protectionist mechanism against the growing power of Chinese economy and Chinese green technologies, it is worth pondering the fate of Africa. With a meager 3% of global economy, no serious defense industry, no "African NATO" to speak of, no real control over its economies, and no control over communication technologies and the production of knowledge and dissemination of information, Africa is extremely vulnerable and up for grab. As some popular wisdom has it "Africans have become capitalists without capital and nationalists without nation; they produce what they do not consume and consume what they do not produce." The solution proposed by the "Washington Consensus" to improve African economies has proven disastrous in many countries. Structural adjustment programs promoted by the World Bank and the International Monetary Funds (IMF) with their cohort of forced privatizations, downsizing of workers and freezing of salaries, and the reduction of budget allocated to education and healthcare, increased the "debt trap," the impoverishment of the population and socio-political instability to the point that, for many Africans, the acronym IMF came to signify "Insecurity, Misery and Famine."

In this situation, can Africa withstand the gathering storm? Is Africa facing a third wave of colonization? Can it survive and thrive in this tumultuous geopolitical Ocean? How? These are the questions this chapter intends to address and in so doing to articulate in broad strokes the contours of an African Philosophy of geopolitics in the 21st century, for as Saint Augustine, that brilliant son of Africa, already articulated in his Political Theology, "kingdoms without justice are mere robberies, and empires are piracy writ large." In this age of "techno-feudalism," blatant political double standards, diplomatic double-dealing, unbridled hyper-imperialism and new forms of empires run by a befuddling cluster of strident plutocrats, unhinged oligarchs, callous autocrats, and mephistophelian politicians, it is well known that beyond moral posturing about democracy, human rights, "world order," and "the rule of law," our geopolitical community is often shaped by Machiavellian *realpolitik*, *Lebensraum* ideologies and the Darwinian "survival of the fittest" strategies, for as Aristotle, that great theoretician of democracy already acknowledged, *"It is the weaker who always seek equality and justice, the strong pay no heed to either."* (Aristotle, Politics 1318b4). Hence arises the nagging question: Quo Vadis Africa?

We shall proceed as follows: after a brief excursus on the state of affairs in our world (Status Quaestionis) which is dominated by the rise of the Chinese question (die Chinesische Frage), we will sketch some guiding hermeneutical principles of geopolitics useful to understand our world, with emphasis on "The Double Helix of the American Geopolitical DNA" and what I summarize as the "decalogue of US Foreign Policy." In the third section we will explore the African tragedy of being caught "between East and West." This will lead to a brief reflection on African concern for neutrality or non-alignment in this age of dangerous competition between Great Powers which divides the world into a titanic struggle between democracies (free world) and autocracies (axis of evil). Finally, we will conclude the study by evoking Pan-Africanism as one significant path for the survival of Africa in the perilous and haphazard geopolitical ecosystem of our time.

1. "Status Quaestionis" and "die Chinesische Frage"

In his recent Farewell Address to the Nation, President Joseph Biden made the following important statement: "You know, when I came to office, the conventional wisdom was that China would inevitably surpass the United States. That's not the case anymore… we've pulled ahead in our competition with China…In the age of A.I., it's more important than ever that the people must govern. And as the

Land of Liberty, America — not China — must lead the world in the development of A.I."[70]

In a world where the US (with around 25% of world Economy) and China (with around 18 % in nominal GDP), dwarf by far all other nations in economic might, these words delivered by the American president on the 10th of January 2025 define the most important geopolitical drama of our time, i.e. the fierce competition between the American hegemon and that China that the West has always feared for centuries. Biden's self-congratulation about winning the competition is not shared by some geopolitical analysts.

"China is a sleeping giant. Let her sleep, for when she wakes up she will shake the world, the world will tremble." This legendary prophecy attributed to Napoleon Bonaparte seems to be in the process of fulfillment in this 21st century with tremendous consequences for the US, Africa and the whole world.

In 1978, Chinese economy was minuscule, equivalent to 5% of the US economy and 80% of Chinese lived in abject poverty. But between 2014 and 2016 China overtook the US. Studies of world economy measured in terms of purchasing power parity (PPP), indicate that since 2016 the US slid to the second rank, while China became the largest economy in the world. As a result, a tumultuous rivalry has emerged between the minority US-led Western world (12 to 15% of world population) and the Chinese-led Global Majority; and Africa is caught in the crosshairs.

As I am concluding this paper President Joe Biden is in Angola for a 3-day visit to sub-Saharan Africa (December 2-4, 2024). The US president is in Angola for the US-backed Lobito corridor Project[71]

---

[70] https://www.whitehouse.gov/briefing-room/speeches-remarks/2025/01/15/remarks-by-president-biden-in-a-farewell-address-to-the-nation/

[71] Anthony Carroll, "What Is Africa's Lobito Corridor?" (Tuesday, June 18, 2024), from https://www.usip.org/blog/2024/06/what-africas-lobito-corridor; also see Readout of the Lobito Trans-Africa Corridor Summit (December 04, 2024), from https://www.whitehouse.gov/briefing-room/statements-releases/2024/12/04/readout-of-the-lobito-trans-africa-corridor-summit/

(including a1,300-kilometer railway) which is viewed by some as the flagship for the G7's new Partnership for Global Infrastructure and Investment which intends to thwart China's Belt and Road Initiative (BRI). An alternative to the Chinese-built TAZARA Corridor (1863 km), the Lobito Corridor is touted as the American way of countering the growing influence of China's BRI in Africa. It is one of the main Western anti-China tools in Africa, and is being saluted with exuberance in Washington DC as a victory in the process of "flipping Angola to the U.S. side."[72] The fact that the Lobito Atlantic Railway concession was awarded in 2022 to a consortium of Western companies has been celebrated as a win against China. It is viewed as an important step in reducing the Chinese grip on "Critical minerals" from Congo (DRC) and Zambia which are judged strategic to US security and vital to US national interests. The fact that the Democratic Republic of the Congo - which was the main cause of the Berlin Conference in 1885 and the colonial occupation of the continent- accounts alone for about 70% of world's production of Cobalt explains why a new scramble for Africa is occurring in the 21st century. The Lobito Corridor includes US investment in the strategic railways intended to channel critical minerals from "the copper belt" of Congo (DRC) and Zambia to the West via the Angolan port of Lobito. This strategic African region contains a vast range of strategic minerals – most notably cobalt, coltan, lithium and germanium - which are critical for electric cars, solar panels, green technologies, green energy generation, and defense industries, including drone technologies and military jets. Rich in Oil and diamond, Angola itself has attracted Russia and China for decades. The competition between the US, China and Russia in Angola and the Democratic Republic of the Congo is a glaring illustration of how Africa is once again a crucial battleground of superpowers.

President Biden and other American officials have publicly proclaimed the importance of Africa to US security and national interests. However, although Biden proclaimed in Angola that the US is "all in on Africa" and pledged lasting U.S. engagement with the continent, top officials from China (and other countries) outdo

---

[72] https://www.csis.org/analysis/biden-goes-angola-beyond-lobito-corridor

American officials when it comes to visiting Africa and receiving African officials. Moreover, in trade matters the influence of the US in African economy has declined while the Chinese influence is growing steadily. In comparison to other trade partners of Africa, exports and imports between the US and Africa represent only about 5% while trade with China counts for more than 15%. China has far surpassed the U.S. as an economic player in Africa, and is now Africa's largest two-way trading partner, hitting $254 billion in 2021, exceeding by a factor of four U.S.-Africa trade.[73] At AGOA's inception in 2000, U.S. commerce with Africa exceeded China's. However by 2022, China had increased its Africa trade 20 times, out-competing both the United States and Britain.[74] In 2020, China was Africa's largest trading partner, with double the foreign direct investment of the United States.[75]

In 2000, China was the leading source of imports for only a few African countries, namely Sudan, Gambia, Benin and Djibouti. But, 20 years later China is now the top supplier of goods for over 30 nations on the continent. The value of Chinese exports to African countries jumped from five billion U.S. dollars to 110 billion.[76] African exports to China also increased, and in 2020, total export value to China reached nearly 62 billion U.S. dollars.

---

[73] Thomas P. Sheehy, 10 Things to Know about the U.S.-China Rivalry in Africa (December 7, 2022): https://www.usip.org/publications/2022/12/10-things-know-about-us-china-rivalry-africa

[74] Thomas P. Sheehy, How America's Trade Program with Africa Bolsters Security and Peace (August 1, 2024): https://www.usip.org/publications/2024/08/how-americas-trade-program-africa-bolsters-security-and-peace

[75] Thomas P. Sheehy, How America's Trade Program with Africa Bolsters Security and Peace (August 1, 2024): https://www.usip.org/publications/2024/08/how-americas-trade-program-africa-bolsters-security-and-peace

[76] China's African Trade Takeover (by *Martin Armstrong*), Jan 25, 2023, from https://www.statista.com/chart/26668/main-import-countries-sources-africa/

However, according to the 2024 US Biennial Report on the Implementation of the African Growth and Opportunity Act, in 2023 US two-way goods trade with sub-Saharan Africa totaled only $47.5 billion.[77] In 2023, two-way U.S.-Angola trade totaled approximately $1.77 billion, making Angola the United States' fourth largest trade partner in sub-Saharan Africa.[78] And yet during that same year the total trade volume between China and Angola reached $23 billion.[79] China-Africa trade reached a record high of 282.1 billion U.S. dollars[80] in 2023, while trade between the US and Africa lagged far behind at $14.2 billion.[81]

It is worth noting that China continues to have influence not only in Africa but also in Latin America, in the US, and in Europe where Germany's main trading partner in 2023 was China with goods worth 254.2 billion euros of exports and imports according to the German Federal Statistical Office.[82]

According to the IMF, over the last 20 years, China has become sub-Saharan Africa's largest bilateral trading partner. Around 20% of the region's exports now go to China and about 16% of Africa's imports come from China.[83] This glaring disparity between China and the US in their trade with Africa is symptomatic of the shifting geopolitical landscape in our time.

This rise of China to global status is now acknowledged all over the world, especially by the World Bank[84] and by political leaders in

---

[77] https://ustr.gov/sites/default/files/2024%20AGOA%20Biennial%20Report%206-27-2024%20PDF.pdf
[78] https://www.whitehouse.gov/briefing-room/statements-releases/2024/12/02/fact-sheet-president-bidens-trip-to-angola/
[79] https://www.ciie.org/zbh/en/news/exhibition/focus/20240318/43375.html
[80] https://www.africanews.com/2024/08/29/chinas-trade-with-africa-hits-119-trl-yuan/
[81] https://ustr.gov/sites/default/files/2024%20AGOA%20Biennial%20Report%206-27-2024%20PDF.pdf
[82] https://www.destatis.de/EN/Themes/Economy/Foreign-Trade/_node.html
[83] https://www.weforum.org/stories/2024/06/why-strong-regional-value-chains-will-be-vital-to-the-next-chapter-of-china-and-africas-economic-relationship/
[84] https://www.worldbank.org/en/country/china

the US and in Europe where Ursula Gertrud von der Leyen, the German politician and 13th President of the European Commission reminded people of this fact in march 2023, in Brussels, in her speech on EU-China relations to the Mercator Institute for China Studies and the European Policy Centre, where she clearly stated the following: "Our relationship with China is one of the most intricate and important anywhere in the world. And how we manage it will be a determining factor for our future economic prosperity and national security. China is a nation with a unique history dating back from early civilization through the rise and fall of dynasties. Its philosophers have shaped culture and society in much of today's world – from Lao Tzu's teachings about living in harmony with nature to the ethical values of Confucius. The Four Great Inventions of Ancient China – the compass, gunpowder, papermaking and printing revolutionized world civilization. But this latest era is in many ways one of the most remarkable chapters in that long, winding and often turbulent history. In less than 50 years China has moved from widespread poverty and economic isolation to be the world's second largest economy, and a leader in many cutting-edge technologies. Since 1978, growth has averaged over 9% per year and more than 800 million people were lifted out of poverty. This is one of the greatest accomplishments of the past half century."[85] And she concludes: "But I also want to say that nothing is inevitable in geopolitics. China is a fascinating and complex mix of history, progress and challenges. And it will define this century."

Likewise, in a speech delivered in May 2022 at Georgetown University on "The Administration's Approach to the People's Republic of China," Secretary of State Antony J. Blinken explained that the US needs to "contain China" because "China is the only country with both the intent to reshape the international order and, increasingly, the economic, diplomatic, military, and technological power to do it." He went on to explain: "The China of today is very different from the China of 50 years ago, when President Nixon broke

---

[85] Speech by President von der Leyen on EU-China relations to the Mercator Institute for China Studies and the European Policy Centre (30 March 2023) https://ec.europa.eu/commission/presscorner/detail/en/speech_23_2063

decades of strained relations to become the first U.S. president to visit the country. Then, China was isolated and struggling with widespread poverty and hunger. Now, China is a global power with extraordinary reach, influence, and ambition. It's the second largest economy, with world-class cities and public transportation networks. It's home to some of the world's largest tech companies and it seeks to dominate the technologies and industries of the future, especially in the critical fields of artificial intelligence, biotechnology, and quantum computing...We used to rank first in the world in R&D as a proportion of our GDP – now we're ninth. Meanwhile, China has risen from eighth place to second."[86] Most importantly, Blinken acknowledged that "China's transformation is due to the talent, the ingenuity, and the hard work of the Chinese people." It is recognized that China's rise rests on 3 major pillars: its vast and extraordinary human resources, its abundant natural resources including the strategic rare earth minerals, and its technological prowess symbolized by the extraordinary achievement of Alibaba, DeepSeek, Baidu, ByteDance, Huawei, Smic, Tiktok, Tencent, Xiaomi, iFLYTEK, Didi Chuxing, SenseTime, BYD, Shenzhen DJI (drone manufacturer), CNSA (Chinese Space Program), Comac, and Sinovation Ventures, among others.

In 2014, the Harvard Business Review published an article explicitly titled "Why China Can't Innovate" which stated the following: "Chinese invented gunpowder, the compass, the waterwheel, paper money, long-distance banking, the civil service, and merit promotion. Until the early 19th century, China's economy was more open and market driven than the economies of Europe. Today, though, many believe that the West is home to creative business thinkers and innovators, and that China is largely a land of rule-bound rote learners—a place where R&D is diligently pursued but breakthroughs are rare."[87] In writing this article Regina M.

---

[86] https://au.usembassy.gov/secretary-blinken-speech-the-administrations-approach-to-the-peoples-republic-of-china/

[87] https://hbr.org/2014/03/why-china-cant-innovate

Abrami, William C. Kirby, and F. Warren McFarlan, reflected a widespread Western view that Chinese are incapable of that brain power which is needed for developing high technology. As some American Presidents, Senators and Congressmen constantly complain, Chinese are capable only of copying or "stealing" Western technology. Less than ten years later, Chinese technological innovations became apparent on the global stage. The United Nations pointed out that in 2016 China received more patent applications than the combined total of applications received by the United States, Japan, the Republic of Korea and the European Patent Office.[88] According to the world intellectual property organization (WIPO), in 2023 China led global patent filings with 1.64 million patents, followed by the US (518,364), Japan (414,413), the Republic of Korea (287,954) and Germany (133,053).[89] In 2018, in their book titled "Innovation in China: Challenging the Global Science and Technology System" Richard P. Appelbaum, Cong Cao, Xueying Han, and Rachel Parker observed that "China is in the midst of transitioning from a manufacturing-based economy to one driven by innovation and knowledge." That same year, Kai-Fu Lee wrote on Chinese technological capability in his book *AI Superpowers: China, Silicon Valley, and the New World Order" (published in 2018)*. And upon the recent rise of DeepSeek, the Bloomberg Businessweek commented: "The Chinese artificial intelligence startup is rocking global technology stocks, raising questions over America's technological dominance."[90] Likewise Chinese high tech has shaken to the core the automobile industry where Germany (with its BMW, VW, and Mercedes-Benz) and the US (with its FORD, and GM) used to reign supreme. Chinese electrical cars reign in the world because of their high quality and cheap cost, a technological feat where many in the

---

[88] https://news.un.org/en/story/2017/12/638432

[89] https://www.wipo.int/pressroom/en/articles/2024/article_0015.html

[90] 27.01.2025 Bloomberg Businessweek
https://www.youtube.com/watch?v=7MQ6sxcRc2k

West have difficulty to sustain the competition. Although some Chinese learned from Tesla and from some German industrialists, now the student has innovated and is about to supersede the master. Between 2020 and 2025 China has firmly established itself as the world's superpower in patent filings and scientific publications, and therefore in technological innovation.

During his visit to China in April 2024, Blinken explicitly acknowledged the growing economic power of China "in a number of key industries that will drive the 21st century economy, like solar panels, electric vehicles, and the batteries that power them." According to Blinken "China alone is producing more than 100 percent of global demand for these products."[91]

Moreover, Europe relies greatly on China in many areas of its economy. A study by the International Energy Agency noticed that China controls about 60 percent of the raw materials essential for green technology production and refines around 90 percent of these elements. This dependence complicates Europe's path toward energy independence. For instance, in 2022, 96 percent of solar panels and 61 percent of wind turbines imported by the EU came from China.

As the green economy grows, Europe's reliance on China increases. The EV sector exemplifies this. Imports of Chinese-made EVs soared from 1.4 billion euros in 2020 to 11.5 billion euros in 2023, representing 37 percent of all EV imports into the EU. In order to avoid repeating the mistakes made with solar panels and wind turbines, the EU has decided to take action by introducing tariffs of up to 45 percent on Chinese-made electric vehicles.

According to Ursula, regarding the raw materials (lithium or rare earth metals) that are vital for Europe's green and digital transition,

---

[91]https://china.usembassy-china.org.cn/secretary-antony-j-blinken-at-a-press-availability-12/

minerals indispensable for wind turbines and solar panels, one country dominates the whole global market: China.

A 2023 European Union study pointed out that China is the world's top supplier of more than 30 Critical minerals, and claims 56% share of global mined supplies of antimony. According to Ursula von Der Leyen, in 2023, the EU relied on China alone for 98% of its rare earth supply, 93% of its magnesium and 97% of its lithium.[92] And she concluded that this is one of the reasons why "it is neither viable – nor in Europe's interest – to decouple from China."

The US also maintains an important trade relation with China, despite all the sanctions. It is therefore fitting to examine the presence of China in Africa in a non-dualistic manner.

The decline of European powers vis-à-vis China and the US, and the anxiety it generates are visible in the difficulties besetting the Germany economy, heretofore revered as the locomotive of Europe and was clearly articulated for the whole of Europe in the Draghi report published on September 9, 2024, at a moment of uncertainty and anxiety about Europe's economic future and standing in the arena of great powers in the 21st century. Ordered by the president of the European Commission Ursula von der Leyen, "The Future of European Competitiveness" (Draghi report) was authored by Mario Draghi (the former president of the European Central Bank, and former prime minister of Italy) who enjoys enormous prestige and legitimacy. Europe is almost absent from the realm of Tech Titans, in our world dominated by the American Magnificent Seven (Alphabet or Google, Amazon, Apple, Meta, Microsoft, Tesla, Nvidia) and the Chinese "GAFAM" (Baidu, Alibaba, Tencent, and Xiaomi), in addition to Huawei and BYD. These are not only the most important technology companies of our time, but also the companies with the most substantial influence on our society.

---

[92] Speech by President von der Leyen on EU-China relations to the Mercator Institute for China Studies and the European Policy Centre:
https://ec.europa.eu/commission/presscorner/detail/en/speech_23_2063

While the US still remains a global leader in science and technology, China is catching up at an extremely rapid pace and has already made significant breakthroughs and strides in twelve important fields, namely, AI, quantum computing, 5G technology, block-chain technology, biotechnology, facial recognition technology, E-Commerce, solar energy, EVs, space programs, drone technology, and robotics.[93] The development of Chinese universities and inventions in science and technology have also been spectacular, most notably in AI, electric cars, EV batteries, solar panel, space technologies, and various areas of electronics with Huawei, BYD, etc. In 2019, China overtook the US with more patent filing. According to a 2023 report by the Griffith University, "China has been dominating global trade in electric vehicles (EV), lithium-ion batteries and solar photovoltaic (PV) as the developed world transitions away from fossil-based systems of energy production."[94]

Car makers in Germany, France and the US acknowledge that their fear of a Darwinian cut-throat competition that is going on in the market place of the automobile industry where China is producing high quality affordable electric cars and China is poised to dominate global vehicle sales.[95] Some point out that Europe is almost ten years behind China in the EVs technology. According to the "Global Solar Power Tracker," the "Global Wind Power Tracker," and the "Global

---

[93] China Is Rapidly Becoming a Leading Innovator in Advanced Industries: https://itif.org/publications/2024/09/16/china-is-rapidly-becoming-a-leading-innovator-in-advanced-industries/

[94] https://news.griffith.edu.au/2024/05/09/chinas-new-three-exports-dominate-the-2023-global-green-transition/

[95] The historic transformation of the automotive industry | Berlin Global Dialogue (DW): https://www.youtube.com/watch?v=xYyLUb7R1DM

Voitures électriques : l'offensive chinoise • FRANCE 24
https://www.youtube.com/watch?v=CcHYYKhwCc0

Voitures chinoises : toujours une longueur d'avance, TF1 INFO :
https://www.youtube.com/watch?v=Rv9Fv-sgAb0

How serious are Europe's car industry problems? | Inside Story (Al Jazeera English): https://www.youtube.com/watch?v=nCeVQgLOTO4

Energy Monitor," China is the world's largest producer of renewable energy and is now constructing almost two thirds of all large scale wind and solar power in the world. China has cemented its position as the global leader in renewables development and continues to lead the world in wind and solar, with twice as much capacity under construction as the rest of the world combined. Home to almost two-thirds of world's utility-scale solar and wind power in construction in 2023-2024, China accounts for 339 GW, while the US accounts only for 40GW and the UK for 10GW.[96]

In such a technological landscape, the Draghi report is a reminder that overstatements that Europe remains wealthy, prosperous and technologically innovative require some caution. The Draghi Report first points out that there has been a dramatic change in the sources of European prosperity by acknowledging that "the era in which the European Union relied on cheap Russian energy, boundless Chinese markets, and U.S. security is over."[97] Subsequently Europe is declining in economic competitiveness and lagging behind the US and China in the fourth industrial revolution. While Europe's competitive gap with the United States and China isn't new, the Draghi report observes that the situation is now reaching a critical tipping point, which requires urgent action to avoid "the death of Europe." The report calls for "buy European" preference. Most importantly, it stresses the need for greater EU strategic autonomy, a more autonomous defense industry, a policy for securing critical minerals, and economic security to reduce susceptibility to economic coercion by other powers, in a world where Europe's amount of money spent on military Defense procurement outside of the European Union is as high as 80 percent, and where over one-third of Europe's corporate "unicorns" (in innovation) relocate abroad, primarily to the United States, due to regulatory, financial, and training barriers.

---

[96] https://globalenergymonitor.org/report/china-continues-to-lead-the-world-in-wind-and-solar-with-twice-as-much-capacity-under-construction-as-the-rest-of-the-world-combined/

[97] The Draghi Report, Commentary by Federico Steinberg and Max Bergmann https://www.csis.org/analysis/draghi-report-strategy-reform-european-economic-model

The European quest for "autonomy" is such that France now has a « ministre de l'économie, des finances et de la souveraineté industrielle et numérique » and a « ministre de l'agriculture et de la souveraineté alimentaire ». And yet any African government that would seek « industrial sovereignty » and « food sovereignty" vis-à-vis the domination of France in African economies would be viewed as a hostile and dangerous government that is threatening and hurting the national interests of France and promoting "anti-French sentiments."

According to Yanis Varoufakis, Europe has failed to make $3.3 trillion of investment in green technologies since 2019, thus "causing it to fall far behind China and the United States" and risking "degeneration into a museum of bygone industries."[98]

The election of Trump in the US sent shock waves of anxiety in Europe.[99] Anxiety and fear amplified by the content and tone of speeches made in Europe in February 2025 by the American Vice-President JD Vance at the 61st *Munich Security Conference* (February 14 to 16, *2025*)[100] and by the US Secretary of Defense Pete Hegseth to NATO members in Brussels (February 12).[101]

In an urgent meeting held in Budapest, Hungry, on the seventh of November 2024, to reflect on the future of Europe, President Macron called Europe to become omnivores to avoid being devoured by carnivores (i.e. US, Russia and China): "We tend to think we should delegate our geopolitics to the United States. Our growth model to our

---

[98] https://www.project-syndicate.org/commentary/europe-lost-its-opportunity-to-pursue-draghi-report-recommendation-by-yanis-varoufakis-2024-09

[99] Trump's victory is an 'existential wake-up call' for Europe: Ex-EU commissioner Moscovici (France 24, English; November 8, 2024) https://www.youtube.com/watch?v=N7ezULjN32I

[100] https://www.reuters.com/world/europe/vance-uses-munich-speech-criticize-europe-censoring-free-speech-2025-02-14/

[101] https://www.defense.gov/News/Speeches/Speech/Article/4064113/opening-remarks-by-secretary-of-defense-pete-hegseth-at-ukraine-defense-contact/

Chinese clients, and our technological innovations to American hyperscalers. That's not the best idea. I believe we can take back control. For me it's simple. The world is made up of herbivores and carnivores, if we decide to remain herbivores, the carnivores will win and we will remain a market for them. I think at the very least, it wouldn't be bad to choose to be omnivores. I don't want to be aggressive, I just want us to know how to defend ourselves and each of these issues. I don't want Europe to become a big stage filled with herbivores. That carnivores will come to devour whenever it suits them."[102]

The fear that Europe risks to die was already expressed by President Emmanuel Macron on the 25th of April 2024 in his "Discourse on Europe" at the Sorbonne university. In this discourse Macron stressed that "There is a risk our Europe could die. We are not equipped to face the risks." He warned that military, economic, trade and other pressures could weaken and fragment the 27-nation EU:

"My message today is simple. Paul VALERY said, at the end of the First World War, that we now know that our civilizations were mortal. We must be clear about the fact that our Europe today is mortal. It can die. And that depends solely on our choices. But these choices have to be made now. Yes, we are at a tipping point, and our Europe is mortal...Sino-American tension has led to an increase in arms spending, technological innovation and military capabilities...The United States of America has two priorities. The United States of America first, and that's legitimate, and then the Chinese question. And the European question is not a geopolitical priority for the years

---

[102] Guardian News, Macron likens Europe to a herbivore as he calls for it to 'take back control': https://www.youtube.com/watch?v=DmVyAGhmAzY

And Macron to Europe: We need to become 'omnivores' after Trump's victory. Europe needs to grow some teeth or risk being eaten by the world's "carnivores," says French president: https://www.politico.eu/article/emmanuel-macron-france-europe-us-elections-donald-trump/

and decades to come, whatever the strength of our alliance... yes, that era when Europe bought its energy and fertilizers from Russia, had its production outsourced to China, and delegated its production to the United States is over."[103]

Likewise recently Dominique de Villepin (former French Minister of Foreign Affairs and former Prime Minister under Jacques Chirac) put it explicitly: "I am a Gaullist, ...I refer you to a wonderful book that has just been published on General De Gaulle, 'L'angoisse et la grandeur'...I belong to a generation that is haunted by the idea of France's disappearance, the idea of its collapse...it's this anguish that inhabits me.... I think that today France is fighting for its survival...the French today are on the verge of collapse...they're worried about their security...they're worried about France's place in the world...and this national humiliation we're suffering from a country that's disappearing off the map... Our country is in danger of collapse and obliteration "[104] Similar views are expressed by Pascal Boniface and Gérard Araud [former Ambassador of France to the United States from 2014 to 2019; former Director General for Political and Security Affairs of the Ministry of Foreign Affairs (2006–2009) and France's permanent representative to the United Nations (2009–2014)].[105]

Understanding this fear is grasping the hermeneutical devise that unlocks the geopolitical mindset and praxis that guide Europe and the United States in their attitude vis-à-vis Africa. When Europe and the US are afraid of China or Russia, their fear affects peace, security and prosperity in Africa. Policies designed by the US and EU to contain

---

[103] Discours du Président de la Republique E. Macron sur l'Europe à la Sorbonne (25 Avril 2024) https://www.elysee.fr/emmanuel-macron/2024/04/24/discours-sur-leurope

[104] In François Bayrou à Matignon : vers une sortie de crise ? - C l'hebdo : https://www.youtube.com/watch?v=EIQWhZBgDgY

[105] Pascal Boniface et Gérard Araud – OTAN, Israël, Syrie, BRICS et l'avenir de la diplomatie française : https://www.youtube.com/watch?v=jQLtVw7QTPM

Russia and China have direct implications for Africa which has become the battleground of powers vying for the control of African critical natural resources.

The conflict becomes more dramatic as China rises as a superpower not only economically but also technologically, and the West loses the ability and capability to control Russia (a superpower in nuclear weaponry) and China (the largest world economy in PPP). Hence the rise in the West of "Die Chinesiche Frage," that terrifying Chinese problem, which is, in some sense, an atavism of European fear of the "yellow peril," inspired in part by the memory of the terrifying power of Genghis Khan (1162 – 1227), Kublai Kan (1215 – 1294), and even the Ulug Ulus of Batu Khan (1205–1255). As historian Jean Delumeau (1923 – 2020) from the College de France already pointed out in his famous book "La Peur en Occident" (Fayard, 1978), fear is a constant feature of Western psyche, fear of the "unknown unknowns," fear of demons, fear of death, fear of foreign diseases, fear of barbarians at the gate, fear of poverty and famine, fear of losing freedom, fear of losing jobs, fear of losing control, fear of African or Asian immigrants, fear of the growth of African population, fear of "the heart of darkness" or fear of the very existence of "African Africa," and, indeed, fear of fear itself.

2. An Overview of Geopolitical Theories Shaping our World and Impacting Africa

Africans do not exist as Leibnizian windowless monads on some Crusoe's island. Indeed, the African is not an abstract being squatting outside the world. In this globalized and globalizing world, a good understanding of the life and the future aspirations of Africans, requires an understanding of the global forces that impact Africa. We need to look for a geopolitical hermeneutical device to unlock the mystery of African constant struggle for dignity and well-being in the long history of constant conquest of the continent by foreign powers.

In the following section we intend to explore some of the major geopolitical theories and doctrines that govern world affairs in our time, shape the thinking of the foreign policy establishments of great powers, and eventually shape the way foreign powers deal with

Africa. Given the important role played by the US as the global superpower par excellence, we shall focus on the US. For the sake of brevity, we will address China and Russia just in a few points. As per EU, European principles are part of the Western crucible of which the US is the pinnacle. However, before a detailed analysis of specific American, Russian and Chinese principles, we shall begin with the overarching "heartland theory" which explains better the global competition and rivalry among the major world powers.

2.1 Geography as destiny

Nations, like individuals, strive for longevity, security, prosperity and posterity. This rests on two important foundations: food security and means of protection against oppressors or foreign invaders. In other words, safe living space and access to indispensable natural resources and fertile arable land. In our time, the US and the EU constantly publish a list of 40 to 50 "strategic and critical" minerals indispensable to the well-being of their population, the flourishing of their economies, and the stability of their governments and their societies. Without these minerals there will be no technological development, no viable economy, no state-of-the-art weaponry. Without them people wages will shrink, markets will be empty, there will be massive job loss; chaos and pitchfork battles in the street will ensue, and it will be the end of civilization as we know it. The fundamental question then is where to find critical natural resources and how to get them regularly. In other words, geopolitics and geopolitical economy deal with the very fundamental question of "survival." That is what power is all about. This is what is at the heart of invasions, conquests, empire building, colonization, globalization and the obsession to force nations "to open up their markets." One can then understand why nowadays China, the US, Russia and the EU for instance as engaged in cut-throat competition for the control of global markets and world's natural resources. It has been well understood for centuries that there is on this planet a landmass that contains more natural resources and the majority of world's population. Some termed it "the heartland," the "pivot area" or the "geographical pivot of world history." Controlling this "Afro-Eurasian land mass" is what global power politics is all about. Articulated between 1987 and 2014 as *The Grand Chessboard* (by Zbigniew Brzezinski) and "Pivot to Asia" by the Obama Administration the American "Grand Strategy" shapes U.S. foreign policy toward China and Russia, and ultimately affects the destiny of Africa. It is rooted in a long tradition of European balance of power which shaped among others, medieval kingdoms and Machiavellian political philosophy, the Thirty Years' War and the ensuing Westphalian equilibrium, the Napoleonic wars, the Prussian empire and Bismarckian *Realpolitik*, and most importantly the British empire where Halford John Mackinder (1961-1947), the director of the Oxford School of Geography (created by the Royal Geographical Society and the university of Oxford) formulated his influential theory according to which who controls the heartland controls the world.

"Geography is destiny." Credited to Napoleon Bonaparte, prior to his army invading Russia, the expression whose roots go back to Plato and Aristotle, plays an important role in geopolitical theorizing and the understanding of the logic that governs the behavior of great powers, and in particular their attitude vis-à-vis Africa.

Coined about the turn of the 20th century by the Swedish geographer and political scientist Johan Rudolf Kjellen (1864-1922), the word "geopolitics" reminds us that in order to better understand the fate of nations we need to analyze the geographic influences on power relations in politics, and most importantly how geographic factors influence international relations in a world where trade, since time immemorial, is central to the pursuit of prosperity and security, and, in so doing generates conflicts among nations in competition. Geography determines people's natural resources, strategic location for economic or political influence, or demographic weight and human resources. Before the Suez Canal, Africa was part of a geographic continuum, the vast uninterrupted landmass called "Afro-Eurasia," a battleground of many kingdoms and empires throughout the ages. Nowadays, Africa is impacted by the tensions and conflicts generated by the struggle between the US, the EU, Russia and China for the control of the Eurasian Heartland. Moreover, because of the abundance of its natural and human resources and its geographic location Africa in general – and the Democratic Republic of the Congo in particular - have been impacted by various foreign powers. From

Pax Romana to Pax Hispanica, from Pax Britannica and Pax Gallica to Pax Americana, Africa has witnessed various forms of international relations that impacted Pax Africana quite negatively.

To better grasp the dramatic conflicts of our time in Ukraine and the Middle East and their impact on Africa, it is worth recalling the classical theory of geopolitics articulated at the height of European colonial empires, most notably the Organic Theory (and Lebensraum) propounded by the German geographer and ethnographer Friedrich Ratzel (1844 - 1904), the "Rimland theory" by Spykman (1893 – 1943) from Yale University and the "godfather of containment theory," and most importantly the "Heartland Theory" by Sir Halford John Mackinder (1861 – 1947) from London School of Economics. They all stressed the strategic importance of the "Eurasian landmass." In his article "The Geographical Pivot of History" submitted in 1904 to the Royal Geographical Society, Sir Halford John Mackinder advanced his heartland theory and extended the scope of geopolitical analysis to encompass the entire globe. In 1919, he stated that "Who rules East Europe commands the Heartland; who rules the Heartland commands the World-Island; who rules the World-Island commands the world." It was understood that any power which controlled the World-Island would control well over 50% of the world's resources.

Access to the natural resources of Africa, Russia, China and the middle East is critical to the global leadership of six major powers in competition: the US/UK anglosphere, the EU, Russia, China, India, and the middle east or the Islamic world with its 3 major actors, Iran, Saudi Arabia and Turkey.

2.2 Geopolitical doctrines of the US

2.2.1 Resources

Influential ideas, theories and perspectives that shape US Foreign Policy (PFP) are produced in a wide range of influential think tanks specializing in U.S. foreign policy and international relations, and war. There is first The Council on Foreign Relations and its powerfully influential Magazine *Foreign Affairs*. Other think tanks of great relevance include: The Atlantic Council, the Woodrow Wilson International Center for Scholars (WWICS), The Rockefeller Institute of Government, the Asia Society Policy Institute (ASPI), the "RAND corporation" (a global policy think tank first formed to offer research and analysis to the United States Armed Forces), The Institute for the Study of War (ISW), Heritage Foundation, The American Enterprise Institute for Public Policy Research, known simply as the American Enterprise Institute (AEI), The Brookings Institution, CATO Institute, and the Hoover Institution (officially The Hoover Institution on War, Revolution, and Peace), National Endowment for Democracy. Some of these think tanks are known for their conservative or quasi-conservative bent.

Guiding principles of US foreign policy can also be gleaned from various official speeches, articles and documents available to the general public on the official websites of the White House, the US State Department, the Pentagon, the US Senate and the US Congress, the Federal Reserve, US Department of the Treasury, US Department of Commerce, the World Bank and the IMF, among others. Beside think tanks and the various Institutions of the US Government, another source of information is found in Universities, especially their Departments of Political Science (most notably the Harvard Kennedy School of Government), their Departments of Economics, their Finance Departments, and their Business Schools. Of particular note here are Harvard University, Columbia University, Yale University, The National Defense University (especially its flagship College of International Security Affairs and its "Center for the Study of Chinese Military Affairs") and the Five military academies of the US (West Point, Naval Academy, Air Force Academy, Coast Guard Academy, and Merchant Marine Academy). The American "Academy of Political Science" is also of interest, especially its *"Political Science Quarterly"* Journal published since 1886.

As per Journals and Newspapers, beside the *"Political Science Quarterly"* and the notorious *Foreign Affairs* Magazine, important geopolitical ideas and geo-economics perspectives are regularly published by mainstream Journalists, scholars, as well as Political officials, investors, leaders in business and the global market, and Nobel Prize-Winning Economists in *The Washington Post, the New York Times, the Wall Street Journal, Bloomberg News (*and its

Bloomberg Businessweek), The Financial Times, Fortune, Forbes, The Economist, The Atlantic or *Politico,* among others. US foreign Policy can also be gleaned from electoral campaigns and especially presidential debates where there are always some explicit questions about foreign policy. Likewise "senate hearings" and debates in the US Congress and the Senate between the ruling Party and members of the Opposition often exhibit criticism that sheds light on US foreign policy.

2.2.2 US geopolitical doctrine and the Decalogue of US foreign policy

To better understand how the United States views its role in the world and the impact of its global leadership on Africa it is worth grasping what I will call the American "geopolitical decalogue" which finds its expression in the constant discourse of "American values," the foundational myths of "the birth of the nation," "the pledge of allegiance," and other symbols of the American Power. I shall call my theory here the *"The Double Helix of the American Geopolitical DNA"* which is expressed in a "double decalogue" of political practitioners. It is a deep faith that guides the foreign policy beliefs of a great many in the US Congress, in the Senate, at the White House, at the Department of State, at the White House, at the Department of Commerce, as well as the work of the vast apparatus of intelligence and security agencies.

To better understand US foreign policy toward Africa, it is crucial to have a clear idea about how the US understands its identity and its role in the world. We can summarize it into a twin-decalogue of US foreign Policy.

The first decalogue pertains to America's self-image, which is articulated in its founding mythologies and its national symbols. It is expressed in ten important notions:

1. "One Nation under God" constantly recited in "the pledge of Allegiance" to the US flag, which is a crucial expression of American patriotic faith and sentiments.

2. "In God We Trust" (inscribed on the dollar bill). It is the preeminent Creed of "Pax Americana" and its "Bellum Justum" toolbox. It is also the expression of faith in the American "DMC-Holy Trinity": Democracy, Military Might, and Capitalism (Free Market economy and its "Mighty Dollar"). "In God We Trust" reminds us that despite claims about the separation between Church and State, American democracy is a "complex affair" where the business of running the American Republic requires some marriage between Church and State in so far as the overwhelming majority of the citizens claim their Christian faith. This means that "American religiosity" is very peculiar in its association of Faith with Capitalism as expressed in the spreading "Prosperity Gospel" and the aspiration to build the Kingdom of God on Earth. The marriage between Church and State is also expressed in the belief that American Militarism and military interventionism in the world is the tool to establish peace and prosperity in the world. American militarism is understood spiritually as a force for global common good, and therefore "morally good." It is a kind of "sacred violence" needed to defeat the autocratic evildoers.

3. Christianity: the US is the largest Christian nation in the world from a demographic standpoint, a Christian nation shaped by "Bible believing citizens"; a nation founded on a Christian Creed and Christian Ethos, by Christian "Founding Fathers" steeped in a Christian worldview, a country where many cities and towns bear Christian or Biblical names.

4. Protestantism ("Capitalism and the Spirit of Protestantism," "Prosperity Gospel"). The US is fundamentally a Protestant country.

5. Evangelical Fundamentalism (Biblical Literalism and Theocratic Proclivities) shapes deeply the American religious ecosystem.

6. the US is defined or described as the "New Israel," or "The New Promised Land"

7. "City upon a hill" (the shining light on the hill, a "beacon of hope" or "beacon of light" for the world) is a dominant description of the US among many conservative Politicians.

8. Manifest Destiny (the US is viewed as a Nation chosen by God, blessed by God, and Destined by God to expand and rule the whole world)

9. American "exceptionalism" (an Exceptional Nation) dominates the vision of many politicians when dealing with foreign nations.

10. the indispensable nation (it is understood that the US indispensable because it is the most democratic nation on earth, the most moral and most compassionate nation, the force for good in the world, the most peace-loving nation, the land of the free and the brave, the richest and most prosperous nation on earth because it is the most blessed by God)

All these notions are rooted in the religious foundation of the country.

Regarding American role in the world, the decalogue of American geopolitics and foreign policy comprises the following ten "articles of faith":

1. The Monroe doctrine,

2. Containment theory (the Truman-Kennan Doctrine)

3. The Obama doctrine and its "Pivot to Asia"

4. Soft power theory

5. The Washington Consensus and its "Market fundamentalism" Creed (rooted in Liberalism, and mainly Neoliberalism)

6. Conservatism

7. Neo-conservatism with its "Wolfowitz-Bush Doctrine" and its "Project for the New American Century"

8. The Clash of civilizations paradigm

9. "Pax Americana" and its Bellum Justum Doctrine which is taught at West point and other American military academies). Pax Americana is grounded in a geopolitical "Missionary categorical imperative" which sees the US as the Beacon of Hope for humankind):

to convert the world to our beautiful "American Values" (i.e. or Western Christian values) and to spread the American gospel of Peace and Prosperity, to spread faith in the American holy DCM Trinity (Democracy, Capitalistic Commerce, and Military Might), a trinitarian faith of Pax Americana, which is itself un updated version of the Livingstonian three C's doctrine of Pax Britannica: to spread to the unfortunate people of the world the blessings of Civilization (by way of a democratic government), Commerce (free market capitalism), and Christianity (Salvation through Western Christian values)

10. The MAGAAF movement (Make America Great Again and America First), which is deeply rooted in Christian Nationalism and in some sense shaped by the Creed, Ethos and the worldview of what many have described as "White Supremacy," a view of racial superiority developed by scientists and philosophers since the Renaissance, but already grounded in Aristotle's "calore-colore" paradigm of geographic determinism.

For the sake of brevity, we shall consider here in some details just a few salient points of this geopolitical chart.

2.2.3 The geopolitical creed of a Christian Nation

The American geopolitical outlook begins with how the US perceives its own identity. A brief glance at the maps of the United States shows that several towns, cities and counties carry names derived from the Bible, from the history of Israel, and from the history of Protestantism and Roman Catholicism, names such as Palestine, Bethesda, Bethel, Jericho, Jordan, Canaan, Salem, Shiloh, Rehoboth, Hebron, Goshen, Nimrod, Nineveh, Ophir, Bethlehem, Nazareth, Jerusalem, Zion, Antioch, Damascus, Bethany, Emmaus, Smyrna, Philadelphia, Los Angeles (full name: *El Pueblo de Nuestra Señora la Reina de los Ángeles*), Sacramento, San Antonio, San Diego, Santa Fe, Santa Cruz, Santa Monica, Santa Ana, Saint Paul, Saint Augustine, Saint Louis, Saint Petersburg, etc.

In the US, God is referred to in the basic documents that define the foundation of the Nation and its identity. The dollar being a global reserve currency, the motto "In God We Trust" printed on the dollar bill proclaims Urbi et Orbi that the US, unlike the French Republic, is a nation founded on belief in God. The very document of the Declaration of Independence makes explicit reference to God: "We hold these truths to be self-evident, that all men are created equal, that they are endowed by their Creator with certain unalienable Rights, that among these are Life, Liberty and the pursuit of Happiness." In a more dramatic language the pledge of allegiance declares that the Republic of the United States is "one nation under God, with liberty and justice for all." But what kind of God are these documents referring to?

According to the Pew Research Center, the US is by far the largest Christian country in the world. In 2011, three American countries - The US, Mexico and Brazil – constituted 24% of the world's Christian population, about the same proportion as all of sub-Saharan Africa (24%) and the whole of Europe (26%).[106]

To better grasp the impact of Christianity on the American spirit and on American Institutions, it is worth noting that Christianity is the most dominant religion in the US. In fact Jews constitute about 2.5 % of US population. Agnostic and Atheists constitute about 10%. All non-Christian believers combined amount to about 6%. Which means that Christians constitute more than 80% of the US population, an overwhelming majority! Within Christianity, Catholic are a minority. Born as the colony of Protestant England, the US remains largely a Protestant country. Since its foundation the country has been run only by 2 Catholics (Kennedy and Biden) out of 47 Presidents. In other words, the US is a Christian nation, and more specifically a Protestant country. Notwithstanding the first Amendment, it is this "Protestant spirit" that shapes in large measure US foreign policy toward Africa, and the way the US reacts to the economic, political or military influence of China and Russia in Africa. Reagan dubbed the Soviet Union and the whole "Communist block" the "evil empire." Bush

---

[106] Global Christianity – A Report on the Size and Distribution of the World's Christian Population

https://www.pewresearch.org/religion/2011/12/19/global-christianity-exec/

talked about the "axis of evil." And when American Senators and Congressmen refer to the threat of "Communist China" they conjure the phantasmagorical mythology of the "devil incarnate," the Godless land of evil dragons, the enemy of America, the enemy of God, the butcher of the Uyghurs and the enemy of the human race. World domination by China would be tantamount to the reign of the anti-Christ. Hence the necessity of crusade to cripple China's economic and technological rise in order to thwart its ambition to become a global hegemon. In this titanic Armageddon struggle between the forces of good and the forces of evil, God is on the side of the United States and Christian West. African countries that chose to do business with China are to be viewed as "useful idiots" or satanic forces of unfreedom which need to be "regime-changed" and crushed mercilessly. Such is the logic of foreign policy in the mind of "Bible believing Christians," especially Fundamentalist Evangelicals.

Within Protestantism, while some among the ruling elite tend to come out of the mainstream cluster of "seven sisters," many ordinary people (and even some politicians) tend to be evangelicals of the fundamentalist bent and "prosperity gospel" orientation.

In 1904 and 1905, German Political economist, jurist and sociologist, Maximilian Carl Emil Weber (1864-1920) composed his book *The Protestant Ethic and the Spirit of Capitalism* (*Die protestantische Ethik und der Geist des Kapitalismus*) in which he explained how the Protestant ethic contributed to the emergence of modern Capitalism not in countries dominated by the Catholic church, but rather where Protestant Churches prevailed. He argued that Calvinist theology and to some degree Lutheran, Baptist, Methodist and Quaker theologies, allowed Protestant promotion of individual freedom, hard work, and moral discipline which led people to develop their own enterprises, to engage in trade in the secular world and to build an accumulation of wealth for investment. Born out of the colony founded by the Pilgrim Fathers who settled in Plymouth (Massachusetts), the US, a country shaped in large measure by Protestants from England, Germany, Netherlands and Scandinavian countries, developed a culture and a form of Capitalism shaped by the Protestant Ethos. More specifically the US is a Protestant country with an influential community of Fundamentalist Evangelicals. As Paul E. Knitter pointed out "To look at American religion and to overlook Evangelicalism and Fundamentalism would be comparable to scanning the American physical landscape and missing the Rocky Mountains... To dismiss Evangelical attitudes as outdated is simply to ignore the fact that these attitudes do represent a strong, and an increasingly louder, voice within the Christian population."[107] A survey by the Gallup organization in 1980 revealed that 40% of the American public claimed to believe that the Bible is the "actual word of God and is to be taken literally, word for word." But what is the fundamentalist vision of the world that has impact on US foreign policy?

In her study of Fundamentalism, Malise Ruthven made the following observation:

"Because of its belief in Manifest Destiny ideology, in literal reading of the Bible, in the Apocalyptic Armageddon war, and its opposition to science, and to Women's right in the Church or in the society at large; because of its "uncritical" approach to moral values, its love for weapons and war, its impact on the environment, its baleful role in US foreign policy toward other nations; because of its support to arms industry, its glorification of the US military and militarism, and its support of US wars against foreign nations, and US economic exploitation of poor nations, America's religiosity is a problem, a major source of instability and violence in the world."[108]

Needless to say that what some people view negatively is perceived positively by Fundamentalist Christians. Since fundamentalists consider themselves to be God's chosen people, they see nothing wrong in their behavior, they see themselves as holy warriors against the forces of darkness. The case of Germany is instructive in this regard. While Max Weber studied the impact of

---

[107] Paul F. Knitter, *No Other Name? A Critical Survey of Christian Attitudes Towards the World Religions.* (New York: Orbis Books, 1985)

[108] Malise Ruthven, Fundamentalism: The Search for Meaning. (Oxford University Press, 2004); pp. 59; 1-34; 216-217.

Protestantism on Capitalism, others focused on Politics and developed the notion of Germany as God's chosen people as clearly formulated by Johann Kessler, a Lutheran pastor in Dresden: "We believe in a world calling for our nation. A nation that God has equipped with such gifts of the Spirit and such depths of mind, that he called to be a bearer of the gospel in the days of the Reformation... God has great things in store for such a nation... We are the tools with which God will construct his Kingdom today. We are the soldiers with which he will win his victory."[109]

This theology of election that pastor Reinhold Dietrich called "the Christianizing of Germanness and the Germanizing of Christianity" led to a formulation of "Christian nationalism" that reverberates in some sense in the American Christian Nationalism well exemplified in the "one nation under God" pledge of allegiance and in the "In God we trust" motto inscribed on the Dollar bill.

To better understand the American attitude and role in Africa, it is worth grasping how America perceives itself and its role in the world in general. American identity and self-consciousness are rooted in "The Spirit of Protestantism" and its intrinsic missionary imperative to "evangelize the world," to save the lost souls, to bring light into darkness. In the US, the evangelization spirit, the passion to proclaim the gospel, goes beyond the religious realm and affects culture, politics and the economy. It is understood that America has been chosen by God to proclaim the good news, not only of the Christian religion, but also the American political system, and Economic model. As a nation chosen by God and blessed with "honey and milk", America has to be faithful. In other words, as a good servant of the Lord, an obedient "servus servorum," America has the duty, indeed the sacred burden to proclaim *Urbi et Orbi* the good news of peace and security through arms trade, the good news of democracy, and the good news of prosperity through capitalism. America has to preach

---

[109] Corrigan, John, et al., *Jews, Christians, Muslims: A Comparative Introduction to Monotheistic Religions.* (Upper Saddle River: Prentice Hall, 1998); p.459.

faith in the sacredness of the free market. Woe to those who will not believe! Damned those who will reject the Gospel!

This secular "missionary zeal" stems from the famous "Manifest Destiny" doctrine, the notion that America, the new Israel, was chosen by God to lead the whole world, to bring to the world the blessings of liberty, democracy, human rights, peace and that Biblical "land of honey and milk" type of prosperity. It is a theory that the U.S. is distinctive, unique, or exemplary compared to other nations, based on its history, culture, and political system. The notion involves a fundamental belief in the superiority of the United States over all nations, morally, spiritually, politically and culturally. From Manifest destiny stem many other views of "American identity" such as "American exceptionalism," and "the indispensable nation."

In 2015, vice-President Dick Cheney published his book (co-authored with his daughter Elizabeth Lynne Cheney) with the explicit title: Exceptional: Why the World Needs a Powerful America. In this book focused on US Foreign Policy Cheney offers an unwavering defense of the virtue of American exceptionalism and explicitly declares that America is "the most powerful, good, and honorable nation in the history of mankind, the exceptional nation."

Prevalent in the US for more than a century, the ideology of American exceptionalism holds that the United States did not make the same mistakes as other world powers. As for indispensability, it is the notion that without American leadership the world will fall into chaos. In 1998, while traveling around the United States making the administration's case for a possible strike against Saddam Hussein, Madeleine Albright declared in an interview: "But if we have to use force, it is because we are America; we are the indispensable nation. We stand tall and we see further than other countries into the future."[110] In other words, the notion of "indispensable nation" justifies the "use of force" in international relations because US military interventions are indispensable for the protection of the common good, for maintaining world peace and protecting weak

---

[110] Secretary of State Madeleine K. Albright, Interview on NBC-TV "The Today Show" with Matt Lauer; Columbus, Ohio, February 19, 1998. From: https://1997-2001.state.gov/statements/1998/980219a.html

nations and weak communities against monstruous predators. The notion of indispensable nation is rooted in an older metaphor used to define the US as a "beacon of hope" or "beacon of light" for the world, an expression similar to the Biblical "shining city upon a hill" popularized by the Presidency of Ronald Reagan (1981-1989), who frequently used it as the characteristic of the "free world" in opposition to the Soviet Union he derided as the "evil empire."

But in the Christian cosmology, America, the nation chosen by God, is a "Force for Good in the World." As such it has the duty to use force to topple criminal dictators, to regime-change non-democratic governments and to wage relentless wars against rogue states in order to establish the common good and ensure world peace and Prosperity for all. More concretely "democracy promotion" and free market are fostered in geopolitics by specific doctrines. The role of the US, its way of assuming its leadership in the world is articulated in various theories that define US foreign policy, most notably the Monroe doctrine, Containment theory, The Obama doctrine and its "Pivot to Asia," the Clash of civilizations paradigm, Soft power theory, Liberalism and Neoliberalism, Conservatism and Neo-conservatism, and finally the "America first" MAGA movement deeply rooted in Christian Nationalism.

2.2.4 The Monroe Doctrine

The Monroe doctrine was enunciated in 1823 by James Monroe, the fifth President of the US from 1817 to 1825, in his annual message to Congress. It is worth noting that at that time the US was still a young, and in some sense, a small and incomplete nation. When the US gained its independence from Britain in 1776, it was a small country, poor and weak politically. When President Thomas Jefferson enlarged the territory with the Louisiana purchase, the vast land was sold to him by Napoleon Bonaparte whose armies still roamed in the Americas. It will take around 60 years of tumultuous expansionism for the US to gain a large territory and an entire century to emerge as an economic power. It is only by the 1880s that the US economy will surpass the economy of Britain, while New York City surpassed London as the world's leading financial center only in the 1920s. It is in this context of a weak, young and insecure country surrounded by

European powers, mainly Spain, France, England, and even Russia, that we can grasp the significance of the Monroe doctrine.

Larger than California, Texas and Montana combined, the large territory of Alaska belonged then to "Russian America." It was a colony of the Russian empire before being bought only in 1867. In total twenty-six states (i.e. more than half of US states) were not yet part of the US and will be admitted to the Union later. That is the case of Arkansas (1836), Michigan (1837), Texas (1845), Florida (1845), Iowa (1846), Wisconsin (1848) California (1850), Minnesota (1858), Oregon (1859), Kansas (1861), Nevada (1864), Nebraska (1867), Colorado (1876), Washington State (1889), Oregon (1889), Montana (1889), North Dakota (1889), South Dakota (1889), Wyoming (1890), Idaho (1890), Utah (1896), Oklahoma (1907), New Mexico (1912), Arizona (1912), Hawaii (1959), Alaska (1959). In other words continental European colonial powers were still having some influence in the Americas despite the independence of some Latin American countries. In this context, the Monroe doctrine came out of US concern that European continent powers such as Spain, France, and even Russia may extend their ambition in their colonies and ex-colonies of the Americas to the point of threatening the interests of the newly independent US nation. The US felt the need to create a "Cordon sanitaire," a kind of buffer zone to protect itself from economic competition, political encroachment and even military interferences of European continental powers in the Americas.

Thanks to the Monroe doctrine, the Americas became the sphere of influence of the US in order to guarantee American "national interests" and "national security". The doctrine established that any attempt by a European power to control any nation in the Western Hemisphere would be viewed as a hostile act against the United States:

In the wars of the European powers in matters relating to themselves we have never taken any part, nor does it comport with our policy so to do. It is only when our rights are invaded or seriously menaced that we resent injuries or make preparation for our defense....

With the existing colonies or dependencies of any European power we have not interfered and shall not interfere. But with the governments who have declared their independence and maintained it, and whose independence we have, on great consideration and on just principles, acknowledged, we could not view any interposition for the purpose of oppressing them, or controlling in any other manner their destiny, by any European power in any other light than as the manifestation of an unfriendly disposition toward the United States.

It is this doctrine that explains the rivalry between the US and Russia in Cuba. It also explains why the US remains hostile to Chinese economic cooperation with countries of Latin America. This Monroe doctrine has implications for Africa. Any African country which would be friendly with countries such as Cuba or Venezuela would be viewed as hostile to the US.

With the collapse of the Soviet Union in 1990-1992, the national interests of the US were extended to the entire planet and the Monroe doctrine went global and found expression in the new logic of total primacy and "full spectrum dominance" or "full spectrum superiority" (FSS) articulated as early as April 2001 by the Pentagon which defined it as "The cumulative effect of dominance in the air, land, maritime, and space domains and information environment, which includes cyberspace, that permits the conduct of joint operations without effective opposition or prohibitive interference." Limiting the ability of any other country to project power globally and to rise as a hegemon capable of challenging the US became a cornerstone not only of the Pentagon but also the US Department of State. In the US foreign Policy, the sphere of influence is not limited to the Americas, but extended to the entire planet. Russian and Chinese influence in Africa is viewed as a hostile criminal activity against US national interests and US security. Moreover, it is viewed as an "anti-West" attitude, an attack on the very survival of the West. In other words, the US is applying its Monroe doctrine when it imposes sanctions, and implicitly or overtly orders African countries to "cease and desist' from doing business or signing military cooperation with Russia and China. However, in the Global South, this notion of "Sphere of Influence" is viewed as a colonialist mindset of those who believe that they own the entire planet as their private property. Even in the West some thinkers have challenged this attitude.

In his 2005 Nobel lecture titled "Art, Truth and Politics," the British playwright Harold Pinter (1930-2008)[111] denounced this "full spectrum dominance" doctrine as a manifestation of problematic American Imperialism because it means "control of land, sea, air and space and all attendant resources."

2.2.5 Containment theory (the Truman-Kennan Doctrine)

Containment was theorized by the American diplomat and historian George Frost Kennan (1904-2005), and applied, in a modified form, by Harry S. Truman, the 33rd President of the United States. It remained the guiding doctrine used by the US to contain the Soviet Union during the cold war. After the collapse of the Soviet Union it was applied to Russia and extended to China. It survives within other new doctrines, especially pivot to Asia and the Project for the New American century articulated by Neocons and applied by Bush in his "Bush doctrine."

Articulated in 1946 by George F. Kennan during the Presidency of Harry Truman (1945-1953), "containment" was a geopolitical strategy for US foreign policy, used during the Cold War to prevent the spread of communism after WWII, by hindering the Soviet capacity for international power projection, while avoiding direct confrontation in hot war. Some of its tenets were incorporated in the Truman doctrine. Nowadays it has been resurrected "to contain China" and any other competitor of the US in global leadership.

"The Truman Doctrine" was announced to Congress in 1947 by President Harry S. Truman who became president upon the death of Franklin D. Roosevelt. A member of the Democratic Party, Truman declared: "it must be the policy of the United States to support free peoples who are resisting attempted subjugation by armed minorities or by outside pressures." The Truman doctrine is an American foreign

---

[111] The Nobel Prize in Literature 2005 . Harold Pinter's Nobel Lecture: Art, Truth & Politics. From:https://www.nobelprize.org/prizes/literature/2005/pinter/lecture/

policy based on American support for democracies or democratic forces against authoritarian regimes. It was used during the cold war as a means to combat the Soviet influence around the globe, by lending American support to nations threatened by Moscow. In Europe it led to the creation of NATO. It is the basis of the American policy of "promoting democracy and human rights" as a way of protecting international peace and American interests throughout the World.

2.2.6 The Obama doctrine and its "Pivot to Asia"

A decade ago, President Barack Obama spoke to Australia's Parliament in November 2011 and spelled out his vision of the U.S. role in Asia: "Our enduring interests in the region demand our enduring presence in the region. The United States is a Pacific power, and we are here to stay... So let there be no doubt: In the Asia-Pacific in the 21st century, the United States of America is all in."[112] This declaration soon became known as the U.S. "pivot to Asia" or "the Obama Doctrine." It is the application to China of the containment theory that was used against the Soviet Union and now Russia. It was reinforced by President Trump and President Biden who applied to China a draconian regime of technological and economic sanctions while reinforcing US military presence in the Indo-Pacific region and arming Taiwan to the teeth as a bulwark against China. According to some geopolitical analysts, Taiwan, Japan, South Korean, Australia, and the Philippines are to China, what Ukraine is to Russia; with Georgia, Armenia and Kazakhstan as a "potential Ukraine."

The Pivot to Asia uses military, economic, and diplomatic alliances, mainly organizations such as The Five Eyes, AUKUS, QUAD, TPP, to contain China. Countries such as Japan, South Korea, the Philippines, Australia, New Zealand and even India play a crucial

---

[112] Remarks By President Obama to the Australian Parliament (November 17, 2011), from: https://obamawhitehouse.archives.gov/the-press-office/2011/11/17/remarks-president-obama-australian-parliament

role as American allies. Some host powerful American military bases that surround China.

It is worth noting that "Pivot to Asia" is perhaps the most important component of the American Grand Strategy in the 21st century because Russia with its 3% of world's GDP is viewed as a lesser threat, while China is viewed as a "mortal threat." With its vast population, its large economy and its stunning technological performance, China is the only country in the world which has the ability to eclipse the US economically and limit US ability to keep projecting its power as the sole global hegemon. Pivot to Asia is therefore the doctrine of the very survival of the US as a global power.

2.2.7 Soft Power

For American grand strategists, the US cannot maintain its global power just by the force of its military. It is important for the US to be "attractive" and to convince other nations to freely accept US leadership as the force for good in the world. This is the point of Soft Power, an area where the US excels more than any other country on earth. US soft power is exercised in a variety of ways, through various institutions and agencies such as the USAID, NED, Fulbright scholarship, Peace Corps, Universities, Churches, Radio and TV programs, Social Medias (Facebook/Meta, Twitter/X, etc), as well as Sport, Hollywood and Music Industry.

Soft power was articulated by Joseph Samuel Nye Jr, a political scientist and former Dean of the John F. Kennedy School of Government. One of the most influential scholars on American foreign policy and international relations, Professor Joseph Nye also served in the US government as Assistant Secretary of Defense for International Security Affairs, and Chair of the National Intelligence Council. He formulated his "Soft Power" theory in his 1990 book, *Bound to Lead: The Changing Nature of American Power* and in his 2004 book, *Soft Power: The Means to Success in World Politics*. He later formulated the notion of "smart power" (a combination of soft power and hard power) which became popular among government officials in the Clinton administration and the Obama administration. According to Nye, soft power is "the ability to get what you want without coercion, using appeal, attraction and persuasion." In politics (and particularly in international politics), soft power is the ability to co-opt rather than coerce (in contrast with hard power) in order to enact change in foreign nations. US soft power rests on three resources: "American culture", "American political values", and "US foreign policies." Soft power helps other nations accept American global leadership, find it credible, legitimate, and morally upright. With soft power, the US intends to obtain the outcomes it wants in world politics because other countries – admiring its values, emulating its example, aspiring to its level of prosperity and openness – want to follow it. In this sense, it is also important to set the agenda and attract others in world politics, and not only to force them to change by the threat of military force or economic sanctions. Soft power is a critical asset of US foreign policy because it produces attraction, which often leads to acquiescence. According to Nye "Seduction is always more effective than coercion, and many American values like democracy, human rights, and individual freedom and economic opportunities are deeply seductive." For Nye, the use of the US military or "hard power" is not sufficient to ensure US global leadership. All over the world American embassies deploy soft power to make American leadership, American democracy, the American economic model and trade with the US more attractive than those of competing powers such as Russia or China. Soft power involves the "battle for the mind." Instead of "arm twisting" it is the power to twist the mind of others in order to obtain desired outcomes by convincing people that "what is good for America, is good for the world." In colonial and neo-colonial military campaigns, soft power is often used as the strategy "to wins the hearts and minds" of the subjugated people. The "winning the hearts and minds" concept was first articulated as a military strategy in the context of French and British colonial empires in Asia. Used in the resolution of wars, insurgency and other violent conflicts, winning the hearts and minds is a strategy which seeks to prevail not by brute force, but by making emotional and intellectual appeals, along with medical, food and financial aid to sway people in favor of the colonizers or occupiers.

Some scholars are of the view that the "winning the hearts and minds" strategy was first promoted by the marshal of France, Louis-

Hubert-Gonzalve Lyautey (1854-1934). A soldier and statesman, General Hubert Lyautey, who built the French protectorate over Morocco, was a devoted believer in the civilizing virtues of colonialism (la mission civilisatrice de la France). As a colonial administrator, Hubert Lyautey used the "winning the hearts and minds" in 1895 to counter the "Black Flags rebellion" during the Tonkin campaign, a war fought between June 1883 and April 1886, in "Indo-China" by French troops against Vietnamese and Chinese troops for the French conquest of Northern Vietnam.

In the British empire, we encounter the "winning the hearts and minds" in the strategy promoted by Field Marshal Sir Gerald Walter Robert Templer (1898-1979). During the *Malayan Emergency* (a guerrilla war waged as an Anti–British National Liberation War from 1948 to 1960), the British decided to give medical and food aid to gain the truth of the Malays and other local people. Shortly after his arrival in Malaya, Gerald Templer defining the "winning the hearts and minds" strategy as follows: "The shooting side of this business is only twenty-five percent of the trouble. The other seventy-five percent is getting the people of this country behind us. The answer lies not in pouring more troops into the jungle but in the hearts and minds of the people."

The US tried and used this strategy in Vietnam war, and has since used it in many places in the world, most notably in Iraq, Syria, and Afghanistan.

Soft power involves the use of universities and scholarships like the Fulbright, the attraction of the symbolic power of the English language, the use of US economic aid, the use of NGO, the marketing of the "American dream," and the symbolic power of the dollar bill; the use of "American values" discourse, most notably the discourse of freedom, human rights and democracy promotion. It also consists in the use of some attractive elements of American culture such as music, Hollywood movie industry, Macdonald, clothing fashion, and Christianity with its vast network of missionaries involved in charity work and preaching spiritual values. Soft power is also carried out by the overwhelming global reach of American media, information channels and communication networks.

In geopolitics, the US soft power reigns supreme above all nations. It helps the US keep its numerous allies, foment rebellions of the oppressed in dictatorial regimes and instigate regime change.

The USAID (established in 1961 by President John F. Kennedy) and the NED (founded in 1983, during the Presidency of Ronald Reagan) have emerged as the most potent and impactful worldwide conduit of US Soft power.

With missions in over 100 countries and an annual budget of $20 to $40 billion since 1961, the United States Agency for International Development (USAID)[113] is probably the world's largest Agency that provides foreign aid and development assistance to people on almost every continent of our planet. Needless to say that it plays a crucial role in "making Americans look generous, compassionate, good and great" in the world, and in so doing saves the "US reputation" from the shortcomings of its foreign policy, the pitfalls of its military interventionism, and the mischiefs of its global corporations, business tycoons and arms traders.

Dedicated to "the growth and strengthening of democratic institutions around the world," the "National Endowment for Democracy" (NED) makes each year "more than 2,000 grants to support the projects of non-governmental groups abroad who are working for democratic goals in more than 100 countries."[114]

Founded with the stated aim of advancing democracy worldwide, by promoting political and economic institutions, such as political groups, business groups, trade unions, and free markets, the National Endowment for Democracy (NED) is viewed by many critics as a potent instrument of U.S. foreign policy helping to foster regime change throughout the world.

In Africa, Soft power enables the US to have a huge competitive advantage over China and Russia. Christianity (mainly Protestantism and Roman Catholicism) is prevalent in many African countries. Moreover, English and French remain official languages used in

---

[113] https://www.usa.gov/agencies/u-s-agency-for-international-development
[114] https://www.ned.org/

schools and universities in the large majority of African countries. American, British and French universities are more attractive to African students and scholars than Chinese or Russian universities. Western cultures and values continue to have a significant "soft Power" impact in Africa. Moreover, another useful soft power consists in the emotional and psychological bond between Africa and the Vast Americanized (or Westernized) African diaspora of the US. The role played by Africans and African Americans in the US Army, in American Music and in American Sport, especially in Olympic games, is a non-negligible aspect of American soft power. For all these reasons, it is easier for many Africans to identify with the US and sing with the Poet Langston Hughes, "I, too, Am America" than to sing "I, too, Am China" or "I, too, Am Russia." The fact that the US is a land of immigrants from its inception and the fact that due to slave trade, African Americans constitute around 14% of the US population gives the US a competitive advantage ahead of China and Russia.

Another important component of American soft power is indeed its economic power. The US is widely viewed as the land of freedom and economic opportunity. This success of American capitalism is grounded in the ideologies of liberalism and neo-liberalism.

2.2.8 The Washington Consensus

At the international level, neo-liberalism found its best expression in the Washington Consensus, a set of American (and Western) economic policies designed by Washington-based Institutions, namely the US Department of Treasury, the World Bank and the IMF for developing countries, especially Africa and Latin America. The British economist John Williamson, who later worked for the World Bank, is credited for introducing the term Washington Consensus in the global economy's lexicon in 1989.

The Washington Consensus developed in the context of debt crisis when, in the early 1980s, many countries became incapable to regularly pay back their rampant debt from loans given by the IMF and World Bank. In this context of "failed and quasi-failed states headed for implosion" the major Western powers, namely the US, Canada, the UK and some major EU members, decided that both the

World Bank and the IMF should play a significant role in the management of that debt and in global development policy more broadly. They maintained that the reduction of state involvement in economic affairs was crucial to development in the global South. Such a neo-liberal stance came to be viewed as a way of depriving countries of their sovereignty.

Hence they recommended prescriptions of trade liberalization, privatization and finance liberalization as a solution to the debt crisis. This constituted the package of economic reforms necessary to fight debt-crisis, to minimize fiscal deficits and minimize inflation in order to stabilize the economy and foster development. Most of these policies came to be known as "structural adjustment programs," a sine qua non condition for any developing country in need of loan from the IMF or the World Bank.

The Washington Consensus is rooted in a dogmatic belief – referred to as Market Fundamentalism - that developing countries should adopt market-led development strategies that will result in economic growth that will "trickle down" to the benefit of all. The "trickle-down" mythology and the empty promises of Privatization Paradise constitute one of the most problematic aspects of neo-liberalism and one of the reasons why some African countries turn away from the West to embrace the new Capitalist Model of the East.

Widely spread during the era of Ronald Reagan (1981-1989), and Margaret Thatcher (1979-1990), these neo-liberal policies were designed to help countries from the global South pay debt, and stabilize their economies, however they produced economic and social mayhem, increased poverty and stifled development in African countries, producing extravagant wealth for a tiny minority and abject poverty for the vast majority. In Africa ordinary people came to call IMF "Insecurity-Misery-Famine".

2.2.9 Neo-Conservatism

Conservatives call for less intervention of the state in economics, less regulation, less taxes and a balanced budget that cuts down government debt by reducing expenses of social services. In the realm of culture and religion, they engage in "culture wars" promote family values, moral values and religious values by combating abortion, safe sex marriage policies and promotes the defense of pure white culture by combatting immigration.

For many Conservatives, pure America is an America that is white and Christian. Hence their slogan "taking our country back." For them America must be governed by Christian men, according to "Biblical principles." As Kevin Phillips pointed out in many of his writings there is a long and powerful tradition of "theocratic tendencies" in the US, spearheaded by Protestants. This "American Theocracy" reached its pinnacle during the Presidency of George W. Bush (2001-2009), the first 21st century US President, and the architect of the "global war on terror." Bush defined himself as a "born again Bible believing Christian" and he shocked many defenders of democracy in the US and in Europe when he declared that he was asking his Father (God) for advice. Bush is widely viewed as a neocon. An updated version of conservatism, neo-conservatism has roots in the reaction to new challenges since the 1960s.

Published in 1979 by Irving William Kristol (1920-2009), "Confessions of a True, Self-Confessed 'Neoconservative'" is one of the major contributions to a movement which include people as disparate as Leo Strauss (1899-1973), Daniel Patrick Moynihan (1927 – 2003), Paul Wolfowitz, Richard Perle, Donald Rumsfeld, Dick Cheney and President Bush, Robert Kagan, Bill Kristol, Paul Bremer, Jeane Kirkpatrick. In Politics neocons have been viewed as war hawks who advocate an aggressive foreign policy akin to neocolonialism under the guise of fighting terrorism.

Established in Washington DC in 1997 by William Kristol and Robert Kagan, and totally focused on US foreign Policy, the neo-conservative think tank called Project for the New American century (PNAC) became the major laboratory of neocon foreign policy considered necessary for the post-cold war era. The think tank called for the global pre-eminence of the US military and increased military spending, and called for the US to be involved in multiple theatres of war. In particular, it called for the removal of Saddam Hussein. Ideas generated by the PNAC from 1997 to 2006 deeply influenced US foreign Policy in the new post-cold era marked by the collapse of the

Soviet Union and the rise of the US as the sole and uncontested global Hegemon.

It is remarkable that of the twenty-five people who signed PNAC's founding statement of principles, ten went on to serve in the administration of US President George W. Bush, including Dick Cheney (vice president), Donald Rumsfeld (secretary of defense) and Paul Wolfowitz (the deputy of Rumsfeld at the Pentagon). Hence what started in 1997 merely as a neocon political theory became official U.S. foreign policy in the Bush administration and Wolfowitz doctrine morphed into "Bush doctrine".

PNAC's stated goal was "to promote American global leadership". These neocons maintained that "American leadership is good both for America and for the world" and that "the only way to guarantee the security and greatness of the United States in the 21st century is to pursue a strong interventionist foreign policy built on "a Reaganite policy of military strength and moral clarity." For the neocon the Us must stop other nations from rising and being able to contest the American global leadership because the US is the force for good in the world. They promoted the American "Grand Strategy" which has as goal to prevent any challenge to the power, position and prestige of the US, and is rooted in the fundamental commitment to maintaining a unipolar world in which the US has no peer competitor (Chomsky 2004: 11-14).

2.2.10 The Clash of Civilizations Paradigm

Published immediately after the collapse of the Soviet Union in 1991, the Clash of Civilizations has been hailed as one of the most influential theories ever devised about foreign affairs, and the classic study of post-Cold War international relations.

Following the dissolution of the Soviet Union, the "Clash of civilizations" paradigm was articulated at the outset of the Post-cold war era, by Samuel Huntington first in his 1992 lecture at the American Enterprise Institute and published as an article in 1993 in the Foreign Affairs under the title titled "The Clash of Civilizations?" It was then expanded into a book published in 1996 under the title *The Clash of Civilizations and the Remaking of World Order.* A sequel focused on the internal situation of the US was published in 2004 under the title *Who Are We? The Challenges to America's National Identity*. This book was based on his article *The Hispanic Challenge* (*Foreign Policy*, March/April 2004). But the issues and challenges addressed by Huntington find an additional illumination in other works covering the same time period, most notably: Arthur M. Schlesinger's The Disuniting of America: Reflections on a Multicultural Society (1992), Francis Fukuyama's *The End of History and the Last Man* (1992), Richard Herrnstein and Charles Murray's *The Bell Curve: Intelligence and Class Structure in American Life (1994)*, and Robert Kagan's *The Jungle Grows Back: America and Our Imperiled World* (2018). Huntington's anxiety about de-Americanization via immigration and multiculturalism is shared with *Patrick J. Buchanan, a Catholic conservative, who wrote abundantly on the subject: A Republic, Not an Empire: Reclaiming America's Destiny, (1999), The Death of the West: How Dying Populations and Immigrant Invasions Imperil Our Country and Civilization, (2002), State of Emergency: The Third World Invasion and Conquest of America.* (2006), *Suicide of a Superpower: Will America Survive to 2025? (2011)*.

Although some thinkers have challenged Huntington's claims, *Clash of Civilization* enjoys great cachet among some key policymakers in the US, and received hefty acclaim from former National Security Adviser Zbigniew Brzezinski as a book that provides "the quintessential insights necessary for a broad understanding of world affairs in our time." Its impact on US foreign policy is non negligible.

Huntington's thesis rests on six major pillars: 1) "the us versus them" worldview (the West versus the Rest), 2) the centrality of cultures in world conflicts, 3) the centrality of "Western values" as universal values that are the hope of humanity's peace, prosperity and well-being, 4) Protestant values as the foundation of American identity and American modus operandi in global affairs, 5) the concept of Modernization as sine qua non for human flourishing, 6) the phenomenon of de-Americanization and de-Westernization as mortal danger to world peace.

With the end of the cold-war, Huntington argues, world politics has entered a new phase where the fundamental source of conflict is no longer primarily ideological nor economic, but cultural. It is the difference among civilizations - with their cultures and religions - that is the main source of conflict in global politics. The problem of the 21st century, therefore, is therefore the clash among civilizations. The reason why the conflicts of the future will occur along the cultural fault lines separating civilizations is due to the fact that differences among civilizations are not only real, but are basic. Civilizations are differentiated from each other by history, language, culture, tradition and, most important, religion. According to Huntington "The people of different civilizations have different views not only on the relations between God and man, the individual and the group, the citizen and the state, but also of the relations between parents and children, husband and wife, as well as differing views of the relative importance of rights and responsibilities, liberty and authority, equality and hierarchy." The fundamental question then is what civilization, culture or religion better? It is in Huntington's answer to this question that resides the specificity of the famous "Clash of civilizations" view of the world and its geopolitical stance. The tragedy of our world, Huntington opines, is the de-Westernization and more specifically de-Americanization of the world. Non-Westerners are returning to their "cultural roots, they are embracing modernity (i.e. economic and technological power) while rejecting Westernization. By rejecting the American leadership and Western cultures and Western values, non-Westerners are leading the world to chaos and misery. This is the case of movements such as "Asianization" of Japan, Hinduization of India, or re-Islamization of the Middle East, and Multiculturalism in the US. Using V.S. Naipaul, Huntington argues that "Western civilization is the universal civilization that fits all men." Most importantly, Huntington's article of faith is that the West is the Best because it produced ideas of "individualism, liberalism, protestant work ethic, constitutionalism, human rights, equality, liberty, the rule of law, democracy, free market, and the separation of Church and State." For Huntington, these are "Western values," ideas that are exclusively Westerners in origin and praxis and "have little resonance in Islamic, Confucian, Japanese, Hindu, Buddhist or orthodox cultures.' He concludes that "the central axis of world politics is the conflict between the West and the Rest and the responses of non-Western civilizations to Western power and values." The problem, he argues is that Non-Western civilizations have attempted to become modern without becoming Western, a situation which makes China the ultimate threat to the US and the EU.

For Huntington, American global leadership is the only hope of humankind. Here he joins Fukuyama. Huntington denounced de-Westernization not only at the Global level but also in the US where he decries multiculturalism. Huntington begins by stating that "The unity of the United States has historically rested on the twin bedrocks of European culture and political democracy." He then goes on to argue that Americans of non-European origin and those who promote multiculturalism are guilty of de-Americanization and de-Westernization and ultimately are a threat to the wellbeing and prosperity of the US. "Multiculturalism," he writes "encourage a clash of civilizations within the United States and encourage what Arthur M. Schlesinger, Jr., terms "the disuniting of America."

The Clash of civilizations is a synthesis and an update of a vision of American identity rooted in a long tradition of spiritual, political and racial superiority that characterizes the West since the golden age of ancient Greece. The fear of non-European immigrants is rooted in 3 centuries of scientific and philosophical racist theories which gave rise to the much feared "replacement theory" articulated by Renaud Camus, Madison Grant, Gobineau, the notorious *Rassenpapst* Hans Friedrich Karl Günther, and a vast galaxy of colorful Eurocentric philosophers, anthropologists, scientists, lawyers, physicians, and theologians since the time of Aristotle.

2.2.11 MAGAAF

Popularized largely between 2016 and 2022 under the leadership of President Trump, *MAGAAF* ("Make America Great Again" and "America First") is the most recent powerful conservative movement in American Politics. It is a synthesis of almost 200 years of conservative ideas and prejudices. It encompasses the soteriological vision of Christian fundamentalism and its missionary zeal, as well as ideas propagated by Huntington's Clash of civilization, the Bell Curve's ideas about the mental and moral incapacity of some races rooted in two centuries of "race studies." Hence its forceful opposition to Affirmative action, abortion, gay marriages, etc. The proclamation that "immigrants poison the blood of America" uttered by the MAGA's High Priest speaks volume on the intellectual heritage of the movement.

For MAGA's authentic believers, the world is divided in two distinct camps: the Best (i.e. West) and the Rest. "America First" movement is grounded in the belief that America is the epitome of the Best, the first and the greatest nation in the history of humankind.

Because of their belief that America is a nation "under Jesus Christ," MAGA believers proclaim their geopolitical gospel according to which the American global leadership is the only beacon of hope for humankind. The implications of "MAGA Gospel" in US foreign policy are staggering, for to oppose American leadership is in some sense to oppose God's will for the wellbeing of humankind.

2.3 Geopolitical Theories and Chinese Foreign Policy

For Westerners China wants to be the new American hegemon, a hegemon worse than the US since it is an authoritarian and autocratic regime impervious to democracy and allergic to human rights, as Professor Mearsheimer the guru of Political Realism, "China cannot rise peacefully, for like all powers in human history it will seek to extend its domination and project its power. For Chinese that smacks of projection since the history of China and its small and weak neighbors speak otherwise. The very fact that China has become the largest economy in the world, in a very brief period of time, without wars of conquest or colonies seems to land credibility to the Chinese spirit and constitutes an important source of its attractiveness.

From a geopolitical standpoint, China's self-image and role in the world is captured in the notion of "Civilizational state" popularized in the West by Martin Jacques' book, When China Rules the world. It is also found in the writings of Zhang Weiwei and Eric Xun Li where it takes the form of "Chinese exceptionalism" which argues that "China's peaceful rise" is evidence of the superiority of the Chinese model. China's understanding of itself and its role in the world is shaped by the long tradition of Taoism and Confucianism and their "Yin-Yang" Spirit, the peaceful coexistence of opposites. In the West, the fear of the rise of China is rooted in Western Political philosophy and its history of gaining wealth and prosperity through conquest and constant wars, according to the motto "peace through strength" itself rooted in the polemological adage of the Roman empire "Si vis pacem, para bellum" or *"Igitur quī dēsīderat pācem, præparet bellum."*

Chinese foreign policy draws from its long tradition of ancestral wisdom articulated in the Analects by Confucius (c. 551 – c. 479 BCE), in The Tao Te Ching, by Lao Tzu, in The Art of Peace, by Sun Tzu (5th century BC), and synthesized in the 20th century in "The Five Principles of Peaceful Co-Existence" which are: mutual respect for sovereignty and territorial integrity, mutual non-aggression, non-interference in each other's internal affairs, equality and mutual benefit, and peaceful coexistence. They were first put fort 1953 by then Chinese Premier Zhou Enlai during his meeting with an Indian Government Delegation. In 1955 the Asian-African Conference convened in Bandung, Indonesia adopted Ten Principles for conducting international relations, inside which the Five Principles of Peaceful Co-Existence were included. These "Five Principles" are not only the basis of the Chinese independent foreign policy of peace, but also constitute important principles in regulating state-to-state relations transcending social systems and ideologies.

2.4 Geopolitical doctrines of Russia

European and American fear of Russia is rooted in the 1917 Russian revolution and its communist ideology of "class struggle" that Lenin and Stalin intended to export to the world according the rallying cry of Marx's Communist manifesto: "Proletarians of all countries unite!" it is this idea of "Russia" that explains in part the Vietnam war, the Angolan war, and US containment policy. Although the current Russian Federation is different from the old Soviet Union, the old image of "Communist Russia" still guides the West in its competition with Russia in Africa. It is however important to consider other aspects of Russian foreign policy.

Like all ancient kingdoms, Russia conquered and expanded its territory since the 10th century AD. From the humble beginning of the Kievan Rus' of Oleg the Wise (r. 879–912) and Vladimir the Great (r. 980–1015), Russia expanded into a vast full-blown empire under Tsars Ivan The Terrible (1533-1584), Peter the Great (1682-1725), and Catherine the Great (1762-1796) before the collapse of the monarchy during the Communist Revolution of Lenin in 1917. However in the 20th and 21st century, Russian foreign policy is, in part, illuminated by Russian fear of foreign invaders attracted by the vast natural resources of the largest country in the world.

Since the 17th century, Russia has been relentlessly invaded by forces from Western Europe. Poland (i.e. the Polish-Lithuanian Commonwealth) invaded Russia and occupied Moscow between 1610 and 1612. During that same period Sweden invaded and captured Novgorod and Pskov during the Ingrian war (1610-1617). A century later, Sweden again invaded Russia during the Great Northern War (1700-1721). In the 19th century France invaded Russia during the Napoleonic Wars (1803-1815). In the Crimean War (1854-56), Russia was attacked by a coalition of Britain, France, Turkey and Sardinia. Britain and France declared war on Russia and in September 1854 the allies landed troops in Russian Crimea, on the north shore of the Black Sea, and besieged Sevastopol for a year. When Russia overthrew the Romanov and established its Communist revolution in 1918, the West intervened with a vast coalition, attacking Russia with troops from Britain, France, Canada, Italy, Greece, the US and some other countries. Finally, in 1941, Nazi Germany launched its famous "Operation Barbarossa" to destroy Russia.

Russian foreign policy is shaped by this historical memory and is rooted in various schools of thought, most notably, the Karaganov Doctrine, the Primakov Doctrine, the Gerasimov Doctrine. In one way or another these doctrines are shaped by "Eurasianism" which has defined the uniqueness of the Russian spirit in Europe. As a popular dictum has it "if in Europe you feel Asian, and in Asia you feel European, it means that you are Russian." A great many European intellectuals have reflected on the singularity of Russia within the European continent. Kipling wrote that "Russians are a racial anomaly." And Winston Churchill thundered: "Russia is a riddle, wrapped up in a mystery, inside of an enigma." In Russia itself the debate over Russian identity divided many schools of thought. Due to its history and geography Russia is "a two-continental State." One third of its geographical area belongs to the Eastern part of Europe and two-thirds to the Northern part of Asia. However, ethnically, over 80% of the Russian people are European Slavs, while less than 20% are Asians. For over two centuries geographical and ethnic differences have served as a breeding ground for discussion among Russian intellectuals, who, up to now, disagree on how to determine to which part of the world Russia belongs."[115] Despite the ongoing debates between "Westernizers" and "Slavophiles," the geographic bi-continentality of Russia and the history of hostility and invasion by voracious conquerors from Western Europe, have led some major thinkers to stress the notion of "Russian uniqueness" known as Eurasianism. Its sees Russia as a unique civilization with a destiny different from that of Western Europe. In recent years, "Neo-Eurasianism" found its expression in the writings of Dugin. Because of the vast territory and natural resources of Russia, the attitude of Eurasianists vis-à-vis Africa has remained different from the colonial and neo-colonial passions of countries such as France, England, Italy, Portugal or Belgium which are bereft of sufficient natural resources.

3. Africa Between East and West

In current geopolitics, Africa finds itself in an awkward situation. Despite all forms of Western sanctions imposed on China and Russia, Europe and the US still continue to trade with those countries. Case in point, speaking on November 8, 2024, about the possibility of European imports of liquefied natural gas from the US, European Commission President Ursula Von Der Leyen explicitly declared: "We still get a lot of [liquefied natural gas] from Russia, and why not replace it by American LNG." European Union (EU) countries exported goods worth over 38 billion euros to Russia in 2023.[116] This led Ousmène Jacques Mandeng (Director of Economics Advisory Ltd

---

[115] https://www.jstor.org/stable/43580581
[116] https://www.statista.com/statistics/1099626/russia-value-of-trade-in-goods-with-eu/

and a Visiting Fellow at the London School of Economics and Political Science) to make the following observation in October of 2024: "The EU has a cumulative merchandise trade deficit with Russia of US$120 billion since Russia's full-scale invasion of Ukraine or 5 percent of Russia's annual GDP. This net transfer of resources to Russia is in stark contrast to the EU's rhetoric, which claims that it will 'remain determined to keep acting to further reduce Russia's sources of revenue and capacity to wage war'. The EU's approach to Russia is self-defeating and risks prolonging the war."[117]

Moreover, according to the United Nations COMTRADE database on international trade, United States Imports from Russia was worth $4.9 Billion during 2023,[118] while Statista noted that in 2023, U.S. imports from Russia amounted to approximately 4.57 billion U.S. dollars.[119] According to the Census Bureau of the US Government, in 2024, U.S. trade in goods with Russia totaled $488 million for US exports to Russia and 2.8 billion for US imports from Russia.[120] Likewise Trade between China and the US continued unabated despite sanctions. While in 2023, China's trade with Africa reached a record $282.1 billion (with $173 billion of exports and $109 of Chinese imports from Africa)[121], in 2024 Chinese exports to the US stood at $ 3.24 trillion and imports at $ 2.36 trillion[122], giving China the advantage of a huge trade surplus.

Likewise, according to the official statistics of the European Commission, in 2023, *China* was the largest partner for *EU* imports of goods (20.5 %), and the third largest partner for *EU* exports of

---

[117] https://blogs.lse.ac.uk/europpblog/2024/10/09/the-eus-continued-trade-with-russia-undermines-its-support-for-ukraine/
[118] https://tradingeconomics.com/united-states/imports/russia
[119] https://www.statista.com/statistics/187732/volume-of-us-imports-of-trade-goods-from-russia-since-1992/
[120] https://www.census.gov/foreign-trade/balance/c4621.html

[121] https://www.weforum.org/stories/2024/06/why-strong-regional-value-chains-will-be-vital-to-the-next-chapter-of-china-and-africas-economic-relationship/

[122] https://tradingeconomics.com/china/balance-of-trade

goods (8.8 %).[123] More specifically, China is the EU's second largest trading partner for goods after the United States, with bilateral trade reaching €739 billion in 2023.[124]

And yet African countries are covertly or overtly constantly threatened with sanctions if they continue to trade with China or Russia. To better understand the African dilemma in this age of intense security competition between the US, China and Russia, let us listen to what the most outspoken guru of the American "political realism" school of thought has to say.

In a 2019 lecture at the Center for Independent Studies (CIS) in Australia, on "Great power politics and security competition between the US and China," John Mearsheimer (professor of political science and international relations at the University of Chicago and author of The Tragedy of Great Power Politics, 2001) warning his Australian audience about trading with China:

"I'm an American and I am rooting for the Americans…The United States is not simply interested in containing China, we are talking about a rollback strategy. The United States does not tolerate peer competitors…Some people say that there is an alternative. You can go with China. You have a choice here. But if you go with China, you understand that you are our enemy. You are then deciding to become an enemy of the United States. If you are trading extensively with China and you are friendly with China, you are undermining the United States in this security competition. You are feeding the beast from our perspective, and that will not make us happy. And when we are not happy you do not want to underestimate how nasty we can be. Just ask Fidel Castro…"[125]

---

[123] https://ec.europa.eu/eurostat/statistics-explained/index.php?title=China-EU_-_international_trade_in_goods_statistics

[124] https://policy.trade.ec.europa.eu/eu-trade-relationships-country-and-region/countries-and-regions/china_en

[125] Australia's Choice: US-China conflict. Can China rise peacefully? | John Mearsheimer & Tom Switzer at the CIS (Center for Independent Studies) in Australia in 2019, from:
https://www.youtube.com/watch?v=JK0oehQVWRo and
https://www.youtube.com/watch?v=YsFwKzYI5_4

All independent countries would like to freely trade with any nation the way Western countries do with the goal of maximizing their national interests and ensuring the well-being of their people. For Africa that requires being mindful of the tragedy of great power politics with its cardinal principle of "spheres of influence." Most importantly it requires a fundamental critical evaluation of the history of Africa's contact with the West and with the East. In other words, what has Africa to gain or lose by siding with one great power or by trying to stay on the sideline, if that is even possible. In a context of asymmetrical power relations, can Africa survive by being politically non-aligned while trading with all powers that are locked in a death struggle for the preservation of their hegemony and their spheres of influence? Is Mearsheimer's warning to Australians relevant to African countries?

Given the strong ties between China and Russia, both prominent BRICS members, we shall address not only China, but also Russia in our discussion of trade between Africa and the non-Western powers which are peer competitors of the US.

3.1 Africa and Russia

With a territory covering 17 million km2- while the US has an area of 9.8 million km2 - Russia is by far the largest country on Earth. It is also endowed with abundant natural resources, most notably gas, oil, and vast mineral deposits. In 2019 for instance Russia ranked first to 10th in world production of such strategic minerals as Uranium, platinum, vanadium, cobalt, gold, diamond, silver, nickel, iron, copper, zinc, molybdenum. According to GlobalData and the Lupicinio International Law Firm[126], Russia was the world's largest producer of diamonds in 2023, and accounted for 32% of global production,[127] followed by Botswana, Canada and the Democratic Republic of the Congo. According to GlobalData, in 2023, Russia was, after China, the world's second-largest producer of gold, accounting for about 10% of global production.[128] Russia is also the

---
[126] https://lupicinio.com/en/russia-importance-of-diamond-industry/
[127] https://www.mining-technology.com/data-insights/diamond-in-russia/
[128] https://www.mining-technology.com/data-insights/gold-in-russia/

world's sixth largest uranium producer and controls about 44% of global uranium enrichment capacity.[129]

With such riches at home, Russia's attitude toward Africa differs in some regards from that of France, Britain, Germany, Italy, Belgium and other countries of West Europe which are extremely poor in mineral resources. At the same time, like Africa, Russia has been visited by the curse of minerals, for it has been a constant object of foreign invasions throughout the ages. One of the features of geopolitics is that both Russia and Africa share some memory of the behavior and strategies of European colonial powers, a memory that cements some affinity between Russia and some African countries in their quest for liberation from colonialism, neo-colonialism, and unipolar hegemony.

Like all ancient kingdoms, Russia conquered and expanded its territory since the 10th century AD. From the humble beginning of the Kievan Rus' of Oleg the Wise (r. 879–912) and Vladimir the Great (r. 980–1015), Russia expanded into a vast full-blown empire under Tsars Ivan The Terrible (1533-1584), Peter the Great (1682-1725), and Catherine the Great (1762-1796) before the collapse of the Romanov monarchy during the Communist Revolution of Lenin in 1917. However, in the 20th and 21st century, Russian foreign policy is, in part, illuminated by Russian fear of foreign invaders attracted by the vast natural resources of the largest country in the world.

Since the 17th century, Russia has been relentlessly invaded by forces from Western Europe. Poland (i.e. the Polish-Lithuanian Commonwealth) invaded Russia and occupied Moscow between 1610 and 1612. During that same period Sweden invaded and captured Novgorod and Pskov during the Ingrian war (1610-1617). A century later, Sweden again invaded Russia during the Great Northern War (1700-1721). In the 19th century, France invaded Russia during the Napoleonic Wars (1803-1815). In the Crimean War (1854-56), Russia was attacked by a coalition of Britain, France, Turkey and Sardinia. Britain and France declared war on Russia and in September 1854 the

---

[129] https://www.reuters.com/markets/commodities/russia-sells-out-vast-kazakh-uranium-deposits-china-2024-12-17/

Allies landed troops in Russian Crimea, on the north shore of the Black Sea, and besieged Sevastopol for a year. When Russia overthrew the Romanov and established its Communist revolution in 1917-1918, the West intervened with a vast coalition, attacking Russia with troops from Britain, France, Canada, Italy, Greece, the US and some other countries. Finally, in 1941, Nazi Germany launched its famous "Operation Barbarossa" to conquer Russia. The fact that Russia lost more than 20 million people in that war against Nazi Germany left some serious scars in Russian psyche.

Since the Ukrainian war the old strategies about dismembering Russia have vociferously resurfaced, with some British leaders talking about "finishing the job." Quite recently, Kaja Kallas (the prime minister of Estonia, and now the EU foreign policy chief) openly called the EU and NATO to work for a Russian defeat, that would lead to "the dismemberment of Russia into mini nation-states"[130] as the only way to eliminate the Russian threat in Europe. Far from being an irrelevant fantasy by some fringe groups, this opinion is part of a vast Western network of associations and think tanks that call for the "decolonization of Russia." In 2022, the "U.S. Helsinki Commission on Security and Cooperation in Europe" organized an entire panel explicitly titled "Decolonizing Russia: a Moral and Strategic Imperative" (Thursday, June 23, 2022).[131] Likewise in 2019, the RAND Corporation published a report titled "Extending Russia, Competing from Advantageous Ground." Covering a wide range of military, economic, and political policy options, including economic sanctions, this report which was sponsored by the US Army Quadrennial Defense Review Office, proposes how to weaken and collapse Russia by causing it to overextend itself militarily or economically. Some scholars trace this "weakening of Russia" theory back to Zbigniew Brzezinski's 1997 book, *The Grand Chessboard: American Primacy and its geostrategic imperatives*. Needless to say

---

[130] https://responsiblestatecraft.org/kaja-kallas/

[131] https://www.csce.gov/briefings/decolonizing-russia-a-moral-and-strategic-imperative/

that such views rekindle Russian fear of invaders from what they now call "the collective West." The existential threat from a coalition of Western countries has a deep seated historical memory in Russian psyche, a memory currently triggered by the vast coalition that actually supports Ukraine.

In other words, Russia and Africa share a common memory of the threat of European colonial powers. The fact that Russia helped some African countries in their struggle to gain independence from European colonial powers and established in 1960 in Moscow the Patrice Lumumba Peoples' Friendship University of Russia contributed to cementing ties between Russia and Africa. In a world where France and Italy had strong communist political parties, and where some leading French or Italian intellectuals were proponent of socialist and Marxist philosophies, Socialism became an inspiration for some African intellectuals and countries, most notably Nkrumah in Ghana, Nyerere's Ujamaa in Tanzania, Kaunda in Zambia, and Senghor in Senegal. As an ideology of liberation, Socialism and Marxism guided many African revolutionaries in their struggle against European colonialism. Since the 1960s, Russia kept diplomatic relations, security and economic cooperation with several newly independent African countries, with strong presence in countries such as Ethiopia, Angola, Algeria, and Egypt. With the collapse of the Soviet Union, Russian influence in Africa declined between 1990 and 2020. But recently in their struggle against French neo-colonial diktat and the continuing presence of French military bases, some countries in "Francophone Africa" have turned toward Russia, most notably Mali, Niger, and Burkina Faso and Russian influence is again growing elsewhere in Africa.

Under Vladimir Vladimirovich Putin a Russia-Africa Summit was established to reinforce cooperation. The first Russia-Africa Summit held in Sochi in 2019 (and co-hosted by Russian President Vladimir Putin and Egyptian President Abdel Fattah el-Sisi) was attended by 43 heads of state or government. During this summit the Russian President explicitly stated his intention to help African states push back against the pressure, intimidation and blackmail used by Western powers against sovereign African governments. The second Russia–

Africa Summit was held in St. Petersburg in July 2023. The fact that Russia and China admitted South Africa, Ethiopia, Egypt, Algeria, Nigeria, and Uganda as members of the BRICS, contributes to the vast movement of emancipation that found expression in the 1955 Bandung Conference and Non-Aligned Movement, and today finds expression in the phenomenon of multipolarity spearheaded by the Global South under the leadership of Russia, China, India and Brazil.

With an African elite trained at the Patrice Lumumba University and elsewhere in Russia, with the "Russia-Africa Summit" and the BRICS, and with a growing economic and military cooperation with the AES block in the Sahel region, and with Algeria, Egypt and Ethiopia, Russia is forging strong ties with Africa and its influence is likely to grow for a forceable future. Most importantly Russia now has its own forms of "soft power" to attract Africans.

3.2 Africa and China

Three important historical facts mark Chinese geopolitics and illuminate Sino-African relations: the silk road (and its modern BRI version), Chinese exploration of the world through Zheng He's seven diplomatic voyages (1405-1433), and the scramble for China.

Although Africa has been deeply impacted by the West over the last five centuries, Sino–African relations should not be viewed as a new phenomenon of the 21st century. It is worth noting that during the 15th century, China preceded Europe in the exploration of Africa. Indeed prior to Columbus' *voyages* (1492–1504) and before the arrival of Diogo Cão at the Congo river in 1482, Chinese Admiral Zheng He made seven diplomatic voyages in the world between 1405 and 1433 and reached East Africa as far as Malindi (near Mombasa). Commissioned by the Ming Dynasty, namely the Yongle Emperor and the succeeding Xuande Emperor (r. 1425–1435), Zheng He's explorations contributed to the establishment of some trade relations between Africa and China. Archaeologists continue to unearth evidence of such a trade in Kenya and some other parts of East Africa.

In the 20th century, in their fight against colonialism and apartheid some Africans got help from China which also established not only diplomatic relations with newly independent African nations but also trade, including financial loans and technical support.

Sino-African relations took off in the late 1950s, when China signed bilateral trade agreements with Algeria, Egypt, Guinea, South Africa, and Sudan. Chinese Premier Zhou Enlai made a ten-country tour of Africa between December 1963 and January 1964, visited Ghana and established close relations with Kwame Nkrumah. In 1971, China received the support from 26 African nations in the UN to take over the seat from Taiwan, prompting Mao Zedong to declare with gratitude: "It is our African brothers who have carried us into the UN".

In its trade with Africa, China got involved, among others, in agriculture, in the construction of Government buildings and in transportation, most notably the long Tazara railway built from 1970 to 1975. With the collapse of the Soviet Union and the end of the cold war, Africa lost its strategic role and was neglected by Western countries. China seized the opportunity to fill up the vacuum. Beginning with the "Going Global" Policy which was launched in 1999 under the presidency of Jiang Zemin (1993 - 2003), China's influence in Africa increased under the Presidency of Hu Jintao (2003-2013) and Xi Jinping (Pdt since 2013). Trade between China and Africa increased by 700% during the 1990s, and China is currently Africa's largest trading partner according to some parameters. Founded in 2000 under the leadership of Jiang Zemin, the Forum on China–Africa Cooperation (FOCAC) remains the primary multilateral coordination mechanism between China and African countries and has been integrated as a major economic and political cooperation platform within the Belt and Road Initiative which was launched in 2013 by Xi Jinping. An important arm of Chinese Foreign Policy, FOCAC is grounded in China's "Five Principles of Peaceful Coexistence" (mutual respect for territory and sovereignty, mutual nonaggression, mutual noninterference in internal affairs, equality and mutual benefit, and peaceful co-existence). At the 2018 FOCAC summit, Xi Jinping emphasized the "Five Nos" which guide its foreign policy in dealing with African countries and other developing countries: (1) non-interference in other countries' pursuit of development paths suitable to their national conditions, (2) non-interference in domestic affairs, (3) not imposing China's will on others, (4) not attaching political conditions to foreign aid, and (5) not seeking political self-interest in investment and financing.

The cooperation between China and Africa is not limited to economic ties and diplomacy. It extends to security, education, cultural exchanges, sport and other spheres. China has received African students since 1958 according to Mao's foreign policy of Afro-Asian solidarity. In 2018, the Chinese government announced at the triennial Forum on China-Africa Cooperation that China would increase its scholarship offerings to African students from 30,000 in 2015 to 50,000. According to the Chinese Ministry of Education 81,562 African students studied in China in 2018. In 2020, according to UNESCO's Global Annual Education Report, China offered 12,000 university scholarships to African students for the next academic year, to support their studies at Chinese universities. Since 1988 China increased the opening of its Chinese cultural centers in Africa. As of 2018, the Confucius Institute had at least 54 locations across Africa, in addition to another 27 Confucius Classrooms in various countries.

In the area of immigration, the phenomenon of "settlers" is such that in 2014, Howard French could publish a book with the telling title "China's Second Continent: How a Million Migrants Are Building a New Empire in Africa." According to Howard W. French an estimated one million Chinese citizens were residing in Africa in 2013. Moreover, it was estimated that about two million Africans were working in China in 2017.

All this shows that the long-standing relationship Africa had with China in the 20th century is being strengthened in the 21st century and expanded to various sectors.

Thanks to FOCAC, BRI and BRICS, China is now deeply involved in Africa, contributes to African development and helps Africa reduce its dependence on Western neocolonial diktat.

In November 2023, the world economic forum acknowledged that, despite Western skepticism and pressures to derail the project, more than 150 countries (from Asia, Africa, Europe and even South America) and 30 international organizations have joined the Chinese

BRI project.[132] Rooted in China's long history of facilitating trade and commerce across the ancient Silk Road routes, the "Belt and Road Initiative" (BRI) or "One Belt and One Road Initiative" was officially unveiled by Xi Jinping in 2013 in a series of speeches made in Kazakhstan and Indonesia.

BRI intends to connect multiple continents across land and sea, and also covers the sky and the internet. Moreover, it includes numerous physical development and financial investment projects ranging from the construction of roads, railways and ports, to satellite networks.

Given that Connectivity is a key driver of economic growth," the BRI fosters international economic cooperation, boosts the flow of goods, capital, technologies and human resources among countries involved, and contributes to the expansion of Chinese influence as a major counterpower to Europe and the US.

It is also worth noting that the integration of some African countries in the BRICS (i.e. South Africa, Egypt, Ethiopia) means that African countries have an alternative to escape undue pressures and sanctions from dominant Western Powers. As we already pointed out, the fact that China has a larger economic footprint in Africa than the US means that African countries are likely to develop further their ties with China despite all the threats from the US or the EU.

As already pointed out earlier China has its own form of soft power, including the growing Chinese Diaspora in Africa and the African diaspora in China. It is worth noting however that one of the important aspects of Chinese soft power is found in the experience with colonialism. Like Africa, China suffered at the hands of European colonial empires, and together China and Africa joined hands in the struggle against colonialism.

---

[132] Spencer Feingold (Digital Editor, World Economic Forum), China's Belt and Road Initiative turns 10. Here's what to know:
https://www.weforum.org/stories/2023/11/china-belt-road-initiative-trade-bri-silk-road/

There is a stark geopolitical contrast between Zheng He's voyages and those of European explorers such as Christopher Columbus (1451–1506), Diogo Cão (1452–1586). While Chinese explored Africa and returned home, Portuguese, Spanish and other Europeans explorers help their countries to occupy African lands and establish slave trade and a harsh colonial regime. According to some historians and geopolitical analysts, China and Russia have the advantage of not having colonized Africa, at least nothing comparable to European's five centuries of subjugation of Africa. Moreover, they supported some African countries in their struggle to gain independence from Western colonialists.

During the ninth FOCAC summit held in 2024 in Beijing, Xi Jinping declared that he has been to Africa 10 times and hosted many African leaders in China. Explaining the uniqueness of the friendship between China and Africa, Xi Jinping stressed the common history of struggle against colonialism: "the cooperation between China and Africa is rooted in our traditional friendship. Since the mid-20th century, we have been fighting shoulder to shoulder imperialism, colonialism, and hegemonism, and advancing hand in hand along the path of development, revitalization, and modernization."[133] What the Chinese President said here is rooted in experience.

An important geopolitical fact is that China, like Africa, had been colonized by European Powers since the Renaissance, a long colonial occupation that lasted more than 400 years!

It is remarkable to note that until 1997 some regions of the Chinese territory were still under European colonial occupation.

It is only in 1997 that 156 years of British colonization of China ended with the handover of Hong Kong from the United Kingdom to China. Two years later, in 1999, the Sovereignty of Macau was

---

[133] Toast by H.E. Xi Jinping, President of the People's Republic of China At the Welcoming Banquet of the 2024 Beijing Summit of the Forum on China-Africa Cooperation; Beijing, September 4, 2024, from:
https://2024focacsummit.mfa.gov.cn/eng/ttxx_3/202409/t20240905_11485532.htm

officially transferred to China, ending the long Portuguese colonization which started in 1557. Prior to the Scramble for Africa and the colonial partition of the continent at the Berlin Conference, there was the "scramble for China" and its partition by Europe, the US and the empire of Japan between 1832 and 1895. During the first and second opium wars (1839-1842 and 1856-1860), Great Britain and then Great Britain and France invaded China and imposed the opium trade. Later, in 1900-1901, the Eight-Nation Alliance invaded China, attacking as a coalition of 45,000 troops from Japan and 7 European nations (Britain, France, Germany, Italy, Austria-Hungary, the United States, and Russia). During this invasion Western forces turned their victory into a punitive colonial expedition, which pillaged Beijing and North China for more than a year. During the second opium war and the invasion by the Eight-Nations Alliance, British, French and other European troops looted Chinese palaces, government buildings, and libraries. They burned down the marvelous imperial summer palace (the fabled "Garden of Eternal Brightness."), destroyed completely the *Yongle Dadian, a collection of* 22,870 volumes that were compiled by 2,100 scholars during the Ming Yongle period (1403–1408). They also destroyed the *Library of the Four Treasuries* (or *Siku Quanshu*) and the books of the Hanlin Academy.

In some African countries there is a political elite which has the historical memory of Russia and China as good friends who came to the rescue of Africa in time of need, especially during the struggle against apartheid in South Africa or against European colonialism in Angola, Mozambique, Algeria and elsewhere. In this context some Africans were trained at the Patrice Lumumba University in Russia, while other freedom fighters received their training in China. Nowadays, China is establishing its Confucius centers in Africa and spreading centers of acupuncture and Chinese massage. a significant number of Africans study medicine or engineering in China which is also receiving African businessmen and businesswomen. There is a growing African Diaspora in China while more than one million Chinese are now firmly established in Africa. A new generation of "African Chinese" babies is emerging in China as it is growing in Africa.

In other words, for some African countries, Western calls to cut ties with their arche-nemesis is unrealistic since the West itself continues its trade and even cultural exchange with China and Russia. Moreover, there is a huge Russian and Chinese Diaspora in the US and in Europe. As problematic as cooperation with China and Russia may be, some Africans benefit from it and therefore are not ready to severe their ties.

3.3 Africa and the West

History shows that, in their 5 centuries of relationship with the West, Africans have been and continue to be caught in the "damned if you do and damned if you don't" dilemma for as Dr. Henry Kissinger (America's eminent diplomat and legendary strategic thinker) stated, "America has no permanent friends or enemies, only interests." In this context how should Africa situate itself vis-à-vis the West?

One important feature of geopolitics in the 21st century is the ubiquitous discourse about "China taking over the whole African continent" as illustrated in various official discourses of the US and the EU and in the titles of various publications such as Xavier Aurégan's "Chine, puissance africaine: géopolitique des relations sino-africaines" (Arman Colin, 2024), and Howard W. French's "China's Second Continent: How a Million Migrants Are Building a New Empire in Africa" (2014).

The growing influence of China and Russia in Africa has generated a "new discourse on Colonialism," ironically spearheaded by French President Emmanuel Macron and other Western leaders who insist that Africa must wake up and beware of the new imperialists and new colonialists from the East and from Russia. They insist that the West is no longer colonialist and that Africa will benefit more from remaining in the Western sphere of influence. For many Western leaders and their dominant school of thought, Africa suffers from the corruption of its own leaders and its lack of values, its "jungleness" to use the language promoted by Borrell. Pan-Africanist intellectuals who denounce Neocolonialism and the presence of French military bases in Africa are viewed as lost souls, useful idiots manipulated by Russian propaganda, bought and paid for by Wagner to spread anti-French sentiments and hatred of the West. Hence the confrontation between two schools of thought that promote irreconcilable narratives. For the proponents of Western civilizing mission, now wrapped in the discourse of democracy promotion, globalization and free market, western colonial powers made a few mistakes here and there, but overall the outcome was great, for as a proverb has it "you can't make an omelet without breaking eggs." This pervasive European mindset is well exemplified in *The Scramble for Africa*, where Pakenham acknowledges colonial violence and its negative impact on Africa, and yet mysteriously concludes with this astonishing claim: "best of all, Europe has given Africa the aspirations for freedom and human dignity, the humanitarian ideals of Livingstone, even if Europe itself was seldom able to live up to them."[134] Thanks to Western enlightenment and benevolent colonization, so the thinking goes, Africans were saved from the darkness of their primitive and chaotic ways and left their state of nature where life was brutish and short. Thanks to Europe, Africans have become civilized, having embraced western languages, western philosophy, Western religion (Christianity), Western mode of political organization (Democracy) and Western values. This school of thought assumes that disconnected from the West, Africa can only slide back to its old ways, and return to barbarism and savagery. These uncivilized and uncivilizeable Africans, we are told, turn toward Russia and China, because in their foreign policy and their dealing with Africans, those backward and purely mercantilist autocracies do not require respect for human rights, democracy and good governance nor adherence to those "universal values" promoted by the West. By turning to China and Russia, Africa, we are told, will miss the path of genuine development because it will fall in the "Chinese debt trap" and in the hands of ruthless Russian imperialists. There is however an alternative view to this way of understanding Africa and African history. This alternative school of thought is made up of some Africans and some Westerners in the old tradition of abolitionists, anti-

---

[134] Thomas Pakenham, *The Scramble for Africa* (New York: Avon Books, 1991), p.680.

imperialists and specialists of post-colonial studies, among others, who challenge the orthodoxy of the apologists of empires by unveiling "how Europe underdeveloped Africa" according to the famous title of Walter Rodney's book.[135]

Africa has been impacted by Europe since the time of Greco-Roman empires. But this impact became generalized and more dramatic over the last five centuries since the Portuguese explorer Diogo Cão (1480–86) reach the mouth of the Congo river in 1482 and Christopher Columbus (1451-1506) landed in the Americas in 1492. Through the ensuing "triangular trade," Europe and the United States of America sealed the fate of Africa till this day, the fate of slave trade, colonialism and neo-colonialism, the fate of dismembering ancient political organizations, the fate of alienation and disorientation of African civilizations and cultures, indeed the fate of "the invention of Africa" at the Berlin Conference (1884-1885) and its lasting consequences. In other words, the issue of African development cannot be properly addressed on the basis of sheer speculation, abstract economic theories or philanthropic propaganda. There is a clear track record pertaining to the history of economic relations between Africa and the West. The fundamental geopolitical question that rises is that of examining what has Africa gained from its 5 centuries of interaction with the West since the famous age of "discoveries." What is the outcome of centuries of "globalization," free market economy, slave trade, colonialism, neo-colonialism, and foreign-backed dictatorships?

Today, after 5 centuries of Western "opening up" of Africa, the continent is the poorest in the world. A report of the world bank revealed in 2024 that among the 26 countries that "are in deeper debt than at any other time in the last 18 years, since 2006" the majority are found in Sub-Saharan Africa.[136] Moreover in 2023, the IMF and

---

[135] Also useful is Howard W. French's Born in Blackness: Africa, Africans and the Making of The Modern World, 1471 to the Second World War (New York: Liveright, 2021)

[136] https://www.dw.com/en/world-bank-poorest-countries-facing-worst-debt-since-2006/a-70487064

the World Bank pointed out that African debt is exacerbated by a higher interest rate environment than in the previous decade, and the average debt to GDP ratio in sub-Saharan Africa has doubled — from 30% at the end of 2013 to almost 60% by the end of 2022. They added that "the cost of servicing this debt has also increased with the ratio of interest payments to revenue more than doubling since the early 2010s, heightening debt sustainability concerns."[137] According to the world Bank excessive public debt is a threat to economic growth; and given that in Sub-Saharan Africa the volume of nominal public debt has more than tripled since 2010, to about $1.14 trillion at the end of 2022,[138] many countries have fallen into external debt distress leading to more impoverishment and social instability. The dramatic debt distress can well be understood when we realized that in 2022 Sub-Saharan Africa as a whole had a meager GDP of only $2.06 trillion.[139] The amount African governments are forced to spend on interest payments is often higher than spending on either education or health. In order to pay debt and "balance the budget," the IMF and the World Bank recommend "structural adjustments" which often target key sectors of social development and well-being, especially retirement programs, Healthcare and Education, throw downsizing or firing of workers, recruitment freezes, wage cuts or salary freezes. Over-indebted, and representing only 3% of the world economy, Africa stands in the Arena of geopolitics and geopolitical economics as a meaningless and powerless entity. As a popular saying has it, "Africans have become capitalists without capital, and nationalists without nation." Moreover "Africans produce what they do not consume and consume what they do not produce."

---

[137] Understanding Sovereign Debt in Africa Options and Opportunities (April 2024)
https://www.imfconnect.org/content/imf/en/annual-meetings/calendar/open/2024/04/16/183749.html

[138] https://www.worldbank.org/en/results/2023/12/15/unlocking-the-development-potential-of-public-debt-in-sub-saharan-africa

[139] https://www.macrotrends.net/global-metrics/countries/ssf/sub-saharan-africa-/gdp-gross-domestic-product

While a great many Africans suffer from food insecurity, the African soil produces countless bananas, cocoa, coffee, tea and other products for the world. Likewise, while Africa is described as the poorest continent in the world, its vast natural resources continue to enrich Western and Asian economies.

Understanding the root causes of this paradoxical tragedy helps to well address the question of whether it makes sense for Africa to trade only with the Western block or to engage with a diversity of trade partners and maintain multipolarity as a guiding framework for its foreign policy and economic interests. One important indicator is the level and nature of trade between Africa and the West. With decades of experience in African trade policy and trade negotiations, David Luke, a Professor and Strategic Director at the London School of Economics' Firoz Lalji Institute for Africa, made the following pertinent observation: "Africa accounts for just 2.3 percent of world trade, and only 3 percent of global GDP, despite the continent being home to around 17 percent of the world's population. The continent similarly accounts for just 2 percent of the EU's trade (in terms of imports and exports). This creates a deeply unbalanced playing field in which the trade policy decisions of the EU matter considerably for Africa, but that of the continent matters relatively little for the EU."[140] In other words, most of the economic programs recommended to Africans turned into "the path to unfreedom."

As Michael Blanga-Gubbay (Senior Research Fellow at the Kühne Center for Sustainable Trade and Logistics at the University of Zurich) pointed out in 2021, African patterns of trade which are characterized by enduring poverty and increased dependency on foreign powers, exemplify well the economic effects of the colonization era and the unsuccessful decolonization: "Africa is a marginal player in global trade. Total trade from Africa to the rest of the world averaged $760,463 million in current prices in the period 2015–2017, compared

---

[140] David Luke, Muddled priorities continue to plague EU-Africa trade policy (May 2023): https://blogs.lse.ac.uk/europpblog/2023/05/26/muddled-priorities-continue-to-plague-eu-africa-trade-policy/

with $481,081 million from Oceania, $4,109,131 million from Europe, $5,139,649 million from America, and $6,801,474 million from Asia. Even with this low share of participation to global trade, Africa depends heavily on trade with the rest of the world, making the continent extremely vulnerable to external trade shocks. More concretely, the share of exports from Africa to the rest of the world ranged from 80 to 90 percent in 2000–2017. The only other region with a higher export dependence on the rest of the world is Oceania. Conversely, the share of intraregional exports in total exports is lowest in Africa, compared with other regions. Intra-African exports were 16.6 per cent of total exports in 2017, compared with 68.1 percent in Europe, 59.4 percent in Asia, 55.0 per- cent in America."[141] The incomprehensible paradox is that while Africa sinks in ever increasing poverty with dysfunctional economic structures and programs, its natural resources are looted to the benefit of foreign nations.

In January 2023 during his visit in Kinshasa, Pope Francis denounced in a stinging language the exploitation of Africa for centuries by Western powers:

"Dear women and men of the Congo, your country is truly a diamond of creation… but it is a tragedy that these lands, and more generally the whole African continent, continue to endure various forms of exploitation. There is a slogan that emerges from the subconscious of many cultures and peoples: "Africa must be exploited". This is terrible! Political exploitation gave way to an "economic colonialism" that was equally enslaving. As a result, this country, massively plundered, has not benefited adequately from its immense resources: paradoxically, the riches of its land have made it "foreign" to its very inhabitants… Hands off the Democratic Republic of the Congo! Hands off Africa! Stop choking Africa: it is not a mine to be stripped or a terrain to be plundered. May Africa be the protagonist of its own destiny! May the world acknowledge the

---

[141] Michael Blanga-Gubbay, Africa's Trade Potential: Escaping the Colonial Past by Building a Self-Sustaining Future:
https://www.kuehnecenter.uzh.ch/impact_series/2021_05_21-04-21-africas_trade_potential.html

catastrophic things that were done over the centuries to the detriment of the local peoples, and not forget this country and this continent."[142]

Likewise, in an extraordinary confession, Jacques Chirac, former President of France, took off the mask of the French "mission civilisatrice" ideology: "We only forget one thing. It is that a large part of the money in our wallet comes precisely from the exploitation, for centuries, of Africa. Not only. But a lot comes from the exploitation of Africa. So we need to have a little common sense. I am not saying generosity. Common sense, justice, to give back to the Africans, I would say, what has been taken from them. Especially since it is necessary, if we want to avoid the worst convulsions or difficulties, with the political consequences that this involves in the near future."[143]

With more than 30 years of experience with French politics, Chirac who was Mayor of Paris from 1977 to1995, Prime Minister (1974-1976 and 1986-1988) and finally President of France from 1995 to 2007, Chirac was well aware of the neo-colonial policies established since General De Gaulle. What President Chirac acknowledged is largely developed by many French writers who have scrutinized French policy in Africa and denounced "Francophonie" and especially the infamous *"Françafrique"* as a relentless continuation of colonialism. Key works in this regard include *Ils savent que je sais tout : Ma vie en Françafrique* (2024) by Robert Bourgi, *Les réseaux Foccart : L'homme de la Françafrique* (2020) by Jean-Pierre Bat, *Katanga ! La guerre oubliée de la Françafrique contre l'ONU* (2024) by Maurin Picard, as well as several works by Antoine Glaser : *L'Afrique sans Africains, le rêve blanc du continent noir* (1995), *Ces Messieurs Afrique 2 : Des réseaux aux lobbies* (1997), *Arrogant comme un Français en Afrique (2016)* and *Nos chers espions en Afrique* (2018).

---

[142] https://www.vatican.va/content/francesco/en/speeches/2023/january/documents/20230131-autorita-repdem-congo.html

[143] https://www.youtube.com/watch?v=oIoLJm2f-fE

This persistence of colonial mindset characterizes a great many Europeans in their dealing with Africa. In October 2022, Josep Borrell Fontelles (EU's High Representative for Foreign Affairs and Security Policy) gave opening remarks to the European Diplomatic Academy in which he made this astonishing utterance: "Yes, Europe is a garden. We have built a garden. Everything works. It is the best combination of political freedom, economic prosperity and social cohesion that the humankind has been able to build - the three things together…The rest of the world is not exactly a garden. Most of the rest of the world is a jungle, and the jungle could invade the garden."[144]

He went on to stress that Europe must tame the rest of the world to avoid being invaded by the jungle: "The jungle has a strong growth capacity, and the wall will never be high enough to protect the garden…The gardeners have to go to the jungle. Europeans have to be much more engaged with the rest of the world. Otherwise, the rest of the world will invade us, by different ways and means." Already in the US Robert Kagan had articulated a similar view in his book with the telling title, The Jungle Grows Back: America and our Imperiled World (2018). It is a view prevalent among neocons and other thinkers who have always maintained that without US global leadership, the world will slide back into primordial chaos, that Hobbesian "Bellum omnium contra omnes" state of nature where life is solitary, nasty, brutish and short.

It is significant that Borrell's discourse on the "fear of the jungle" comes at a time when the growing anti-immigrant wave in Europe and the US has resurrected the "replacement theory" and its corollary xenophobia articulated for centuries by Renaud Camus, Madison Grant, Gobineau, the notorious *Rassenpapst* Hans Friedrich Karl Günther, and a vast galaxy of colorful Eurocentric philosophers, anthropologists, scientists, lawyers, physicians, and theologians since the time of Aristotle. Borrell's speech stands as a peculiar case of the performance of "memory as a public discourse," an atavism of

---

[144] Borrell, Josep. "EU Ambassadors Annual Conference 2022: Opening speech by High Representative Josep Borrell"
at https://www.eeas.europa.eu/eeas/eu-ambassadors-annual-conference-2022-opening-speech-high-representative-josep-borrell_en

"colonialism's culture" and "the rhetoric of empire" so well-articulated by Aimé Césaire (2013), Kwame Nkrumah (1965), Cheikh Anta Diop (1967), Jean-Paul Sartre (2006), to name but a few. For many analysts of geopolitics, Borrell just stated bluntly and blatantly what many think sotto voce in most Western ruling classes. Borrell is no exception in this regard, nor is his opinion the voice of an inoffensive fringe in Western intelligentsia. Similar abstruse and obtuse views of "alterity" and "subalternity" are found in ubiquitous "values discourses" relentlessly proclaimed *urbi et orbi* by Ursula von der Leyen, David Maria Sassoli (President of the European Parliament, 2019–2022), NATO leaders, and countless public intellectuals, historians, journalists, and politicians in the West, especially in post 9-11 era. On July 27, 2007, French President Nicolas Sarkozy delivered at Cheikh Anta Diop University in Dakar a conspicuously neo-colonial discourse that many viewed as scandalous for the continent and blasphemous to the memory of Cheikh Anta Diop. Echoing that "Grand Manitou" of Eurocentric historians from Oxford, professor Hugh Redwald Trevor-Roper, Sarkozy stated that "the tragedy of Africa is that the African has not fully entered into history... Africans have never really launched themselves into the future...for thousands of years the idea of progress never found its place in Africa." (Adi 2018:19). What Borrell and Sarkozy illustrate is the enduring presence in our "post-colonial" age of tacit colonial axioms of the imperial imagination about the "ignoble savages." Borrell's "Jungle perception" of the non-Western world is what I have termed "the Hegelian Paradigm." It is an exemplary case of epistemic violence. It is a dogmatic and relentlessly scornful refusal to acknowledge the obvious existence of values in non-Western cultures and social organizations. This peculiarly dualistic view of the world, and Africa in particular, goes back to Aristotle's "calore-colore" paradigm. The Hegelian paradigm rests on colonialism, racism and geographic determinism which claims that people living in warm climate under the tropics are deficient in intellect and moral character (Bancel 2002, Bernasconi 2003, Colas 2004, Eze 1997, Goldberg 1993, Herrnstein 1994, Levin 1997, Mudimbe 1994, Outlaw 1996). Deemed essential to Western construction of its identity, the Hegelian paradigm was repackaged by several philosophers, theologians and scientists since the Renaissance and systematically articulated by Georg Wilhelm Friedrich Hegel (1770-1831) in his Philosophy of world history, in a section titled "the Geographic Basis of History."

This "Hegelian Paradigm" reverberate in the recent declarations of Presidents Macron and Sarkozy as well as Joseph Borrell and illustrate well that intriguing confession made by the French writer *Régis Debray* in his oeuvre *"Aveuglantes Lumières"* (Gallimard 2006): "the European has removed his colonial helmet, but his head remains colonial." As Alain Dreneau commented in 2008, "In the mind of the West, which still wants to confiscate the word 'humanity' for its own benefit, the whole colonialist ideology remains in place of the vanished colonial helmet. This West, whose practice constantly belies the values it proclaims, forces the South into misery and despair, while at the same time claiming to give moral lessons to the whole world".[145]

Even Samuel Huntington, the high priest of Westernization, confessed that "The West won the world not by the superiority of its ideas or values or religion [...] but rather by its superiority in applying organized violence...Westerners often forget this fact; non-Westerners never do." (Huntington 1996: 51). Likewise the French general Vincent Desportes (former Military attaché in the French embassy in the USA, and former director of the Ecole de guerre and affiliate professor at Sciences Po – Paris) recently declared in an interview to Pascal Boniface:

"Basically the supremacy of the West was established by the cannon, by the power of Western cannon. It was like that, ask the conquistadors...but then we said that we had the moral right to do it, because our values are pure etc... But today our values, our world order, our culture are rejected because we're not clear.... we do not have the moral clarity to see what's good and what isn't... and since our business isn't clear, well, it's all rejected... Are our democracies the envy of the world today? well, no!... look at our French democracy,

---

[145] https://www.temoignages.re/international/monde/ils-ont-enleve-le-casque-en-dessous-leur-tete-reste-coloniale,33904

which can't even govern itself...look at the American democracy, which is dividing America in two...the system we wanted to sell to the whole world is no longer the envy of the world...and this is one of the great weaknesses of the North compared to the global South...the global South is a geopolitical fact... the will now is to de-Westernize the world...and for us, it's the de-Francization of Africa...We've been thrown out of Senegal like dirt...and our last plane left N'Djamena,three days ago... The global South is not united...it's not a power...but we mustn't despise it...you know how much we despised Russia from 1989 onwards...You know, wars are often the fruit of this attitude of contempt for other nations..." [146]

The problematic impact of Western civilizing mission on Africa through colonial enterprise has been object of countless scholarly studies since the twilight of colonial empires. Among the classics on the genre significant studies include, among others, Ngũgĩ wa Thiong'o's Decolonising the Mind (1986), Aimé Césaire's Discourse on Colonialism (1950), Frantz Fanon's The Wretched of the Earth (1961), Jean-Paul Sartre's Colonialism and Neocolonialism (1964), Walter Rodney, How Europe Underdeveloped Africa (1972), Joseph Conrad's Heart of Darkness (1902), Thomas Pakenham's The Scramble for Africa (1991) and Sven Lindqvist's Exterminate All the Brutes: One Man's Odyssey into the Heart of Darkness and the Origins of European Genocide (1996), Basil Davidson's African Slave Trade: Precolonial History 1450-1850 (1961) and African Civilization Revisited: From Antiquity to Modern Times (1991), Cheikh Anta Diop, The African Origin of Civilization: Myth or Reality (1974) and Civilisation ou barbarie: anthropologie sans complaisance (1981), and the 8 volumes of UNESCO's General History of Africa.

Colonial violence is widely symbolized in the Algerian war, and most importantly in 2 gruesome genocides that occurred at the outset of the 20th century, namely the Namibian genocide and the Congolese

---

[146] L'ère du basculement géopolitique. Avec Vincent Desportes | Entretiens géopo Podcast "Comprendre le monde" - Entretiens géopo (18.12.2024), from : https://www.youtube.com/watch?v=YbCc9w2AISo

genocide, which paved the way for the despicable butchery of world war I and world war II.

The genocide of the Nama and Herrero in Namibia has been studied by many experts including German scholars. Important books include among others Jürgen Zimmerer and Joachim Zeller's *Genocide in German South-West Africa: The Colonial War of 1904-1908 and its Aftermath* (2008) and Klaus Bachmann's *Genocidal Empires: German Colonialism in Africa and the Third Reich* (2018).

Caroline Elkins captured well the brutality of British colonialism in her book *Imperial Reckoning: The Untold Story of Britain's Gulag in Kenya* (2005) which won the Pulitzer prize. The savagery of the genocidal regime of Belgian King Leopold II regime in the Congo is well articulated in the blistering "Casement Report" (1904) by Sir Roger David Casement, in Joseph Conrad's *Heart of Darkness* (1899), in Mark Twain's *King Leopold's Soliloquy* (1905), in Edmund Morel's Red Rubber: *The Story of the* Rubber *Slave Trade Which Flourished on the Congo for Twenty Years, 1890-1910*, in Conan Doyle's *The Crime of the Congo* (1908) and Adam Hochschild's *King Leopold's Ghost: A Story of Greed, Terror and Heroism in Colonial Africa* (1998). After the independence of the Congo (DRC) in 1960, Belgium continued its hostility that led to the brutal assassination of Patrice Lumumba, according to a practice already well established in French colonies which witnessed the assassination of Félix-Roland Moumié (1925 – 1960), Ruben Um Nyobè (1913 – 1958), Thomas Sankara (1949-1987) and many other freedom fighters.

The assassination of Dr. Félix-Roland *Moumié*, Ruben Um Nyobè, Patrice Émery Lumumba, Bantu Stephen Biko, Thomas Sankara, and many other freedom fighters, the constant fomenting of political or constitutional coups, the support and protection of selected and elected African dictators, the safe protection in Western banks of billions of dollars stolen from Africa by dictators and other politicians constitute a well-known modus operandi of Western powers in Africa and their constant double standards and double talks about democracy, human rights and development. The violent elimination of anti-colonialist and anti-imperialists found its famous cynical expression in the legendary words of Hillary Clinton. Speaking with laughter about the killing of Gaddafi during a NATO military campaign, using the parody of the famous "veni, vidi, vici" uttered by Gaius Julius Caesar (100 BC – 44 BC), Hillary Clinton sung in an interview on CBS News: "We came, we saw, he died!"[147] the killing of Gaddafi did not establish democracy in Libya, it rather created a huge chaos that has destabilized several countries in the Sahel region, in West Africa and even in Central Africa.

A growing number of people in the globe South say that the US builds military bases and drops bombs while China builds roads and bridges as the U.S. Vice President-elect J.D. Vance, recently recognized in an astonishing confession: "We have built a foreign policy of hectoring, and moralizing and lecturing countries that don't want anything to do with it, the Chinese have a foreign Policy of building roads and bridges and feeding poor people, and I think that we should pursue a diplomacy of respect, and a foreign policy that is not rooted in moralizing, but is rooted in the national interests of this country."[148]

In the age of internet, tik tok, and independent youtubers, the flow of information has enhanced African awareness of the pitfalls of Western benevolence. This is why some Africans are now turning toward various partners and find it unwise to put all their eggs in one single basket.

The evaluation of this impact of the West on Africa has been captured and expressed by two schools of thought and two different narratives. The dominant Western discourse is that of "civilizing mission" paradigm nurtured by the theory of evolution, Christian missiology and its soteriological ideology, and numerous studies that promoted philosophical and scientific racism. According to this school of thought the West helped Africans become fully humane but introducing in Africa civilization, economic development, democracy,

---

[147] CBS News. https://www.youtube.com/watch?v=6DXDU48RHLU
[148] J.D. Vance on US Foreign Policy:
https://www.facebook.com/NationalErInterest/videos/vp-elect-jd-vance/428783476692505/

human rights, logic, rationality, "true religion," high moral standards and "good values" (i.e. Western values).

Already at the close of the 19th century, the Polish novelist Joseph Conrad who witnessed instances of genocide perpetrated in the Congo by the regime of King Leopold II began questioning the civilizing mission ideology in his legendary "Heart of Darkness."

A century later, the indignation of this son of Apollo Nałęcz Korzeniowski, will emerge in another Polish writer, Karol Józef Wojtyła, known as Saint John Paul II. This Polish Pope who led the Catholic Church from 1978 through 2005, and visited Africa nine times, initiated the process of asking for forgiveness for the evil committed by the West against Africa. He made apologies for Catholicism's role in enslaving Africans. During a meeting in 1985 with intellectuals and Catholic students in Yaoundé (Cameroon), the Polish pope addressed the painful history of slavery: "Throughout history, people belonging to Christian nations have unfortunately not always behaved well, and we ask for forgiveness from our African brothers who have suffered so much, for example, from the slave trade." Likewise, in 1992, during a visit on the island of Gorée (Senegal), a historic site of the French slave trade in the 17th and 18th centuries the Pope addressed to God the following prayer: "From this African sanctuary of black pain, we implore heaven's forgiveness."

History shows that, in their 5 centuries of relationship with the West, Africans have been and continue to be caught in the "damned if you do and damned if you don't" dilemma for as Dr Kissinger already pointed out from his long geopolitical experience, "to be *America's* enemy is dangerous, but to be *America's friend* is fatal."

"We do not look West or East, we look forward." With this dictum Nkrumah defined what remained a memorable geopolitical path for Africa. Africa cannot prosper by trading one master for another, but by pursuing a "strategic autonomy" and some form of "economic sovereignty," which implies freely trading with various nations by embracing multilateralism and multipolarity. Africa has a long history of interaction with both East and West.

Anti-imperialist and anti-colonialist "axis of resistance" comprises the analysis and critique of Power articulated not only by those discounted as a marginal fringe of outliers, but also by a small but powerful galaxy of authoritative "public intellectuals" and other thinkers from the academia, the military, the intelligence services, the business world, and even government officials, senators and parliamentarians, as well as leaders from mainstream churches. Some have found their voices amplified by the new medias of independent journalists and youtubers. Well documented examples of imperialism, neocolonialism and all manners of pseudo-democratic modes of governance are also constantly voices in the US and in Europe by some members of the opposition in various debates in the Senate, in the Congress and other Parliaments, as well as during electoral campaigns. It is an open secret that many democracies are not democratic, and that oligarchs and plutocrats use democracy promotion as smokescreen to hid hegemonic ambitions, like the civilizing mission ideology of colonial era.

As the official documents of cooperation between Africa and other powers such as the US, the EU, China or Russia, clearly indicate foreign partners are self-interested in their dealing with the continent. It is therefore important that Africa avoids siding with one block against another as President Sall observed, "Africa has suffered enough from the burden of history… It does not want to be the home of a new Cold War but a pole of stability and opportunity open to all its partners on a mutually beneficial basis." And further, he reminded foreign partners that "Africa…wishes to engage with all its partners in reinvented relationships, which transcend the prejudice that who is not with me, is against me."

Africans are deeply aware that both China and the US pursuit first of all their own national interests in Africa. The truth of the matter is that so far Africa remains in a precarious situation despite the presence of multinationals from the East and from the West.

Speaking at Harvard T.H. Chan School of Health, in March 2024, Ms. Fatima, the first Lady of Sierra Leone summarized well how a great many Africans understand the issue of trade with the West or the East. She first observes that, in the name of democracy, foreign powers instigate chaos so that African presidents cannot properly govern their countries. Instead of investing in development, they have to spend their limited resources to first establish peace in their countries:

"When you look at what Sierra Leone has to offer, when it comes to our natural resources, the kind of mineral resources we have, for example, is enough to take care of everybody in the country. Unfortunately we are not given the free will to make decisions on our own mineral resources. There is always big brother who decides and when you fight and say no we are not going to do this, they use the system to stop you. It's either they set you up with the opposition and they will be supporting the opposition against you from the back, or they cause unnecessary chaos in your country so that you are not able to even govern your own people, they will do things so that you cannot function properly. Of course a country that does not have peace cannot develop. You have to have peace before you talk about development.

She then goes on to explain how Africans do not own their natural resources and cannot achieve genuine development because of foreign interference and looting of African wealth:

I will give you a simple example about Sierra Leone. Every mining company that is in Sierra Leone today is owned by a foreigner, if it is not the Chinese, it is the Americans or the British. Our electricity BUBUNA is run by the British and we still do not have light. If you don't have electricity how can you talk about education, how can you talk about healthcare facilities.

With all the minerals we have why can't we even have proper drinking water? Before my husband came to power, they said that Sierra Leone was benefitting about 0.0001%. What is that? Basically a company can take as much as $100 million out of the country in terms of minerals and then just give ten thousand dollars to the country. Now what will $10,000 do for our health system or our education system. These are the things, I believe, that are stopping Africa from progressing. We don't have a say...I don't know why we celebrate independence, because we are not free. I am not speaking on behalf of the government of Sierra Leone nor am I speaking on behalf of his excellency the President. I am speaking as Fatima, as a citizen who believes that things need to change...I speak on behalf of the people because I understand what people go through. I am not paid a salary, so I cannot be fired either. That is the advantage of being the first Lady. I believe that what is happening in Africa needs to change and to change now.... You know this divide and rule, if you are close to China, we are not coming to your country, if you are close to America we will not come to your country. Look the fight that is there between Europe, England, America, China, Russia, is not a Sierra Leonian fight. That's not our problem. We are fighting for our daily bread, we want to have education, health facility, we are looking for a government structure where one single person cannot be the dictator of the nation, that is what we are looking for. And in that process we are going to be ally with everybody who wants us to grow. But if we ally ourselves with someone, and the other person feels offended... that is his problem. I am not restricted in where I should go or who I should talk too. In Africa you cannot have a leader who is assertive and knows what his people want, a leader who wants to change what is happening. The moment you have that he becomes everybody's target. Then they find reasons to slow you down, the reasons to stop you, and they use that system of corruption, they use corrupt people, negative people, they use unpatriotic citizens to come after a government which is doing what is right for the people."[149]

The exploitation of African natural resources by way of neo-colonial violence finds its paradigmatic case in the DRC, the proverbial "heart of Darkness" as Helen Epstein rightly pointed out: "Beneath Congo's soil lies an estimated $24 trillion in natural resources, including rich supplies of oil, gold, diamonds, the coltan used in computer chips, the cobalt and nickel used in jet engines and car batteries, the copper for bathroom pipes, the uranium for bombs and power plants, the iron for nearly everything. This wealth is the

---

[149] Empowering girls in Africa: A Q&A with Sierra Leone First Lady Fatima Maada Bio https://www.youtube.com/watch?v=mMuk82iVUxw

https://www.hsph.harvard.edu/event/empowering-girls-in-africa-a-qa-with-sierra-leone-first-lady-fatima-maada-bio/

source of untold suffering. Today, more Congolese are displaced from their homes than Iraqis, Yemenis, or Rohingyas. Yet their miseries are all but invisible, in part because the identities and aims of Congo's myriad combatants are mystified by layers of rumor and misinformation, which serve the interests of those profiting from the mayhem."[150]

For 30 years, from 1960 to 1990, covert operations, coups and assassination of leaders viewed as hostile to Western national interests wreaked havoc in newly independent African countries throughout the heyday of the cold war. Meanwhile in post-colonial era African economies continue to be torpedoed, sabotaged or hijacked by powerful Western nations through a variety of mechanisms including debt traps by the IMF, privatizations and structural adjustment programs of the "Washington Consensus," and manipulation of the cost of African raw materials on the global market. And the saga continues, would argue some activists.

Despite a few bright spots here and there, in comparison to the rest of the World, Africa is still the heart of Darkness, a land where for the vast majority of the population life is "nasty, brutish and short." The immigration crisis is a good case in point. The fact that thousands of young Africans drown in the Mediterranean Sea trying to escape from their motherland is a telltale sign of the grim reality of life under the tropics, the tale of the sorry state of affairs in what is still a gloomy world. In other words, the story of African development under Western leadership and economic aid has proven highly problematic and that explains why many African countries are not trying to diversify their partnership.

A remarkable fact is that over the past two decades, Africa's trade partnerships have significantly shifted from Europe and the US to Asia.

---

[150] Epstein, Helen, "Give Congo Back to the Congolese" in New York Review of Books, February 23, 2018

We have already pointed out that the US accounts only for about 5% of trade with Africa. However, even Europe which, due to its colonial legacy, remains a major trading partner has now fallen behind Asia. In 2021, for instance, Asia accounted for over 40% of both Africa's exports and imports, surpassing Europe in both categories. Between 2014 and 2023, the share of Europe in Africa's trade averaged 26.8 percent compared with about 48 percent in the 1990s, while China and India accounted for a combined share of about 23 percent of African trade in 2023.[151] While the European Union (EU) remains the largest single market for African goods and the largest source of African imports, China has become the leading trading partner in terms of individual countries, in both exports and imports. Despite being (still) Africa's biggest trade partner, the EU funded only 6% of African infrastructures in 2019, while China funded 20.8% of them.[152]

Does it mean that Africa should completely sever its ties with the West and side with China and Russia? Such an option would not be realistic for several reasons. A genuine understanding of geopolitics requires an acknowledgement of realpolitik which requires an understanding not only of apparent weaknesses of the West, but also a grasp of its real power.

From Oswald Spengler's *The Decline of the West (Der Untergang des Abendlandes, 1918-1922),* to Patrick J. Buchanan's *The Death of the West (2001),* and Emmanuel Todd's La *Défaite de l'Occident (2024),* many have sang the requiem of the West to no avail. Joseph Nye's *"Is the American Century Over?"* (2015) and Josef Joffe's "The Myth of America's Decline" (2013), remind us that it is premature to talk about the end of the American century. Between the jeremiads of right-wing ethnonationalists who lament the old good days of their

---

[151] https://media.afreximbank.com/afrexim/African-Trade-Report_2024.pdf

[152] Michael Blanga-Gubbay, Africa's Trade Potential: *Escaping the Colonial Past by Building a Self-Sustaining Future.* Form: https://www.kuehnecenter.uzh.ch/impact_series/2021_05_21-04-21-africas_trade_potential.html

privileges and the anti-cassandra over-optimists, a careful reflection is needed regarding the evolution and the metamorphosis of the American hegemony. History shows that the "rise and fall of great powers" is a law of nature as old as humanity itself. However, Rome was not built in one day nor did it collapse in one day. Current rhetoric about the end of the American empire is certainly untethered to the whole truth. When Rome fell at the hands of Barbarians in 476, Europe entered a period of crisis called by historians "dark ages" that lasted for an entire millennium. The economic, political, cultural, and intellectual order established by the Greek philosophers and the Roman senators collapsed. Warlords, diseases, misery and ignorance plunged the whole society in that Hobbesian state of nature where life became solitary, nasty, brutish and short. Then during the Renaissance Europe bounced back and conquered the world. In other words, we have seen this movie before. It would be a very dangerous mistake to underestimate those that poets call the "children of Vikings and Vandals, Visigoths and Ostrogoths." The West has already proven – after the pessimism generated by world war I and world war II - that it has a tremendous capacity of resilience and renewal. Certainly the West and the US, in particular, face serious challenges now. However, the fundamentals of their power are still strong, and talks about the end of Western dominance are rather wishful thinking at this stage of the geopolitical game. Despite all the noise about de-dollarization and the decline of the West, the West remains strong with an extensive power projection covering the whole planet. There is not yet any serious global alternative to dollar. Chinese elites that trade with the US need a stable dollar for the stability of world economy. The same is true for other BRICS members. The strong bond between North America and Europe, makes it difficult for the BRICS and the incoherent Global South to easily and quickly overthrow the Western System. If the US accounts only for about 4.2% of world population, it is still huge with its European allies, and even its Asian allies, most notably Japan, South Korea, Australia, New Zealand, the Philippines, and even to some degree India. That is a lot of people in the Western block. In formerly colonized African and Asian countries, an important segment of the ruling elite remains staunchly pro-Western in virtue of their education, their economic privileges, or their

Christian faith. The US and Europe constitute a vast market with tremendous economic power and technological know-how. Moreover, together, the US and Europe, still control vast segments of the economic sector in Africa through Western multinational companies and loans from the IMF and the World Bank. On the Security front, the West is still dominant in arms trade, and the defense budgets of the US and Europe dwarf by far those of China or Russia. According to a leading global defense review, among the top 5 largest military budgets in the world, with a defense budget of $895 billion in 2024, the US alone constituted about 62.3% of world's defense budgets, superseding by far China ($266.8 billion or 18.6%) and Russia ($126 billion or 8.8%).[153]

Needless to say that in these matters of military budgets and arms production, Africa remains a meaningless entity, easily up for grab by any adventurous conquistador. Moreover, NATO and its global expansion constitute a formidable war machine, the proverbial invincible armada at this juncture. Assisted by its Think tanks, its NGOs, its "intelligence agencies," its Christian networks, its vast libraries, its universities and its vast army of anthropologists and other researchers, the West has a good understanding of the weaknesses of almost any society on the planet and can deploy the *"divide et impera"* strategy more efficiently than any other competing power.

According to a well-established track record, documented by many historians and in the memoirs written by important figures in the military and political establishments, the West, when facing its foes or peer competitors, has a formidable "nuisance capacity" with many tools in its toolbox. Expert in the "Carrot and Stick" strategy since the time of Roman emperors, the West knows too well not only how to manufacture consent but also how to manufacture discontent and enlist disgruntled insiders to weaken societies and governments, and how to "extend its competitors" to the breaking point, instigate coups and rebellions, foment civil wars, and engineer regime change.

The US remains the only hyperpower with unparalleled capacity of military power projection covering the entire planet, with incredible

---

[153] https://www.globalfirepower.com/defense-spending-budget.php

dominance of the sea and the air. While the US, surrounded by two big oceans, is relatively secure in its borders, Russia and China are geographically more vulnerable to foreign attacks. Moreover, they are surrounded and contained by a vast geopolitical belt of American allies and American military bases. In GDP terms, the US alone accounts for about 25% of the global economy, while Russian GDP accounts for about 3% of world economy. According to the Institute for Security Studies (headquartered in Pretoria), "Russia's trade volume with Africa in 2022 (US$18.4 billion) was lower than the continent's traditional partners, such as China (US$199 billion), Italy (US$76.3 billion), France (US$67.8 billion), the US (US$65.7 billion) and Germany (US$45 billion); and African imports from Russia were under 2% which is very low in comparison to other global trade partners."[154]

This means that while Russia can assist Africa in security matters with its powerful military industry, its contribution to economic and financial development will remain limited for some time. The recent collapse of the Syrian regime of president Bashar al-Assad has shown the limits of Russian power as well as the weaknesses of the "Axis of Resistance." On the economic side, many African countries are still vastly controlled by the IMF, the World Bank and Western companies. Most importantly the mind of many people is heavily formatted by information produced and distributed by Western information technologies in a world where the West invented, owns and controls not only communication satellites, but also google, Wikipedia, Meta, X (Twitter), YouTube, social medias and various news channels. In other words, in the area of "Infowars" and "epistemic violence," the West has a tremendous advantage.

The US also enjoys a tremendous influence with its soft power, an area where Russia and China lag far behind. Africa is closer to the US via Christianity, Universities, a large elite trained in the West or Western academic framework. The symbolic power of language is also of great importance. Africa is largely divided into Francophone Africa and Anglophone Africa, with Portuguese being spoken in

---

[154] https://issafrica.org/iss-today/russia-s-growing-influence-in-africa-calls-for-more-balanced-partnerships

Angola and Mozambique. A great many Africans are fluent in Western languages, while those who master Russian or Chinese are a tiny minority. Indeed, French and English still remain official languages in a great many African countries. Many Africans regularly consume Western media available in Western languages more than those from China. Most importantly the largest African diaspora is in the US, the Caribbean, the UK, France, Belgium, and some other Western countries. Moreover, the African diaspora in the Americas (mainly Brazil and the Caribbean) is shaped by Western culture more than by Russian or Chinese cultures. There is also the psychological connection shaped by family ties and friendship among some people.

In other words, what Africa needs is not decoupling from the West, but de-risking! At the present time the network of relations between Africa and the West is so deep, so pervasive and so old that decoupling for the majority of the African people or leaders is almost an impossibility. But this bond is likely to progressively weaken as the economic power of the West dwindles in a world of globalization where the BRICS and multipolarity may offer an alternative to Africans who want to free themselves from the ubiquitous economic, military, political and cultural yoke of the West.

Most importantly an alienated Africa cannot defend itself and thrive. Foreign powers do not only intend to dominate Africa politically and militarily in order to better loot African natural resources, they have also always struggle to "colonize the mind." This is why the African Union promotes not only Pan-Africanism, but also the philosophy of "African Renaissance" which calls for a "reafricanization" through a rediscovery of "African values." For the sake of brevity, we shall address this issue just in a few points here.

Borrell's "jungle worlview" overlooks almost a century of Western and African scholarship that systematically debunked racist mythologies and their "manufactured barbarism" articulated by Eurocentric thinkers to justify colonial conquest and the looting of African natural resources. African values, now largely described as "Bumuntu" or "Ubuntu" are well known to scholars. Africa, the cradle of Humanity, played a crucial role in the creation of world civilization (exemplified in Africa in the ancient civilizations of ancient Egypt,

Nubia, Mali, or the Great Zimbabwe) and greatly contributed to world spirituality, science and technology. The decolonization of knowledge pertaining to African history has been well established in countless volumes produced by Western Africanists such as Basil Davidson.

Basil Risbridger Davidson (1914 – 2010), Harold Courlander (1908-1996), Melville Jean Herskovits (1895-1963), French Egyptologists Serge Sauneron (author of The Priests of Ancient Egypt) and Christiane Desroches-Noblecourt (the queen of European egyptology, who authored *Gifts from the pharaohs: how Egyptian civilization shaped the modern world*, 2007). Most important studies by African and African American scholars are found in The Kemetic school of African Egyptologists (most notably works by Cheikh Anta Diop and Theophile Obenga), the Afrocentric school of Molefi Kete Asante, the monumental eight volumes of the UNESCO's *General History of Africa*, and the Encyclopedia "Africana" edited by the Harvard team of Henry Louis Gates and Kwame Anthony Appiah, to name but a few in a vast panoply of outstanding scholarship.

We shall not dwell on this topic here. I have written elsewhere a detailed overview of "Bumuntu Values." (Nkulu-N'Sengha, 2011). Suffice it to recall what Pope John Paul II acknowledged during the first African Synod of Bishops held in Rome in 1994:

"Although Africa is very rich in natural resources, it remains economically poor. At the same time, it is endowed with a wealth of cultural values and priceless human qualities which it can offer to the Churches and to humanity as a whole...Africans have a profound religious sense, a sense of the sacred, of the existence of God the Creator and of a spiritual world. The reality of sin in its individual and social forms is very much present in the consciousness of these peoples, as is also the need for rites of purification and expiation."[155]

---

[155] Maura Browne, ed., *The African Synod: Documents, Reflections, Perspectives*. (Maryknoll: Orbis Books, 1996); p. 245.

As R. Bastide observed in his work on *Le Candomblé de Bahia,* "among the Yoruba and Fon there is an entire civilization of spirituality comparable to that of the wood carvings and bronzes of Benin.'[156] And Yoruba and Fon people are not an exception in this regard in Africa. In the current dark age of geopolitical brute force, Africa needs to rediscover its "Civilization of spirituality" in order to promote that sense of dignity and sanity so indispensable for survival.

4. Conclusion: where do we go from here?

The reality of current geopolitics offers Africa a clear choice: Pan-Africanize or Wither away!

In 2013, Africa celebrated the Golden Jubilee of the formation of the OAU in 1963. At this occasion, in their "50th Anniversary Solemn Declaration," African heads of state and government reaffirmed their commitment to the "ideals of Pan-Africanism" and their strong commitment "to accelerate the African Renaissance by ensuring the integration of the principles of Pan-Africanism" in all the policies and initiatives of the African Union (AU).[157] They also reminded us explicitly that it is the philosophy of Pan-Africanism that led to the independence of Africa and the creation of the Organization of African Unity (OAU) by guiding African struggle against slavery, colonialism, apartheid and cultural genocide.

Moreover, according to the African heads of state and government, Agenda 2063, the AU's blueprint or strategic framework for African development over the next 50 years (2013-2063), is "a concrete manifestation of the pan-African drive for unity, self-determination,

---

[156] Bastide, Roger, Le Candomblé de Bahia, cited by Zahan, Dominique, *The Religion, Spirituality, and Thought of Traditional Africa* (Chicago: The University of Chicago Press); p.126.

[157] https://au.int/sites/default/files/documents/36205-doc-50th_anniversary_solemn_declaration_en.pdf

freedom, progress and collective prosperity pursued under Pan-Africanism and African Renaissance."[158]

In other words, far from being superficial abstract cogitation by some isolated arm-chair intellectual dreamers, Pan-Africanism is an existentialist philosophy at the core of "African Humanism" (Bumuntu) and African geopolitical Philosophy. It is a crucial heuristic code for African survival and well-being in a world of constant danger from foreign powers vying for the vast strategic resources of the continent.

A cursory glance at the history of Africa since the creation of OAU indicates that Africa is far from the needed Pan-African unity. Conflicts in the Horn of Africa, civil war in Sudan, tensions between ECOWAS and the AES polities, conflicts in Mozambique and in Central Africa, most notably between Rwanda and the DRC, are just a few examples in the litany of internal strife and glaring African weakness and wickedness that cry out to heaven and urgently call for Pan-African remedy.

In the 21st century, it is a United Europe that each African country has to deal with. When France, for example, intervenes in Africa, it comes with soldiers from other NATO members, and even in the economic realm some agreements are signed as "EU." This is for instance the case of the Memorandum of Understanding on Sustainable Raw Materials signed in February 2024 between Rwanda and the EU.[159]

In these conditions isolated African countries find themselves in asymmetrical power relations vis-à-vis the EU, the US, China, Russia or India. This is why Pan-Africanism is necessary for meaningful cooperation between Africa and foreign powers.

"2015-2024" was proclaimed in December 2013 the "International Decade for People of African Descent" by the UN

---

[158] https://au.int/en/agenda2063/overview

[159] https://ec.europa.eu/commission/presscorner/detail/en/ip_24_822

General Assembly (resolution 68/237). The goal of this proclamation is to foster "recognition, justice and development" of People of African descent. Now that this decade has ended, it is fitting to reflect on the fundamental philosophy of Pan-African consciousness that is so essential to the liberation and development of the African people in Africa and the Diaspora.

In the first half of the 20th century, some African intellectuals from the Americas, Europe and Africa developed the philosophy of Pan-Africanism in response to the danger of slave trade and colonial oppression. We can grasp the meaning and scope of Pan-Africanism in various texts published since the time of abolitionists Ottobah Cugoano (1757-1791) and Olaudah Equiano (1745-1797), and most notably in the documents of the first 5 major Pan-African Congresses held in the wake of the first world war, between 1919 and 1945, under the leadership of William Edward Burghardt Du Bois (1868 –1963) and Georges Padmore (1903-1959), and in the 6th Pan-African Congress held in Tanzania in 1974. In light of these congresses, we can summarize the key points of the Pan-African movement as follows:

1) Affirmation of African agency through the motto "Africa for the Africans"

2) Unity of the African continent in one polity: "The United States of Africa"

3) Moral, spiritual and cultural renaissance of Africa

4) Moving Africa from tribalism to nationalism

5) Faith in Democracy

6) Affirmation of Non-violence and rejection of violence

7) Planetary solidarity in a world where "We are all African" as paleontologists and geneticists have proven.

8) Economic development of Africa

9) Neutrality regarding the political ideology of the Western Capitalist bloc and the regime of Moscow or the Beijing Model.

These points summarize in broad strokes the answer to the fundamental question, "What is Pan-Africanism?" They reverberate in an updated way in the "Seven Aspirations" of the Agenda 2063 articulated by the African Union. This is so precisely because several decades after the early Pan-African congresses the struggle remains *mutatis mutandis* the same, against an almost similar danger.

Since its inception, the twenty-first century has emerged as a bewildering whirlpool of polarizing geopolitical and social forces which indicate that the world is at a problematic, if not, dangerous crossroad. The 2001 tragedy of "9-11" and its ensuing global war on terror, the 2007–*2008* Global Financial Crisis, Covid-19, the Russian-Ukrainian war, and the recent "Gaza vs Israel Nakba" illustrate well the pathology of a world which has moved from the Kabuki theater of corrupt politics to the tears and fear of a real Greek tragedy. With the progressive dwindling of the problematic "world order" established in the wake of the second world war, the world is now in search of a new equilibrium, while the increasing competition between global powers vying for the dominium of the world is increasing chaos and mayhem. In this arena of the battle between the hegemonic forces of unipolarity and neo-colonialism and the advocates of multipolarity and strategic autonomy the survival of microscopic polities and powerless nations is in serious jeopardy. Fragmented by the colonial legacy into 55 incoherent and unstable nations, Africa discovers the drama of *realpolitik* in a world dominated by political, demographic, economic or military juggernauts such as China, India, Russia, EU, the US, and an increasingly frightening NATO. Swimming in this Kafkaesque ocean of economic sharks, Africans discover that they have become capitalists without capital and nationalists without nation in a competitive Crusoeist global market of conscious and unconscious cruelty, calculating taciturnity and "Hasbarahic" narratives of economic aid to development, democracy and human rights from the very powers that pursue their interests with a Machiavellic zeal.

Generally speaking, Africans still consume what they do not produce and produce what they do not consume – be it in the agricultural realm or in the area of minerals. Despite its widely sought out natural resources, the reality of Africa in this first half of the twenty-first century is that its position in the global economy is peripheral. With few exceptions, African countries are marginal to global economic transactions, and their impact on the decisions that shape the global economy is negligible. Time to quit the foggy kingdom of magical thinking about the histrionic "African century" mythologies, and face the reality of a dire predicament in this era of a "New Scramble for Africa"! Having negligible military power and less control over their economies, a great many African political officials exercise "nominal suzerainty" over what is, for all intents and purposes, neo-colonies. It becomes self-evident that unity is *a sine qua non* for survival, for as a powerful Latin American slogan - popularized in protest song by the Chilean Sergio Ortega Alvarado - has it: *El pueblo unido jamás será vencido!* In other words, for Africa, as our political and intellectual forebears understood it in light of the tragedies of past centuries, Pan-Africanism is the key to the kingdom of survival, the key to salvage the continent from those who ubiquitously savage it mercilessly: Pan-Africanize or die in painful agony!

Africa has several countries with less than ten million people, some even have less than one million people. Several others are so geographically minuscule that they cannot properly satisfy the economic and security needs of their population. Even large countries with sufficient human and natural resources have to face the harsh reality of interdependence in the global economy where rules are fixed by the powerful. This is well understood by a great many nations as we see in the development of Pan-Arabism, Pan-Slavism, Pan-Americanism, the creation of the European Union, etc.

Home to vast natural resources defined by the European Union, the US and some other powers from the East and the West as "critical" and "strategic" minerals for their prosperity and security, Africa finds itself in a precarious situation as the battleground of rapacious and brazen foreign interests. This is to say that the struggle for genuine independence and human flourishing is not over, for the same danger that led our forefathers and foremothers to articulate the philosophy of Pan-Africanism, to create the OAU and to struggle against the colonization of the mind is still alive. Perhaps even more menacing that ever. As historians have it, "Barbarians are at the gate," and even already inside the gate and inside the African head! Barbarians that attack African values, Barbarians that sow divisions and destroy African solidarity and hospitality, Barbarians that kill African prosperity and posterity, Barbarians that destroy hope in the future... enemies of African States, enemies of the human race, enemies of Humanity as a whole....architects of chaos and selfishness... Barbarians here, Barbarians there, misandrist Barbarians everywhere....The history of Africa is a long trail of tears in the never ending struggle to overcome the violence of dangerous and misanthropic Barbarians. This is why Pan-Africanism calls for "African Renaissance," involving the revival of ancestral values of human dignity, now widely known as "Bumuntu" or "Ubuntu," values as old as humanity itself in a continent which is the cradle of humankind and civilization. The call to Pan-Africanism is therefore a call to leave behind the ways of Barbarians and become fully humane, by transcending cronyism, tribalism, ethnocentrism, sexism, racism, jingoism, religious ostracism and political persecution. Without Pan-African unity and solidarity, Africa will remain powerless and subsequently wealthless and worthless. In this globalized and globalizing world, the challenges of our time impose upon Africans a clear choice: Pan-Africanize or wither away in the swamp of superfluousness!

REFERENCES

Allison, Graham, *Destined for War: Can America and China Escape Thucydides's Trap? (Houghton Mifflin Harcourt, 2017).*

Bat, Jean-Pierre, *Les réseaux Foccart: L'homme de la Françafrique* (Nouveau Monde Editions, 2020).

Bourgi, Robert, *Ils savent que je sais tout: Ma vie en Françafrique* (Max Milo Editions, 2024).

Brzezinski, Zbigniew, The Grand Chessboard: American Primacy and its geostrategic imperatives. New York: Basic Books, 1997.

Carter, Jimmy, Our Endangered Values: America's Moral Crisis. (New York: Simon and Schuster, 2005).

Césaire, Aimé. 2013. *Discours sur le colonialisme, Suivi de Discours sur la Négritude*. Paris : Présence Africaine.

Chomsky, Noam, Hegemony or Survival: America's Quest for Global Dominance (Metropolitan Books, 2003); republished by Haymarket Books in 2024.

Chomsky, Noam, World Orders Old and New (Columbia University Press, 1996).

Chomsky, Noam, Profit Over People: Neoliberalism and Global Order (Seven Stories Press,1999).

Chomsky, Noam, Imperial Ambitions: Conversations with Noam Chomsky on the Post-9/11 World (Metropolitan Books, 2005).

Chomsky, Noam, Manufacturing Consent: The Political Economy of the Mass Media (Pantheon Books, 1988), in collaboration with Edward S. Herman.

Chomsky, Noam, The Prosperous Few and the Restless Many (Odonian Press, 1994).

Chomsky, Noam, Requiem for the American Dream: The 10 Principles of Concentration of Wealth & Power (Seven Stories Press, 2017).

Chomsky, Noam, Deterring Democracy (Haymarket Books, 2024), first published in 1991.

Chomsky, Noam, Pirates and Emperors, Old and New: International Terrorism in the Real World (Haymarket Books, 2015), first published in1986.

Chomsky, Noam, The Political Economy of Human Rights, Volume I: The Washington Connection and Third World Fascism (Haymarket Books, 2014), first published in 1979.

Chomsky, Noam, The Political Economy of Human Rights, Volume II: After the Cataclysm: Postwar Indochina and the Reconstruction of Imperial Ideology (Haymarket Books, 2014), first published in 1979.

Chomsky, Noam, *American Power and the New Mandarins (*New York: Pantheon Books, 1969).

Diesen, Glenn, *The Ukraine War & the Eurasian World Order* (Clarity Press, 2024)

Diop, Cheikh Anta. 1967. *Antériorité des civilisations nègres: Mythe ou vérité historique?* Paris: Présence Africaine.

Diop, Cheikh Anta. 1991. *Civilization or Barbarism: An Authentic Anthropology*. New York, NY: Lawrence Hill Books.

Engelhardt, Thomas M., *The World According to Tomdispatch: America in The New Age of Empire* (Verso, 2008).

Engelhardt, Thomas M., *The United States of Fear* (Haymarket, 2011).

Engelhardt, Thomas M., Shadow Government: Surveillance, Secret Wars, and a Global Security State in a Single Superpower World. (Haymarket, 2014).

Fukuyama, Francis, The End of History and the Last Man (Free Press, 1992)

Good, Aaron, American Exception: Empire and the Deep State (New York: Skyhorse Publishing, 2022).

Hedges, Christopher Lynn, *American Fascists*: The Christian Right and the War on America (2007).

Huntington, Samuel P., The Clash of Civilizations and the Remaking of World Order (Simon & Schuster, 2011)

Huntington, Samuel P., Who Are We? The Challenges to America's National Identity. (New York: Simon and Schuster, 2004)

Jacques, Martin, When China Rules the World: The End of the Western World and the Birth of a New Global Order (Penguin, 2012)

Johnson, Chalmers Ashby, (2004). Blowback; The Costs and Consequences of American Empire (2nd ed.). Holt Paperbacks.

Johnson, Chalmers Ashby, (2004). The Sorrows of Empire: Militarism, Secrecy, and the End of the Republic, Metropolitan Books.

Korten, David C., When Corporations Rule the World (Kumarian Press, 1995).

Le Gouriellec, Sonia, Géopolitique de l'Afrique (Paris : Que sais-je, 2022).

Maddison, Angus, The World Economy: Historical Statistics (OECD, 2004).

Maddison, Angus, Contours of the World Economy 1-2030 AD: Essays in Macro-Economic History (Oxford University Press; 2007).

Mander, Jerry and Edward Goldsmith, eds., The Case Against the Global Economy: *And for a Turn toward the Local.* (San Francisco: Sierra Club Books, 1996).

Nkulu-N'Sengha, Mutombo. 2011. "Bumuntu Memory and Authentic Personhood: An African Art of Becoming Humane." In Tom Spencer-

Walters, ed., *Memory and The Narrative Imagination in the African and Diaspora Experience.* Troy, MI: Bedford Publishers.

Nkrumah, Kwame. 1965. *Neo-Colonialism, the Last Stage of Imperialism.*

Nye, Joseph S. Jr., Soft Power: The Means to Success in World Politics (PublicAffairs, 2004).

Nye, Joseph S. Jr., Is the American Century Over? (Polity, 2015).

Nye, Joseph S. Jr., A Life in The American Century (Polity, 2024).

Piketty, Thomas, *Capital in the Twenty-First Century* (Cambridge, MA: Belknap Press, 2014).

Piketty, Thomas, *Capital and Ideology* (Harvard University Press, 2020).

Phillips, Kevin, American Theocracy: The Peril and Politics of Radical Religion, Oil, and Borrowed Money in the 21st Century (2006).

Phillips, Kevin, The Cousins' Wars: Religion, Politics and the Triumph of Anglo-America (1999).

Phillips, Kevin, The Politics of Rich and Poor: Wealth and Electorate in the Reagan Aftermath (1990).

Phillips, Kevin, Bad Money: Reckless Finance, Failed Politics, and the Global Crisis of American Capitalism (2008).

Phillips, Kevin, Wealth and Democracy: A Political History of the American Rich (2002).

Phillips, Kevin, American Dynasty: Aristocracy, Fortune, and the Politics of Deceit in the House of Bush (2004).

Ruthven, Malise, Fundamentalism: The Search for Meaning. (Oxford University Press, 2004); pp. 59; 1-34; 216-217.

Sachs, Jeffrey (2020). *The ages of globalization : geography, technology, and institutions.* New York: Columbia University Press.

Sachs, Jeffrey (2018). *A new foreign policy : beyond American exceptionalism*. New York: Columbia University Press.

Sachs, Jeffrey (2011). *The price of civilization : reawakening American virtue and prosperity* (1st ed.). New York: Random House.

Sachs, Jeffrey (2005). *The End of Poverty: Economic Possibilities for Our Time*. New York: Penguin Press.

Sachs, Jeffrey, ed. (1989). *Developing country debt and the world economy*. Chicago: University of Chicago Press.

Sartre, Jean-Paul. 2006. *Colonialism and Neocolonialism*. New York, NY: Routledge.

Stiglitz, Joseph E. (2002). *Globalization and its discontents*. New York: W.W. Norton & Company.

Stiglitz, Joseph E. (2006). *Making globalization work*. New York: W.W. Norton & Company.

Stiglitz, Joseph E. (2010). *The Stiglitz report: reforming the international monetary and financial systems in the wake of the global crisis*. New York, New York London: The New Press.

Stiglitz, Joseph E.; Sen, Amartya; Fitoussi, Jean-Paul *(2010). Mismeasuring our lives: why GDP doesn't add up: the report*. New York: *New Press*: Distributed by Perseus Distribution.

Stiglitz, Joseph (2010). *Freefall: America, free markets, and the sinking of the world economy*. New York, NY: W.W. Norton & Company.

Stiglitz, Joseph E. (2012). *The Price of Inequality: How Today's Divided Society Endangers Our Future*. New York: W.W. Norton & Company.

Stiglitz, Joseph E. (2015). *The great divide: unequal societies and what we can do about them*. New York: W.W. Norton & Company.

Stiglitz, Joseph E. (2019). *People, Power and Profits: Progressive Capitalism for an Age of Discontent*. Allen Lane.

Stiglitz, Joseph E. (2024). *The Road to Freedom: Economics and the Good Society*. W. W. Norton & Company.

Tarnas, Richard, The Passion of the Western Mind: Understanding the Ideas That Have Shaped Our World View (New York: Ballantine Books1991).

CONCLUSION

The cooperation between Africa and China has evolved into a multifaceted relationship encompassing economic, political, and technological dimensions. This partnership, while offering significant opportunities for development, also presents substantial challenges that require careful management to ensure that it benefits both Africa and China in a sustainable and equitable manner.

One of the central themes of this book is the economic impact of China's involvement in Africa, particularly in terms of infrastructure development. As discussed in several chapters, including the analysis of the Sino-Congolese trade relations and China's role in Africa's science and technology sectors, Chinese investments have played a pivotal role in bridging Africa's infrastructure gap. Projects ranging from roads and railways to educational infrastructure have been financed and constructed by Chinese companies, often at a pace and scale unmatched by other international partners. These developments have facilitated economic growth, improved connectivity, and provided access to new technologies, which are critical for Africa's long-term development.

However, the book also highlights the complexities and potential downsides of this cooperation. A significant concern is the sustainability of the debt incurred by African nations to finance these large-scale infrastructure projects. As discussed in the chapter on the political economy of Africa-China trade relations, the terms of many Chinese loans are often opaque, and there is growing anxiety about the potential for a debt crisis in some African countries. This issue is particularly pressing in resource-rich nations like Angola and the Democratic Republic of Congo, where resource-backed loans could tie up valuable natural resources for decades, limiting the economic options for future generations.

Moreover, the book raises critical questions about the broader developmental impacts of China's engagement in Africa. While Chinese investments have undoubtedly improved physical infrastructure, the benefits have not been evenly distributed across all sectors or populations. The chapter on Sino-Congolese trade, for instance, points out that local industries and labor markets often do not benefit as much as they could from these investments. The reliance on Chinese labor and materials limits the job creation potential and technology transfer to local communities, leading to concerns that China's involvement in Africa could resemble exploitative practices reminiscent of colonial times.

Environmental and social impacts are also significant issues discussed throughout the book. Several chapters, including those focused on China-Africa science and technology cooperation, argue that many Chinese-funded projects proceed with insufficient regard for environmental sustainability and the social implications for local communities. Large infrastructure projects, such as dams and mining operations, have led to the displacement of populations and the destruction of natural habitats, raising questions about the long-term sustainability of these developments.

On the geopolitical front, China's growing influence in Africa is reshaping the continent's international relationships. The book underscores how China's non-interference policy while appealing to many African governments, especially those with authoritarian tendencies, may undermine efforts to promote good governance, human rights, and democratic accountability in the region. This concern is particularly salient in countries where China's support has enabled regimes to sidestep international pressure for reforms, as seen in the chapter discussing the implications of China's foreign policy on Africa's political landscape.

Looking forward, the future of Africa-China cooperation will depend on how both parties navigate these challenges. For African countries, it is imperative to engage with China in a way that maximizes developmental benefits while minimizing risks. This requires stronger governance frameworks, greater transparency in dealings with Chinese entities, and a strategic approach to managing debt and investment. The book suggests that African nations must prioritize their long-term interests, ensuring that partnerships with China do not compromise their sovereignty or developmental goals.

For China, continuing to improve its approach to environmental sustainability, local job creation, and technology transfer will be crucial. The book advocates for a shift towards more equitable and sustainable practices that would enhance the perception of China as a partner rather than a new colonial power. This would involve China adopting higher standards of corporate social responsibility and ensuring that its investments contribute positively to Africa's broader social and economic landscape.

In conclusion, Africa-China cooperation holds immense potential for driving development on the continent, but it also comes with significant risks. The book provides a nuanced analysis of these dynamics, highlighting the need for both Africa and China to address the challenges head-on. By fostering a partnership that prioritizes sustainability, equity, and transparency, both regions can ensure that their relationship supports economic growth while also promoting broader social and environmental well-being.